THE CIVIL CONDITION
IN WORLD POLITICS

Bristol Studies in International Theory

Series Editors: **Felix Berenskötter**, SOAS, University of London, UK, **Neta C. Crawford**, Boston University, US and **Stefano Guzzini**, Uppsala University, Sweden, PUC-Rio de Janeiro, Brazil

---

This series provides a platform for theoretically innovative scholarship that advances our understanding of the world and formulates new visions of, and solutions for, world politics.

Guided by an open mind about what innovation entails, and against the backdrop of various intellectual turns, interrogations of established paradigms, and a world facing complex political challenges, books in the series provoke and deepen theoretical conversations in the field of International Relations.

Also available

Snapshots from Home
Mind, Action and Strategy in an Uncertain World
By **Karin M. Fierke**

What in the World?
Understanding Global Social Change
Edited by **Mathias Albert** and **Tobias Werron**

The Idea of Civilization and the Making of the Global Order
By **Andrew Linklater**

Find out more

bristoluniversitypress.co.uk/
bristol-studies-in-international-theory

Bristol Studies in International Theory

Series Editors: **Felix Berenskötter**, SOAS, University of London, UK, **Neta C. Crawford**, Boston University, US and **Stefano Guzzini**, Uppsala University, Sweden, PUC-Rio de Janeiro, Brazil

Coming soon

Praxis as a Perspective on International Politics
Edited by **Gunther Hellmann** and **Jens Steffek**

Broken Solidarities
How Open Global Governance Divides and Rules
By **Felix Anderl**

Pluriversality and Care
Rethinking Global Ethics
By **Maggie FitzGerald**

Find out more
bristoluniversitypress.co.uk/
bristol–studies–in–international–theory

Bristol Studies in International Theory

Series Editors: **Felix Berenskötter**, SOAS, University of London, UK, **Neta C. Crawford**, Boston University, US and **Stefano Guzzini**, Uppsala University, Sweden, PUC-Rio de Janeiro, Brazil

---

International advisory board

Find out more
bristoluniversitypress.co.uk/
bristol-studies-in-international-theory

THE CIVIL CONDITION IN WORLD POLITICS

Beyond Tragedy and Utopianism

Edited by
Vassilios Paipais

BRISTOL
UNIVERSITY
PRESS

First published in Great Britain in 2023 by

Bristol University Press
University of Bristol
1-9 Old Park Hill
Bristol
BS2 8BB
UK
t: +44 (0)117 374 6645
e: bup-info@bristol.ac.uk

Details of international sales and distribution partners are available at bristoluniversitypress.co.uk

British Library Cataloguing in Publication Data
A catalogue record for this book is available from the British Library

ISBN 978-1-5292-2417-7 hardcover
ISBN 978-1-5292-2418-4 paperback
ISBN 978-1-5292-2419-1 ePub
ISBN 978-1-5292-2420-7 ePdf

Cover design: blu inc, Bristol
Front cover image: © NicoElNino / istock

Contents

Notes on Contributors

Chris Brown is Emeritus Professor of International Relations at the LSE. He is the author of numerous articles and book chapters, and *International Society, Global Polity* (2015), *Practical Judgement in International Political Theory* (2010), *Sovereignty, Rights and Justice* (2002), *International Relations Theory: New Normative Approaches* (1992), editor of *Political Restructuring in Europe: Ethical Perspectives* (1994) and co-editor (with Terry Nardin and N.J. Rengger) of *International Relations in Political Thought* (2002) and (with Robyn Eckersley) of *The Oxford Handbook of International Political Theory* (2018). His textbook *Understanding International Relations* 5th edition (2019) has been translated into Arabic, Chinese, Euskara, Portuguese, Thai, and Turkish.

Sophia Dingli is Lecturer at the School of Social and Political Science, University of Glasgow. Her work is at the intersection of critical theory and political realism. Her work focuses on silence and silencing in politics, and she has also published work on gender and security, states of exception and peace theory. Her work has appeared in *Politics, Journal of International Political Theory, European Journal of International Relations*, edited volumes, and online forums.

Ian Hall is Professor of International Relations at the Griffith Asia Institute, Griffith University, Queensland. He is also Academic Fellow of the Australia India Institute and a co-editor (with Sara E. Davies) of the *Australian Journal of International Affairs*. He has written or edited several books, including *Modi and the Reinvention of Indian Foreign Policy* (2019), and articles in various journals, including the *European Journal of International Relations, International Affairs*, and *Third World Quarterly*. His research and teaching focuses on Indian foreign and security policy, and the history of international thought.

Caroline Kennedy-Pipe is Professor of International Security and International Relations at Loughborough University. She has published on the Cold War, the War on Terror and contemporary security challenges. She is currently a Visiting Fellow in the Danish Institute of Advanced Studies

(DIAS) at the University of Southern Denmark working on climate change and its effects on the business of war.

Anthony F. Lang, Jr is Professor of International Political Theory at the School of International Relations, University of St Andrews. His research focuses on the intersection of politics, law, and ethics at the global level through such topics as universal values, global constitutionalism, international legal theory, and the just war tradition. He has published three single-authored books, edited nine, and published numerous articles, book chapters, and reviews. His publications can be found at www.st-andrews.ac.uk/ir/people/lang/ and he tweets @ProfTonyLang.

Valerie Morkevičius is Associate Professor of Political Science at Colgate University, Hamilton, New York. Her work focuses on the intersection between strategy and ethics, and the applicability of traditional just war thinking to contemporary challenges. She is the author of *Realist Ethics: Just War Traditions as Power Politics* (Cambridge University Press, 2018).

Noël O'Sullivan is Research Professor of Political Philosophy at the University of Hull. His undergraduate and postgraduate study was at LSE and Harvard. His monographs are on *European Political Thought since 1945* (2004), *The Philosophy of Santayana* (1992), *The Problem of Political Obligation* (1986), *Fascism* (1983), and *Conservatism* (1976). He has in addition edited volumes which include *The Place of Michael Oakeshott in Contemporary Western and Non-Western Thought* (2017), *The Concept of the Public Realm* (2010), and *Political Theory in Transition* (2000). His work has been translated into Chinese, Czech, Dutch, French, Italian, Persian, Serbo-Croatian, and Spanish.

Vassilios Paipais is Lecturer (Assistant Professor) in International Relations at the University of St Andrews. He is the editor of the 2019 Special Issue 'Political theologies of the international: the continued relevance of theology in international relations' in the *Journal of International Relations and Development*, the author of *Political Ontology and International Political Thought: Voiding a Pluralist World* (Palgrave Macmillan, 2017), and the editor of *Theology and World Politics: Metaphysics, Genealogies, Political Theologies* (Palgrave Macmillan, 2020) and of *Perspectives on International Political Theory in Europe* (Palgrave Macmillan, 2021).

Kate Schick is Senior Lecturer in International Relations at Te Herenga Waka, Victoria University of Wellington. Her research lies at the intersection of critical theory and international ethics. She is particularly interested in the way critical theories highlight our mutual vulnerability and interdependence, and in their countercultural critique of the pursuit of invulnerability and self-sufficiency. Kate is author of *Gillian Rose: A Good Enough Justice* and co-editor of *The Vulnerable Subject: Beyond Rationalism in International Relations* (with Amanda Russell Beattie), *Recognition in Global Politics* (with Patrick Hayden), and *Subversive Pedagogies: Radical Possibility in the Academy* (with Claire Timperley).

John–Harmen Valk is University Lecturer (Assistant Professor) at Leiden University. His research interests lie at the intersection of international relations, political theory, continental philosophy, and the philosophy of religion. He has recently published work on the place of religious symbolic expression in the thought of Hans Morgenthau.

Richard Whatmore is Professor of Modern History at the University of St Andrews and Co-Director of the St Andrews Institute of Intellectual History. He is the author of *Republicanism and the French Revolution* (Oxford, 2000), *Against War and Empire* (Yale, 2012), *What is Intellectual History?* (Polity, 2015), *Terrorists, Anarchists and Republicans* (Princeton, 2019), and *History of Political Thought. A Very Short Introduction* (Oxford, 2021).

Michael C. Williams is Professor at the Graduate School of Public and International Affairs and holds the University Research Chair in Global Political Thought at the University of Ottawa. His primary interests are in International Relations theory, including the place of classic political theory in IR. His current research explores the impact of contemporary radical conservative movement on international order and foreign policy. His publications include *Security Beyond the State: Private Security in International Politics* (2011), with Rita Abrahamsen, *The Realist Tradition and the Limits of International Relations* (2005), and *Culture and Security: Symbolic Power and the Politics of International Security* (2007), and *Realism Reconsidered: The Legacy of Hans J Morgenthau in International Relations* (2008).

Acknowledgements

This is a book inspired by Nick Rengger and the intellectual legacy he left behind. Nick was nominally Professor of Political Theory and International Relations at the University of St Andrews but his remarkable knowledge of several other fields, such as History, Theology, Classics, Literature, and the broader Human Sciences, set him apart as a genuine *homo universalis*. To use the title of one of his favourite films featuring Paul Scofield, he was '*A Man for All Seasons*'. Perhaps among the last of a generation of academics with a humanist orientation who are rapidly becoming an eclipsing breed. I will always remember our endless conversations on topics as diverse as philosophy, politics, theology, cinema, art, history, and literature. I would learn from him insatiably as every conversation was a *muesis* (the Greek word for mystical initiation) into an exciting realm of intellectual pleasures, witty remarks, pithy comments, and good humour, often spurring me to look something up, a monograph, a film, a novel, a piece of poetry or music.

Nick's generosity was legendary as was his disregard for the trivialities of academic life. He belonged to a generation of scholars that lamented the rampant bureaucratization and corporatization of contemporary academic life and had no time for it. As a scholar, he had so few insecurities about his intellectual abilities that sharing widely his expertise and knowledge was an act of returning to the world the charisma that was amply given to him. Nick was a natural optimist of the will and pessimist of the intellect. Like one of his favourite philosophers, Michael Oakeshott, he was a fine mixture of good old English scepticism with strong doses of Epicurean hedonism, but also someone who cared deeply about the future of our societies and the importance of the values and practices that bind us. He used to repeat, with that familiar twinkle in his eye, that he was a Tory anarchist or a Bohemian nihilist, fully enjoying the paradoxical sound of it as well as the bafflement he caused to his interlocutors. His irresistible desire for a punchy quip apart, this self-description revealed all that was endearing about Nick, his love of freedom combined with his care for his fellow human beings, for he was a deeply affectionate and compassionate man without being sentimental, and someone who lived the life of the mind without being otherworldly. The embodiment of a true φιλόσοφος, as one of his doctoral students aptly put it.

For me, Nick was a mentor and a paragon of scholarship, intellectual integrity, and academic ethos. This book is just a small token of my gratitude and admiration. Gratitude is also owed to his widow Vanessa and his two beloved daughters, Corinna and Natalie, about whom he always talked with boundless affection. I thank them deeply for sharing their intimate memories of Nick and for helping me gain a broader picture of his personality. Special thanks go to my dear colleague at St Andrews, Tony Lang, who in May 2019 put together a colloquium in honour of Nick's work at St Andrews where first iterations of some of this volume's chapters were presented. Tony offered useful advice in all the stages of the preparation of this volume. Both Tony and I are also very grateful to one of Nick's last PhD students, Antonio di Biagio, who helped with the organization of the St Andrews colloquium. Thanks also go to John-Harmen Valk with whom I organized a couple of British International Studies Association (BISA) panels on Nick's work in 2019. Caroline Kennedy-Pipe was always there to share delightful stories of Nick's mischievous and playful nature along with moral and intellectual support. Nick Wheeler, Kate Schick, John-Harmen Valk, Noël O'Sullivan, Sophia Dingli, Richard Whatmore, Adham Saouli, and especially Ian Hall, offered their invaluable feedback and good humour during the process of putting this volume together and I am grateful for that. Finally, I would like to thank the BSIT series editors for pushing me to refine the volume as well as Stephen Wenham and Lorna Blackmore at Bristol University Press for their efficiency and support. Nick gained his first permanent academic post at Bristol, and so publishing this volume with BUP is a particularly fitting tribute.

Nick was not given the time to complete his work, but this book is a testament to the fact that what he left behind is worth preserving and engaging. This is a book about civility as an ethos of conversation between individuals, not necessarily between cultures. Conversation not merely for the purpose of understanding one another – since communication is not a panacea and often leads to misunderstanding and conflict, as Augustine knew all too well – but for the sheer joy of sharing thoughts, sentiments, stories, and even jokes. Nick believed in the power of thought and goodwill between well-meaning persons but had no illusions about the dominant tendencies in our cultures that keep us suspicious and contemptful of one another or plunge us into fear and despair. Yet, he insisted that such uncivil passions remain a choice, not a destiny. In the turbulent pandemic and post-pandemic years that seem to lie ahead, this is a lesson to be heeded.

Vassilios Paipais
Edinburgh, September 2021

1

Introduction: Rengger's Anti-Pelagianism: International Political Theory as Civil Conversation

Vassilios Paipais

Introduction

The late Professor Nicholas John Hugh Rengger (1959–2018) was a scholar of extraordinary range and voracious intellectual appetite. Rengger may have formally carried the title of Professor of Political Theory and International Relations at the University of St Andrews but, beyond Political Theory and International Relations (IR), his work and research interests spanned the fields of Intellectual History, Philosophy, Classics, Theology, Literature, and the broader Human Sciences. His unusual scholarly breadth and ability to converse across disciplines marked him out as one of the last of an eclipsing species of academics who used to embody the Renaissance ideal of the *homo universalis* within academia and the world of the intellect, in general.[1] This book is inspired by Rengger's enduring legacy and impact as a teacher and scholar, and by the way he put his cross-disciplinary talents in the service of bringing the broader social and political theory but also more humanist

---

[1] Rengger had unusually broad intellectual and aesthetic interests in a variety of topics, making no distinction between high and popular culture. He was an avid reader of fiction (he loved spy novels and Tolkien's world) and a lover of poetry, a connoisseur of classical music, a fan of Western films (John Wayne movies especially), an amateur singer and actor in his undergraduate years. He was a person who embraced life and the imagination in their plural interconnections. I am thankful to Vanessa and Corinna Rengger for sharing their memories of Nick.

disciplines, such as philosophy, theology, and the history of ideas, into the study of international politics.

The various chapters in this volume assess the many aspects of Rengger's work and legacy but focus on three main areas that constitute the driving ideas behind his contribution to the political theory of IR and the problem of world order: his Augustine-inspired idea of an 'anti-Pelagian imagination' favouring a sceptical, non-utopian, anti-perfectionist response to the ethico-political dilemmas of the contemporary liberal world order; his Oakeshottian argument for a pluralist 'conversation of mankind' that could sustain an ethos of civility in world politics; and his ruminations on war as the uncivil condition in world politics coupled with his critical engagement with the just war tradition as an institution of civil world order.[2] Civility and anti-Pelagianism, two central concepts in Rengger's work that will be the focus of this chapter, express a poetic re-imagining of world order that transcends both tragic realism and liberal utopianism, denying neither the fragility of the civilizing impulse in world politics nor the resourcefulness and the creativity of the human spirit in inventing new, imaginative ways to contain the modern world's destructive tendencies.

From political theory to international political theory

Undoubtedly, one of Rengger's enduring legacies within IR is his original contribution to the creation of the subfield of International Political Theory (IPT). His background in the history of political thought, moral philosophy, and political theory equipped him with the ability to contribute significantly to the emergence and evolution of IPT in the late 1980s/early 1990s, but also to the renewal of IR theory through the (re)introduction of normative, philosophical, and historical concerns to its subject matter.[3] Rengger, in other words, did not see IPT merely as a small niche production at the margins of IR, or another name for 'international ethics', but primarily as a way of doing IR theory and a key dimension of theorizing international relations.

Rengger, however, did not enter academia as a scholar of IR, an academically unremarkable discipline in his early days anyway, but came

---

[2] Rengger's understanding of a civil world order and his concomitant idea of an anti-Pelagian imagination that sustains a sceptical ethos of civility in world politics will be fully addressed further on. Both ideas are developed in his two last books: Nicholas Rengger, *The Anti-Pelagian Imagination in Political Theory and International Relations: Dealing in Darkness* (London and New York: Routledge, 2017) and Nicholas Rengger, *Just War and International Order: The Uncivil Condition in World Politics* (Cambridge: Cambridge University Press, 2013a).

[3] Chris Brown et al., eds, *International Relations in Political Thought: Texts from the Ancient Greeks to the First World War* (Cambridge: Cambridge University Press, 2002).

to the study of international relations through cognate fields. He obtained his first degree in Politics at Durham University where he was taught, among others, by Henry Tudor, Noël O'Sullivan, and David Manning (see Kennedy-Pipe in this volume), and later earned his PhD in Political Theory from the same institution under the supervision of Professor Alan Milne. Part of a generation of academics that were experiencing a sea change in British academia following the neoliberal Thatcherite reforms of the early 1980s, he turned to the then burgeoning field of IR under the pressures of the profession. As Chris Brown informs us in his chapter, IR was fast becoming a popular discipline and Rengger was happy to respond to the rising demand for teachers in a rapidly growing field. There were probably, however, intellectual reasons too for his shift to IR. Early on, he realized that some of the questions that for him constituted 'the tasks of political theory'[4] could not be answered without due consideration of the problem of order both in its domestic and its international dimensions, although for Rengger this traditional IR distinction obscured more than what it revealed.[5]

Having arrived in IR with a strong background in the humanities, in political and social theory, and in the history of political thought, Rengger never accepted its mainstream self-image as a positivist discipline. He was rather more comfortable to describe it as an interdisciplinary field of inquiry, a meeting place of diverse knowledge areas such as history, philosophy, law, and political theory among others, a view akin to the traditional way the field was envisaged and taught in Britain and Europe before the rise of the scientific/rationalist approaches. He had nothing against the latter, but he strongly advocated a pluralist discipline celebrating its methodological diversity and its increasingly plurivocal and self-reflexive nature.[6] Indeed, as part of a group of academics with a similar profile that founded the new discourse of IPT, Rengger taught the field how to practise interdisciplinarity

---

[4]   In a much more optimistic tone than what will become the tenor of his later work, Rengger defined those tasks in his first monograph borrowing from John Dunn's thought: 'The purpose of political theory is to diagnose practical predicaments and to show us how best to confront them. To do this, it needs to train us in three relatively distinct skills. Firstly, in ascertaining how the social, political and economic setting of our lives now is and in understanding why it is as it is; secondly, in working through for ourselves how we could coherently and justifiably wish that world to be or become; and thirdly in judging how far, and through what actions, and at what risk, we can realistically hope to move this world as it now stands towards the way we might excusably wish it to be.' Nicholas Rengger, *Political Theory, Modernity and Postmodernity: Beyond Enlightenment and Critique* (Oxford: Blackwell, 1995a), p. 14.

[5]   See Nicholas Rengger, *International Relations, Political Theory, and the Problem of Order: Beyond International Relations Theory?* (London; New York: Routledge, 2000a).

[6]   Nicholas Rengger, 'Pluralism in international relations theory: three questions', *International Studies Perspectives* 16, 1 (2015a), pp. 32–9.

by integrating broader insights from the humanities and the domains of intellectual history and social and political theory into the study of IR theory.

An original contributor to the critique of the positivist dominance in IR, displayed in his 1988 discipline-defining critical dialogue with Mark Hoffman in the pages of *Millennium*,[7] he was never a thinker one could pigeonhole or readily pin down. His forays into normative IR and critical theory[8] were always launched from a distinctly sceptical disposition he came to describe as the 'Anti-Pelagian Imagination' against the pretentions of rationalism and abstract analytical reasoning in political theory and IR. At the same time, his strong advocacy for a genuinely pluralist and diverse field of IR that would embrace contributions from different cultural, geographical, and methodological traditions was reflected in his treatment of IR as an interdisciplinary terrain of pluralist conversation and his later interest in comparative political theory.[9] While not by training a postcolonial scholar, he had an intuitive appreciation of the multiple and diverse sites knowledge may originate from and was always eager to engage in conversation with non-Western traditions of philosophical and political thought as part of his overarching humanist orientation.

Importantly, Rengger's pluralism pertained not only to his appreciation of diverse disciplinary approaches and geo-cultural epistemologies, but also to his broad-minded approach to the activity of theorizing. Recently, Felix Berenskoetter has highlighted the necessity, and relative neglect or decline within IR, of 'deep theorizing', a mode of contemplative theorizing that examines the human condition and agency in the various spatiotemporal and normative contexts that shape its ontologies and motivations.[10] Rengger had been an early proponent of that type of theorizing in IR, refusing to relegate theory to either an exclusively explanatory, interpretive, or normative function. For Rengger, IR theory should perform all those functions without prejudice or disciplinary angst. What interested him most was not theory

---

[7] Nicholas Rengger, 'Going critical? A response to Hoffman', *Millennium: Journal of International Studies* 17, 1 (1988a), pp. 81–9; see also Nicholas Rengger and Mark Hoffman, 'Modernity, Postmodernism and International Relations', in Joe Doherty, Elspeth Graham, and Mo Malek (eds), *Postmodernism and the Social Sciences* (Basingstoke: Palgrave McMillan, 1992), pp. 127–47.

[8] Nicholas Rengger, 'Serpents and doves in classical international theory', *Millennium: Journal of International Studies* 17, 2 (1988b), pp. 215–25; Nicholas Rengger and Ben Thirkell-White, 'Still critical after all these years? The past, present and future of Critical Theory in International Relations', *Review of International Studies* 33, S1 (2007), pp. 3–24.

[9] Nicholas Rengger, 'Between transcendence and necessity: Eric Voegelin, Martin Wight and the crisis of modern international relations', *Journal of International Relations and Development* 22, 2 (2019a), pp. 327–45.

[10] Felix Berenskoetter, 'Deep theorizing in International Relations', *European Journal of International Relations* 24, 4 (2018), pp. 814–40.

as a demarcation exercise, agenda-setting device or even merely a cognitive endeavour, but *theorizing* as both an intellectual and an aesthetic activity (although, rather distinctly, not a practical one). The self-understanding of IR theories and their often-parochial claims to exegetic primacy were, in that respect, secondary. What mattered most to Rengger was their ability to open up new vistas of thinking old problems and to sharpen our imagination and creativity in challenging theoretical orthodoxies or scholarly taboos.

Rengger shared with other critically minded contemporary IR theorists not only a pluralist sensibility, but also an interest in the diverse ways theoretical creativity can be practised in IR.[11] His principal way of pursuing theoretical creativity and expanding the borders of the discipline's theoretical and moral imagination involved delving into the history of ideas to resurrect forgotten conceptual resources that challenge the field's theoretical complacencies and divest it of its presentist illusions by re-aligning theoretical production with the richness of diverse intellectual traditions and global histories. Like Socrates, Gadamer, and Oakeshott, he also believed that moral and cognitive progress is achieved in dialogue and that a civil conversation, not so much between cultures but between honest, well-meaning individuals, is possible and needs to be engaged, not only for the knowledge gains one might derive from it, but simply for the fun of it. It is to these two aspects of his theoretical imagination that the rest of the chapter will turn.

Rengger's civil conversations

The theme of a civil 'conversation of mankind' is one that pre-eminently runs through Rengger's corpus, a corpus greatly influenced by the British political philosopher Michael Oakeshott. Oakeshott's influence on Rengger is duly explored in the volume, particularly with regards to Rengger's endorsement of Oakeshott's emphasis on civility, plurality, and individuality in the establishment of a 'conversation of mankind'. Indeed, in his plea for a nomocratic, as opposed to a teleocratic, model of civil association as the most appropriate response to the ills of violence and conflict in the late-modern era,[12] Rengger appealed to Oakeshott's distinction in order

---

[11] For a good overview of how theoretical creativity is practised in IR by a series of contemporary IR theorists, see Christine Sylvester, 'Creativity' in Aoileann Ni Mhurchu and Reiko Shindo (eds), *Critical Imaginations in International Relations* (Abingdon: Routledge, 2016), pp. 56–69.

[12] In his *On Human Conduct* (Oxford: Clarendon Press, 1991 [1975]), Michael Oakeshott famously distinguished between 'nomocratic' and 'teleocratic' regimes. Teleocracies seek to impose an abstract vision of human flourishing (a philosophical goal or *telos*) onto contingent historical circumstances (law and philosophy shape history). Nomocracies, more modestly, rather than attempting to reconstruct their societies, seek to protect the traditional liberties and social norms of their citizens, their nomos (law reflects history).

to disclose a particular image of human beings as well as the resulting joys that could arise from its recognition. The image was one 'of self-employed adventurers of unpredictable fancy' who, with certain rules of civility, could become 'convives capable of answering back in civil tones with whom to spend an eternity in conversation'.[13]

This image of conversation with convives of unpredictable fancy infused both the work and the life of Rengger. It is impossible to convey to the reader who was not fortunate enough to meet him, the unbelievable joy Rengger derived from an intellectual encounter, the erudition and rhetorical flair of his interventions, and the immense impact that he himself exerted on his interlocutors. Indeed, he can safely be counted among those larger-than-life intellectual figures, such as Isiah Berlin, Martin Wight, or Michael Oakeshott indeed, whose measure of influence on their contemporaries cannot solely be based on the volume of the work they left behind; even more so for Rengger since he did not have the time to complete his work nor the temper or the inclination to establish or head schools of thought.

Apart from his published work, Rengger practised his idea of civility by engaging in incessant conversations either in classrooms where he had been a charismatic teacher adored by his students or in conference rooms and pubs debating with his colleagues, usually over more than a few glasses of red wine. In all those social spaces, Rengger argued with conviction but with no fanaticism, engaging in debates just for the pleasure of it without necessarily seeking to convert his interlocutors or force an image of reality on them, just hoping to infuse them with the spirit of conversation, which for Rengger meant an openness to the multi-perspectival nature of 'civil' thought serving the plurality and unpredictability of life.

The definition of civility in his work was markedly taken from Oakeshott but carried, both for him as for Oakeshott, Augustinian overtones:

> Civil understandings of politics require ... an Augustinian recognition of the limits of our knowledge and a humility towards our capacity to alter the conditions of our existence – an 'anti-Pelagian' recognition if you will – and that accommodates us to the continuing importance of charity and mercy and the possibilities that exist for us to make spaces for these and related virtues in our world. Teleocratic understandings, however, close off such options and emphasize the common purposes that would of necessity trump the plurality and many-sided 'uncentredness' of a genuinely 'civil' international order.[14]

---

[13] Oakeshott, *On Human Conduct*, p. 324; Rengger, *Just War and International Order*, p. 174.

[14] Rengger, *Just War and International Order*, p. 175.

Rengger thought the search for the civil condition in world politics was best served by what he called a modern 'anti-Pelagian imagination', employed as the title and leitmotif for the collection of essays included in his last published book.[15] The challenge in the late-modern era, as Rengger saw it, was to identify an alternative to both the narratives of progress and tragedy (or of optimism and pessimism) that represent two dominant framing devices for the study and practice of international politics. For Rengger, an alternative could be found in a form of sceptical, anti-perfectionist, non-utopian, pluralist sensibility vis-à-vis the modern dilemmas of political theory and international relations. Such a mode of inhabiting, or comporting to, the world would seek to eschew both an unwarranted overconfidence in human capacity to achieve uninterrupted progress as well as surrendering to tragic pessimism that risks becoming merely the mirror image of what it rejects.[16]

The anti-Pelagian imagination

Rengger employed the idea of an 'anti-Pelagian imagination' as an umbrella term that covers a variety of ethico-political approaches that hold in common a set of sceptical, non-utopian, anti-perfectionist responses to the dilemmas of political theory and international relations. Rengger described it as a 'sensibility', rather than a coherent theoretical framework or position, that allowed him to focus on a diverse array of 'sceptical, anti-perfectionist, non-utopian assumptions that *inform* theoretical reflection on human activities (including politics) without being *reducible* to any particular "theory" (or even a group of "theories")' (emphasis in original). It is a term consciously chosen because he believed it allowed him to transcend the divisions that plague contemporary political thought 'at whatever level, "right"/"left", "conservative"/"radical", "realist"/ "liberal" and so on'.[17] It is also a term that is equally defined by what it stands against, various forms of what Rengger called, with Oakeshott, 'modern Pelagianism'.

The latter, for Rengger, were secularized echoes of an ancient Christian heresy that believed salvation to be possible through one's own unaided efforts rather than through God's grace. Pelagius, the man behind the moniker, was a 4th- to 5th-CE-century British monk who opposed Augustine's doctrine of original sin by defending the capacity of human beings to achieve perfection

---

[15] Rengger, *The Anti-Pelagian Imagination*.
[16] See Nicholas Rengger, 'Tragedy or scepticism? Defending the anti-Pelagian mind in world politics', in Toni Erskine and Richard Ned Lebow (eds), *Tragedy and International Relations* (Basingstoke, UK; New York: Palgrave Macmillan, 2012a), pp. 53–62.
[17] Rengger, *The Anti-Pelagian Imagination*, p. 4.

untainted by a congenital enslavement to sin.[18] To be fair, for Pelagius, the issue at stake was the preservation of the human capacity to respond to God's call for salvation (what in patristic sources is often called *synergy*), rather than some prideful affirmation of human self-assertion – which reflects a rather modern sensibility. Even so, after Pelagius' condemnation and excommunication in 418 CE, Augustine's more sceptical view of human nature progressively became part of a tradition of political thought that reads the human predicament as condemned to 'deal in darkness', in Oakeshott's pithy phrase. In fact, rather than a distant theological debate between Augustine and Pelagius, the main source of Rengger's anti-Pelagianism seems to be Oakeshott's reading of modern political thought as in risk of falling victim to two equally undesirable tendencies: Pelagianism and antinomianism:[19]

> Pelagianism because we are misled into thinking that we can will the human condition to completion, but we cannot; anti-nomianism because we are easily misled into thinking that there must be a 'true' or 'correct' political order, accessible to our understanding, which is distorted or suppressed by the actually prevailing order.[20]

The reason, then, Rengger resorted to a rather antiquated theological term, for some plagued by pretentious obscurity (see Brown in this volume), was not his adherence to some form of historical essentialism. Rather, Oakeshott's use of the term to describe 'dispositions' or dominant *trajectories* in modern political thought since the 17th century provided Rengger with the conceptual tools to launch a blanket critique of a range of approaches spanning from ideal theory in contemporary political philosophy to cosmopolitanism, liberal internationalism, and radical progressivism in IPT. Rengger claimed that all those modern anti-Pelagians that he examined in his work, thinkers as diverse as Jean Bethke Elshtain, John Gray, Leo Strauss, and Judith Shklar, seemed to agree more on the Pelagian intuitions they sought to oppose rather than on working out a robust anti-Pelagian position. What is more, Rengger's main argument in his *Anti-Pelagian Imagination* book was that 'modern anti-Pelagianism' is an inherently unstable sensibility, constantly

---

[18] See Vassilios Paipais, 'First image revisited: human nature, original sin and International Relations', *Journal of International Relations and Development* 22, 2 (2019), pp. 364–88.

[19] A doctrine that has religious roots and is usually associated with the rejection of rules. For Oakeshott, however, antinomianism bore a specific meaning targeting those who argue that inherited, traditional rules should be challenged and overturned on the way to a better order.

[20] Michael Oakeshott, *Religion Politics and the Moral Life*, edited by Tim Fuller (New Haven, CT: Yale University Press, 1993), p. 20.

running the danger of tipping over to Pelagian optimism or turning into its negative mirror image, a form of anthropological or metaphysical pessimism that precludes any possibility of social or political amelioration.

Instead, in a manner not dissimilar to Augustine's, Rengger's scepticism resisted both Pelagian optimism and modern forms of Gnosticism, a term that was (re)introduced in modern debates on the crisis of liberal modernity by Hans Jonas and widely, as well as controversially, popularized by Eric Voegelin.[21] Voegelin's polemical use of the term 'Gnosticism' stemmed from a – similar to Oakeshott's – anti-perfectionist impulse. Yet, Voegelin employed it as a diagnostic tool of modernity's nihilistic tendencies, calling out what he termed the 'political religions' of the 20th century (Liberalism, Socialism, Fascism) for wreaking havoc by attempting to 'immanentize the eschaton', that is, bring heaven on earth. By reading modernity as a secularized Gnostic heresy, Voegelin condemned not only totalitarian politics or the modern liberal order, but almost all forms of modern politics which he saw as irredeemably tainted by the utopian Gnostic temptation of projecting intra-mundane salvific doctrines (akin to Oakeshott's teleocracies) as ultimate truths.

Rengger did not use the term 'Gnosticism' as centrally as he employed 'Pelagianism' in his work, nor did he entirely agree with Voegelin's inconsistent use of the term.[22] Rather, Rengger's understanding of the term was closer to Augustine's who associated the Gnostics with the denigration of the world of creation and the identification of material reality with evil. For Rengger, then, it represented a type of teleocratic pessimism, a kind of dogmatic anti-perfectionism as dangerous and misguided as utopianism. Rengger found those Gnostic tendencies more pronounced in some modern anti-Pelagians (for example, John Gray or Morgenthau and the IR realists) who seemed to buy into the tragic vision of the word as an inexorable existential predicament.[23] While he admired the early IR realists, such as

---

[21] Hans Jonas, *The Gnostic Religion: The Message of the Alien God and the Beginnings of Christianity* (London: Routledge, 1992); Eric Voegelin, *The New Science of Politics: An Introduction* (Chicago: University of Chicago Press, 1952). The term 'Gnosticism' emerged in 18th-century France and is usually employed to denote the Gnostic systems of the 2nd and 3rd centuries CE, particularly those of Basilides, Valentinus, and Mani. The term 'Gnosis' is known in Ancient Greek and Latin texts as opposed to the use of the term 'Gnosticism', which seems to be related to 20th-century religious and philosophical polemics rather than its late antiquity referent. See Yotam Hotam, 'Gnosis and modernity: a post-war German intellectual debate on secularisation, religion and "overcoming" the past', *Totalitarian Movements and Political Religions* 8, 3–4 (2007), pp. 591–608. See also Vassilios Paipais, 'Overcoming 'Gnosticism'? Realism as Political Theology', *Cambridge Review of International Affairs* 29, 4 (2016), pp. 1603–23.

[22] See Rengger, 'Between transcendence and necessity'.

[23] Nicholas Rengger, 'Tragedy or scepticism? Defending the anti-Pelagian mind in world politics', *International Relations* 19, 3 (2005a), pp. 321–8.

Morgenthau, Niebuhr, and Herz, as well as political theory realists, such as Raymond Geuss, Bernard Williams, and Glen Newey, for their anti-perfectionist and non-utopian insights, he refused to concede some of the bleaker or more dogmatic implications of their vision. Aspects of the realist sensibility seemed to conflate a statement about how human beings relate to the world with how the world is. Rengger's scepticism would have none of that realist pessimism; both Pelagianism and Gnosticism in this respect were two equally teleocratic positions (although driven by polar-opposite teleocracies) towards which modern anti-Pelagians seemed to gravitate.

This ambivalence at the heart of modern anti-Pelagianism had, for Rengger, philosophical roots. It was grounded in the very nature of modernity. Indeed, the study and impact of the debates around the nature and character of modernity was a central part of Rengger's investigations since his doctoral dissertation.[24] Subsequently, his first two monographs touched on aspects of what he termed the 'hybridity of modernity' or 'the hybrid character of our moral world'.[25] Rengger thought that one should approach modernity both as a mood and as a socio-cultural form. The two dimensions do not always, or necessarily, conflate or overlap but must be thought together. Rengger believed that the failure of modern Pelagians – namely Enlightenment rationalists or even critical theorists and postmodern critics of modernity – to escape what Adorno and Horkheimer called 'the dialectics of Enlightenment', had to do with their inability to disentangle the idea of modernity as a mood from the one as a socio-cultural form and the narrow definition of the modern ethos they often adopted.[26]

---

[24] Nicholas Rengger, *Reason, Scepticism and Politics: Theory and Practice in the Enlightenment's Politics*, PhD diss., Department of Politics, University of Durham, 1987.

[25] Rengger, *Political Theory, Modernity and Postmodernity*; Nicholas Rengger, *Retreat from the Modern: Humanism, Postmodernism and the Flight from Modernist Culture* (London: Bowerdean Publishing Company, 1996a); Nicholas Rengger, 'On theology and International Relations: world politics beyond the empty sky', *International Relations* 27, 2 (2013), pp. 141–57.

[26] An example of this incongruence is that while modernity as a socio-cultural form, chiefly reflected in the creation of independent sovereign states as expressions of distinct national wills, was arguably superseded by forms of socio-political organization that serve more transnational economic and social needs, the dominant form of modernity as a mood, namely the rise of scientific and philosophical rationalism with Galileo and Descartes in the 17th century culminating in the dominance of instrumental rationality in late modernity, is still the engine behind the supranational functionalist forms of social and political organization that for some have signalled the end of modernity as a socio-cultural form (that is, the nation-state). At the same time, modernity itself can be viewed as encompassing a far broader vision of rationality. Toulmin, for example, whom Rengger cites approvingly, would argue that so-called postmodern thinkers, such as Heidegger, Wittgenstein, and Rorty, have a lot more in common with the 16th-century Renaissance humanists than often acknowledged and that rather than seen as anti- or postmodern, they should rather be read as reviving a path to modernity not taken. See

Rengger argued that modernity as a mood, at least since the 17th century, is characterized by a constitutive rift between nature and convention coupled with a resignification of what 'nature' stands for in scientific, social, and political discourse. This new reality was expressed in the 17th-century revolutions spearheaded in physics by Galileo, Kepler, and Newton, in philosophy by Descartes, Locke, and Leibniz, and in moral philosophy (political and social theory) by Hobbes. Inspired by John Milbank's theological critique of modernity,[27] Rengger would describe this predicament in his later work as modernity's 'hybrid', blending ambiguously a morally realist universalism and a voluntarist nominalism.[28] It is worth quoting him at length here as this is a central plank in his thought:

> international relations in the modern world – and indeed a good deal of politics in general – is effectively a hybrid between a system built on will and artifice yoked together with a rhetoric that effectively assumes the older 'realist' transcendent conception of reality. One can see this in many respects throughout the seventeenth and eighteenth centuries, where the likes of Grotius and Vattel (Kant's 'sorry comforters') consistently try and emphasise the voluntaristic character of human agency with a sense of transcendent truth. And the whole history of the idea of Natural Law from the thirteenth century to the present is clearly marked by this dilemma. Hobbes is in this, as in many other things, the most far-sighted and the most consistent of his contemporaries in refusing the hybrid and saying point blank that (for example) the 'Mortall God', the Leviathan, creates what is good and what is just, rather than as the – now intellectually hollowed out – tradition of Natural Law would suggest discovers what is good and what is just … Can one coherently have a fully and only constructed and artificial sense of agency and society and a belief that anything is universal?[29]

Rengger, *Political Theory, Modernity and Postmodernity*, pp. 48–52, and Stephen Toulmin, *Cosmopolis: The Hidden Agenda of Modernity* (Chicago: University of Chicago Press, 1992).

[27] John Milbank, *Theology and Social Theory: Beyond Secular Reason*, 2nd edition. (Oxford: Blackwell, 2006).

[28] 'A realist ghost in a nominalist machine', as Rengger put it, largely siding with insights offered by Michael Gillespie and Charles Taylor. Here, Rengger refers to metaphysical, not IR, realism. Metaphysical realism is the doctrine, with origins in medieval debates, that universals, such as humanity, justice, or 'redness' (the property of being red) are ontologically real entities in which particular objects participate. The opposite doctrine is nominalism arguing that universals are but mental names (*nomina*) that do not pre-exist but only follow after (*post-res*) the existence of particular entities which are the only ones considered real. See Michael A. Gillespie, *The Theological Origins of Modernity* (Chicago and London: University of Chicago Press, 2008) and Charles Taylor, *A Secular Age* (Cambridge, MA: Belknap Press of Harvard University Press, 2007).

[29] Rengger, 'On theology and international relations', p. 144.

For Rengger, then, the 'hybrid' gives rise to irresolvable tensions in modern thought between politics and morality, law and justice, faith and reason. In IPT, this is translated as the tension between universalism and particularism, or in English school terms, a more solidarist commitment to human rights vs a pluralist allegiance to the idea of unconditional sovereignty.

To Rengger's mind, however, both particularistic and universalistic tendencies are grounded on teleocratic visions of international order, both promoting 'common purposes' of different kinds and so ending up being two sides of the same coin. The civil vision Rengger would favour becomes almost a drowned-out possibility with a slim chance of actualization (see also Williams in this volume). Nevertheless, Rengger emphatically insists that, despite the current dominant teleocratic tendencies in world politics, expressed either through realist pessimism, nationalist ideologies, or liberal internationalism, these remain a 'choice, not a destiny',[30] and that re-imagining the principles upon which world order is constructed to make room for civility and individuality should be the moral task of international thought. Ultimately, for Rengger, the different vision of the world the anti-Pelagian imagination offers, is a moral one. The basic features of the world remain unchanged but are now 'viewed from the perspective of a different scale of values.'[31]

Scepticism, civility, and world order

One central issue that the majority of the chapters in this volume raise in different ways is that on closer inspection Rengger's work is marked by a potential tension between his early emphasis on judgement and the possibility of practically oriented reason having an influence on the world of praxis (action), and his later Oakeshottian position that the realms of theory and practice should be kept separate and that every effort to conflate the two would only result in fuelling teleocratic tendencies in world politics. The first position is evident in his doctoral dissertation and his books up to *International Relations, Political Theory and the Problem of Order*. His explorations in these works were driven by his concern with the 'tasks of political theory' and how the latter can help us not only reflect on the world and its problems, but also instruct us as to the best ways of living well together in this world. This was a central concern of ancient and medieval political thought that Rengger shared in his early work. In those early articulations, civility meant for him a comportment or ethos

---

[30] Rengger, *Just War and International Order*, p. 158.
[31] Rengger, *The Anti-Pelagian Imagination*, p. 168.

that appeared a lot more affective and embodied fusing practical reason and rules of conduct that are experienced not as abstract commands but as historically embedded habits.[32] Indeed, as part of his regard for virtue ethics and pre-modern political thought, Rengger was equally open-minded to aspects of Alasdair McIntyre's traditionalist critique of modernity and John Milbank's post-liberal effort to reconcile faith and reason or, negatively, to divest us of our illusion that modern reason may occupy a place of neutrality or ground some version of common morality.[33]

Intellectual appreciation aside, however, late Rengger was arguably reticent to abandon his increasingly overshadowing Oakeshottian scepticism for a post-liberal or a neotraditionalist alternative.[34] He would, nevertheless, insist that he carried his scepticism lightly as part of an Oakeshottian pluralist disposition whereby discourses such as art and religion belong to the poetic mode of experience (or 'voice' of civilization) while philosophy's task is to examine the presuppositions underlying those aspects of practical (or poetic, as a later addition to the Oakeshottian modes of experience) activity that can be religious, aesthetic, or political.[35] To quote from Oakeshott's *On Human Conduct*, philosophy proper is an inquiry 'in which questions are asked not in order to be answered but so that they may themselves be interrogated with respect to their conditions'.[36] This sharp Oakeshottian distinction between the products of the intellect (poetry or philosophy) and the world of action (politics) is a theme that pervades Rengger's later work, and especially the essays included in the *Anti-Pelagian Imagination*.

To further clarify that peculiar Renggerian distinction that seems to be the object of criticism for a number of chapters in this volume, one has to appreciate the reasons behind his reluctance to mix poetry, philosophy, and politics. With Oakeshott, Rengger argued that there was a language for history, one for science, one for art, and another for politics; they each captured part of experience, but no single one captured all of it and, therefore, no single one should dominate the conversation. Furthermore, Rengger defended the Oakeshottian sensibility of the 'religious man', in contradistinction to the 'worldly man', as a type of anti-rationalistic,

---

[32] Rengger, *Political Theory, Modernity and Postmodernity*, pp. 153–62.

[33] Alasdair McIntyre, *After Virtue: A Study in Moral Theory* (London: Duckworth, 1981) and Milbank, *Theology and Social Theory*.

[34] See Nicholas Rengger, 'Post-secular global order: metaphysical not political?' in Luca Mavelli and Fabio Petito (eds), *Towards a Post-secular International Politics: New Forms of Community, Identity, and Power* (London: Palgrave, 2014), pp. 65–80.

[35] Nicholas Rengger, 'The boundaries of conversation: a reply to Dallmayr', *Millennium: Journal of International Studies* 30, 2 (2001), pp. 357–64 and Michael Oakeshott, *Experience and Its Modes* (Cambridge: Cambridge University Press, 2015 [1933]).

[36] Oakeshott, *On Human Conduct*, p. 11.

pluralistic Self that 'sees all things in the light of his own mind, and desires to possess nothing save by present insight'.[37] The religious man is the lover of the life of the present open to a poetic understanding of existence that learns how to favour the standards of the Self over the standards of the World, not vice versa.

That is, however, emphatically not the task of theory or philosophy. Rather, the latter remains compartmentalized as an activity of thought. Surely, an activity of thought that does not impose itself on – or seek to capture – life, yet also one that does not necessarily (perhaps only contingently so) connect with it, either. In Rengger's own words:

> [theory has no] necessary connection with what goes *in* [the] world. The task of theory one might say – if, indeed it can be seen as a 'task' at all – is simply to *be* theoretical; to follow the argument wherever it goes and to be as honest as one can be about one's assumptions, presuppositions and conclusions. [emphasis in original][38]

A limitation that perhaps Rengger's thought here shares with George Santayana's,[39] whom Rengger admired, is that both would regard thinking, whether in science, art, or politics, as an activity of the spirit (*psyche*) to be kept apart from the effects upon it of social influences they would both regard as 'contagion'. This is understandable as a critique of social conformism (or of teleocracies of the conservative or the progressive kind), but it leaves the relationship between thinking and 'society' or 'culture' unspecified. If life is not thought, what is this peculiar activity called 'thought' that is separate from life? Or, otherwise put, can theory and practice, mind and life, be so securely sequestered?

This is a distinctly modern or, rather, an early modern (humanist) disposition that accords primacy to the critical function of thought as the relentless interrogation of the grounds of knowledge and the presuppositions of life. Indeed, one that views epistemological scepticism as the engine behind the development of modern philosophy, from Machiavelli and Montaigne through Descartes and Hobbes to Kant and Nietzsche (either as something to be contained for reasons of social utility or something to be accorded free rein). Rengger entertained a special fondness for the 16th-century Renaissance humanists (Erasmus, Rabelais, Montaigne, Bacon), and

---

[37] Oakeshott, *Religion, Politics and the Moral Life*, p. 38.

[38] Rengger, *The Anti-Pelagian Imagination*, p. 16.

[39] See his approval of Santayana's claim that 'scepticism is the chastity of the intellect' and his argument for a 'sceptical, anti-perfectionist political philosophy' in his 'Dystopic liberalism' essay in Rengger, *The Anti-Pelagian Imagination*, p. 77.

their Pyrrhonian scepticism, singling out especially Montaigne, a devout Catholic whose scepticism did not clash with his faith.[40] While he never offered a systematic account of the sources of his scepticism, Rengger's work is replete with approving references to the early modern humanists whom he saw as the ideal epistemological subjects combining religious faith with intellectual honesty and employing an understanding of reason and rationality that was yet untainted by Cartesian rationalism and the 'theory-centred' style of philosophy that became the touchstone of modern philosophy post-1650s.[41]

Rengger's own scepticism then was grounded on his critical reading of the conditions that enabled the break with a pre-rationalist modern ethos in the early 1600s. His guide to the intellectual and social changes that led to the decline of more contextual forms of moral reasoning was the work of Stephen Toulmin and Albert Jonsen on medieval and early modern casuistry.[42] According to Toulmin and Jonsen, but also to a host of modern neo-Aristotelians, pre-eminently among whom Alasdair McIntyre and Martha Nussbaum, the Aristotelian emphasis on *phronesis* or practical wisdom prioritizing contextualized, practically minded reason was abandoned in favour of more abstract, context-independent, universal forms of reasoning.[43] Rengger thought that many of the problems associated with contemporary political and IR theory were directed related to the uncontested dominance of such forms of instrumental, abstract theorizing that neglected a more practically oriented style of theorizing with its concomitant emphasis on habits of thought and practice, concrete thinking, practical judgement, and rhetorical persuasion.[44]

Along with the humanist pre-rationalist ethos, Rengger appreciated what Quentin Skinner has called the 'subordinate ideology' in the history of political thought, the kind of civic republicanism, and the concomitant

---

[40] Like Oakeshott and Montaigne, Rengger liked to think we need both scepticism and some measure of faith. In his non-dogmatic, almost ironic, religious traditionalism he could be described as an 'aesthetic Anglican', paraphrasing one of his favourite thinkers, George Santayana, who used to describe himself as an 'aesthetic Catholic'. Rengger would often repeat to me Santayana's witticism: 'there is no God and Mary is His mother'.

[41] Toulmin, *Cosmopolis*, p. 11.

[42] Albert R. Jonsen and Stephen Toulmin, *The Abuse of Casuistry: A History of Moral Reasoning* (Berkeley: University of California Press, 1988).

[43] McIntyre, *After Virtue*; Martha Nussbaum, *The Fragility of Goodness: Luck and Ethics in Greek Tragedy and Philosophy* (Cambridge, Cambridge University Press, 2001 [1986]).

[44] Rengger, *Political Theory, Modernity and Postmodernity*; Nicholas Rengger, 'Practical judgement: inconsistent – or incoherent?' in Mathias Albert and Anthony F. Lang Jr (eds), *The Politics of International Political Theory: Reflections on the Works of Chris Brown* (Basingstoke: Palgrave, 2019b), pp. 55–68; Rengger, *International Relations, Political Theory, and the Problem of Order*, p. 199.

spirit of religious tolerance, that preceded the consolidation of the absolutist state in Europe after the religious wars.[45] His nomocratic vision of world order was not anti-statist *per se* but lamented the unchallenged dominance of state sovereignty as the constitutive principle of international organization over the last two hundred years.[46] Rengger thought that the teleocracy of the nation state, no less than that of its utopian critics, impoverished our ethical horizons and bred disaster, moral hypocrisy, and barbarism.

Unsurprisingly, then, given his avowed preference for a pluralist conception of world order, Rengger was attracted to neomedieval ideas of world ordering.[47] Like Martin Wight's theological critique of modern culture, Rengger's questioning of the sovereign state system and the liberal world order's totemic status had theological underpinnings. His chosen entry point here was the work of John Milbank and Stephen R.L. Clark, both of whom offered a post-secular vision of world order based on a revival of Christian Platonism (or the medieval Aristotelian-Platonic synthesis) that authorizes a strong metaphysical realism, quite an unpopular outlook in the modern secularized, post-metaphysical academy.[48] Rengger had no reservations engaging with the work of two unconventional thinkers, outside IR proper, that seemed to contest the traditional manner in which international order has been routinely conceptualized in political theory and international relations through the idolizations either of absolute state sovereignty, of individual rights, or of the forces of capitalist rationality. They both envisage not only a post-sovereign conception of world order but a post-liberal one too, mixing a strong emphasis on the classical idea of common good with institutional proposals favouring a highly diffuse, functionally differentiated social and political order populated by local, regional, and corporate (in the pre-capitalist sense) bodies where the

---

[45] Quentin Skinner, *The Foundations of Modern Political Thought: Volume 2, The Age of Reformation* (Cambridge: Cambridge University Press, 1978).

[46] Nicholas Rengger, 'European communities in a neo-medieval global polity: the dilemmas of fairyland?' in Morten Kelstrup, Michael C. Williams (eds), *International Relations Theory and the Politics of European Integration* (London: Routledge, 2001b), pp. 57–71, which also explains Rengger's reservations against the English School of International Relations regarding the School's statist orientation. For Rengger (cf Hall in this volume), that made the international society tradition 'ethically profoundly confused at best and dangerous and harmful at worst'.

[47] For Rengger's distinction between world order and the 'ordering of ends' which expresses a more pluralist, multi-layered conception of world ordering, see Rengger, *International Relations, Political Theory, and the Problem of Order.*

[48] Rengger, 'Post-secular global order: metaphysical not political?'

continuously revisable structures of power and authority are grounded on non-coercive, virtuous hierarchies.[49]

Rengger viewed those experiments in reimagining the contours of our contemporary world order favourably. He also thought that actual examples of a possible return of neomedieval international organization, such as regional supranational bodies, like the EU, or post-sovereign international institutions, had already been raising interesting questions about trust, legitimacy, and authority that could bring some of the contradictions of teleocratic world ordering to the fore.[50] But one could never be sure whether he endorsed those developments unreservedly, how a nomocratic neomedievalism would look like, or whether his discussion was simply part of his fascination with the world of the intellect, part of a civil 'conversation of mankind' with no immediate or necessary connection to the world of action. Yet, if the nomocratic model of civility seems to have little purchase in the world we live in and if every attempt to bring it into existence risks resurrecting the phantoms of teleocracy, one wonders how one can escape this aporia. Different aspects of this question as well as different discussions of its implications can be found in the chapters by Valk, Schick, Brown, Kennedy-Pipe, and Williams.

An illustration of this aporia can also be traced in another of his lasting contributions to IPT, his critical engagement with the just war tradition. Rengger was among those critics of the ongoing revamping of the just war tradition over the last 50 years and, especially, of the direction contemporary just war theory has taken after 9/11.[51] He believed that the

---

[49] John Milbank, *Beyond Secular Order: The Representation of Being and the Representation of the People* (Chichester: Wiley Blackwell, 2013); Stephen Clark, *Civil Peace and Sacred Order*, (Oxford: Clarendon Press, 1989); John Milbank and Adrian Pabst, *The Politics of Virtue: Post-Liberalism and the Human Future* (London; New York: Rowman and Littlefield, 2016).

[50] Nicholas Rengger, 'The ethics of trust in world politics', *International Affairs* 73, 3 (1997), pp. 469–87; Rengger, 'European communities in a neo-medieval global polity'. Rengger's nomocratic vision shares affinities with the neomedieval political theory of Otto von Gierke and the English school of legal pluralism. Gierke's 'theory of association', popularized in the Anglophone world by the historian J. Neville Figgis, appealed to the medieval legal tradition according to which the state was merely a 'corporation of corporations': the state (*civitas*) was itself composed of many associations (*universitates*). According to this view, the state has no business in dictating the good form of life to society; its role is merely to assure that individuals and groups pursue their interests and values in a rightful way. See Otto von Gierke, *Community in Historical Perspective*, edited by Antony Black (Cambridge, UK: Cambridge University Press, 2002).

[51] Although Rengger routinely denied that 9/11 constituted such a break with previous eras so as to justify a more permissive attitude towards the use of force (in general, his realist/sceptical sensibility had a hard time accepting dramatic claims of uniqueness about specific historical eras), it may have signalled a break in his own work which arguably took a more pessimistic turn after his disillusionment with the progressive liberal humanitarianism of

recasting of a tradition of ethical reasoning that used to be about restraining violence – primarily intelligible within a late medieval framework, struggling to accommodate even the requirements of 'responsible statecraft' – into a rationalist, juridical apparatus that justifies a more permissive attitude to the use of force, constituted a perversion of that tradition.[52] And yet, even though he never refused that in some cases the use of force can be justified and should be considered, Rengger would not always be clear on how to balance a qualified defence of the just war tradition, as practised in an inescapably teleocratic world, with a more civil or nomocratic reading of the tradition that rejects 'permissive' renditions of just war thinking in favour of accounts that bring it closer to what amounts to a 'realist pacifism'.[53]

The enigma of Nicholas Rengger[54]

Rengger's ambiguity, or perhaps playfulness, is not circumstantial nor, I would argue, an accidental feature of his *oeuvre*. As many of his readers would attest, the experience of reading Rengger can often be frustrating. Despite being a superb writer with a remarkable ability to make difficult ideas crystal clear to the reader, his argumentative style was often evasive and elusive, promising clarifications or future elaborations that were never delivered, leaving loose ends and offering accounts of his position that appeared tantalizingly vague or equivocal. He himself would characteristically address those complaints

---

the 1990s. I owe this point to Ian Hall. See Rengger, *Just War and International Order*, pp. 6, 17–18.

[52] Nicholas Rengger, 'On the Just War tradition in the twenty-first century', *International Affairs* 78, 2 (2002), pp. 353–63; Nicholas Rengger, 'The judgment of war: on the idea of legitimate force in world politics', *Review of International Studies* 31 (2005b), pp. 143–61.

[53] Nicholas Rengger, 'The greatest treason? On the subtle temptations of preventive war', *International Affairs* 84, 5 (2008), pp. 949–61 (955); for the idea of a 'realist pacifism', see Jeremy Moses, 'Peace without perfection: the intersections of realist and pacifist thought', *Cooperation and Conflict* 53, 1 (2018), pp. 42–60.

[54] The section title is adapted from Michael Nicholson's homonymous title referring to Martin Wight, a figure with whom, and here I concur with Ian Hall, Rengger shared considerable affinities of outlook, temper, and argument. See Michael Nicholson, 'The enigma of Martin Wight', *Review of International Studies* 7, 1 (1981), pp. 15–22. Rengger also shared with Wight, as well as with another major figure of the British Committee on the Theory of International Politics, Herbert Butterfield, the tendency to be a contrarian as his acrimonious confrontations with Onora O'Neill and Jean Bethke Elshtain could attest. See Nicholas Rengger, 'Just a war against terror? Jean Bethke Elshtain's burden and American power', *International Affairs* 80, 1 (2004), pp. 107–16 and Rengger, *The Anti-Pelagian Imagination*, pp. 54–8. A friendlier take would be that Rengger saw himself as a Socratic gadfly, after the Greek philosopher he admired and whose dialogic ethos and practice he tried to emulate – inimitable as he was in everything else – in his scholarship and teaching.

by promising future works where all these ambiguities would be ironed out and due clarifications would be offered. Alas, he was not able to deliver on his promise; but I think there was something deeper going on in his reluctance to make his argument conventionally rigorous and unequivocal. Rengger did not believe in fixed positions or iron-clad arguments nor that conversations should have a predetermined *telos*. Above all, he was reticent to adopt an argument that would bring the discussion to a premature close.

In her chapter, Kennedy-Pipe mentions an occasion in which Rengger had applauded the arguments of two debating academics, making a case for and against the then prospective Iraq war 'with equal gusto explaining later that both had made compelling cases'. I believe this is a good illustration of the enigma of Nicholas Rengger. One could read this incident as an example of his inconsistencies or unresolved contradictions, or perhaps even of epistemological *epoché* (a refusal to let reason pronounce authoritatively on practice). It would serve us better, however, I think, if we appreciated it as a performative, practical manifestation of what he meant by the need to promote civility in world politics, namely value toleration, generosity of spirit and forbearance over ideological fanaticism, the force of persuasion over the persuasion of force, reasonable disagreement over violent confrontation, and the delight of conversation – often for the sake of it – over the shallowness of dogmatism.[55] In a world riven by religious frenzy and populist anger, ideological polarization and new forms of dogmatic intolerance, economic stagnation, ecological degradation, delusions of sovereignty, fantasies of national superiority, and popular endorsement of infantile or farcical politics, civility has indeed become a rare virtue and is likely to remain so. But if we do not want to make this situation our destiny, we may have to engage in Rengger's play, heeding the wisdom of the past but allowing it no absolute control on imagining the future.

Outline of the chapters

In their chapter, Dingli and O'Sullivan question the coherence of Rengger's anti-Pelagianism. While they are sympathetic to his search for an alternative to both Pelagian optimism and tragic pessimism, they raise doubts about the origins of Rengger's non-realist anti-Pelagianism in Oakeshottian idealism. Their principal objection is that Rengger's attempt to provide

---

[55] This pluralist spirit of conversation explains Rengger's positive disposition towards agonistic democratic theorists like William Connolly, Chantal Mouffe, and James Tully. As Dingli and O'Sullivan argue in this volume, a closer engagement with that strand of pluralism might have benefitted Rengger's argument on civility. I think Rengger would have found much of their pluralism sympathetic, but he would have probably remained unconvinced by the Pelagian tendencies in their thought.

his anti-Pelagian vision with a philosophical justification that rests on the Oakeshottian modal differentiation between theory and practice risks reproducing a purist otherworldly Pelagianism. For Dingli and O'Sullivan, Oakeshott's model of conversation may resist facile appropriation in the service of cosmopolitan purposes, but it rests on an aesthetic sensibility that is divorced from the world of practice and so is hardly amenable to serve as a ground for an anti-Pelagian ethos in politics. Alternatively, and in contrast to Oakeshott's more apolitical leanings, they propose what they term 'a more viable anti-Pelagian position' that places prudence, legitimacy, and a preoccupation with the political at the centre of anti-utopian, anti-perfectionist thought. In so doing, they demonstrate how Rengger's thought intersects fruitfully with agonistic perspectives that his Oakeshottian allegiances prevented him from pursuing.

A sense of dissatisfaction with Rengger's Oakeshottian scepticism is the driving sentiment behind John-Harmen Valk's chapter, too. Valk turns his attention to an arguably blind spot in Rengger's *oeuvre*, the lack of systematic treatment of the work of Max Weber, despite the fact that Weber could be counted among the 20th century's most prominent anti-Pelagians. Weber's disenchantment thesis and dissection of rationalist modernity resonates with Rengger's Oakeshottian critique of rationalism in politics, a sentiment he also shared with IR realists, such as Hans Morgenthau. Valk notes that Rengger and Weber overlap in their diagnosis of modern rationalism as the main culprit behind the decline of the spirit of brotherliness in modern social and political relations. Virtues such as humility, mercy, and charity became almost anti-political, wedded to private, personal relations between human beings and expelled from the realm of politics governed in late modernity by universal norms and codes, bureaucratic depersonalized processes, and standardized procedures. Valk praises Rengger's aesthetic sensibility, or what the latter calls, with the Oakeshott, the poetic voice of civilization, but he also flags up an abiding contradiction between Rengger's emphasis on practical judgement and his insistence on separating theory from practice. If poetry and politics can't mix, then the political significance of an ethics of brotherliness, which rest on a desire to live well together, is strangely declared irrelevant to politics. This is a step that even Weber does not take, insisting rather that an ethics of responsibility in politics does not preclude an ethics of ultimate ends, only that the former serves as a check on the latter. Through a Ricoerian reading of Weberian ethics, Valk shows how Weber's ethics of responsibility presuppose the dignity of mature persons, Weber's *virtuosi* of religion, who exemplify an ethics of brotherliness in personal relations. For Valk, the lives of exemplary figures embody the poetic and the practical in a manner that brings the imagination and religiously mediated desires to bear on the world of action. The ethics of responsibility is then not merely the expression of a heroic will, practised in a void, but a poetically disclosed *ethos* that predisposes action in particular directions. For Valk the possibility of such a synthesis is more evident in the early Rengger who was more concerned with how rhetoric, habit, and the aesthetic imagination can strengthen the capacity for practical judgement, rather than the late Rengger of anti-Pelagian scepticism that seemed to fall back on the Oakeshottian modal distinction between aesthetics and politics.

The arguably aporetic structure of Rengger's anti-Pelagian scepticism is at the centre of Kate Schick's friendly fire. In principle, Schick is inspired by Rengger's anti-Pelagianism for refusing to settle with the 'logic of the world'. For the Oakeshottian Rengger, knowledge has no direct relation to action, and therefore moral and political theory should rather be understood as 'world-disclosing' as opposed to 'action-coordinating'. Schick agrees with Rengger' scepticism against those progressives who employ theory as a guide to action to ameliorate the world's ills or those realists who are too quick to embrace the dominant standards of the status quo. Yet, she finds Rengger's compartmentalization of theory from practice too divorced from the world of praxis. For her, it is the work of Gillian Rose that is closer to expressing a more consistent anti-Pelagian sensibility without the risk of appearing too removed from the present world as it is. That world, for Rose's radical Hegelianism, is the realm of deep relationality and vulnerability where human beings live out their fragmented, compromised, divided political lives rooted in intertwined histories and structures. For Rose, engagement with such a world should indeed resist being captured by the false logics of this world, but not from a position of cheerful detachment from the risks and aporias associated with the challenges of ethical and political life. For Schick, Rose's embrace of the aporetic structure of our ethical entanglements requires a commitment to risk-taking and an openness to the possibility of failure or of an only 'good enough justice' in our 'dealing with darkness' in this world. Ultimately, Schick may be convinced of the necessity of an anti-Pelagian ethos in politics but questions the capacity of Rengger's Oakeshottian scepticism to be as world-disclosive as it claims to be.

In his chapter, Ian Hall interrogates Rengger's affinities with the English School (ES) of IR. As Hall notes, Rengger had mixed feelings about the ES despite sharing some of its philosophical commitments. On the one hand, he found the international society tradition 'ethically profoundly confused at best and dangerous and harmful at worst'. He also believed that those who tried to take the School to a more progressive direction, like the ES solidarists, were overstating their case as the early ES theorists like Manning, Wight, and Bull were more conservative, intellectually and ideologically. On the other hand, he sided with the School's avowed preference for a historicist and normative mode of analysis, termed the 'classical approach', as opposed to the more science-based methodologies that were dominating mainstream IR at the time. That said, Rengger did not think that the School's main unit of analysis, the international society with its emphasis on a society of states, was a particularly coherent or helpful starting point. Privileging the state in an environment where the distinction between the domestic and the international was increasingly making less sense was diminishing the School's analytical value. The Rengger project, as Hall calls it, expounded a political theory always informed by the contextual, historical, and cultural circumstances that determine our engagement with the world, but not restricted by the boundaries of the state. Such an orientation increasingly led Rengger to a preoccupation with the question of international order, a long-standing theme of his work. It is here that Hall locates affinities between Rengger's contextualism and the early ES, especially Wight's, interpretivism. Other than a common project, Rengger and the early ES seem to share 'a point of view' that is historical with the same 'pervading moral concern'. Hall shows how the late anti-Pelagian Rengger reconnected with some of the themes of the early ES thinkers, like Wight and Butterfield, even endorsing elements of their apocalyptic tone in their shared anti-perfectionism. Not unlike Brown and Kennedy-Pipe in this volume, Hall describes a moodier late Rengger who seemed more settled in his anti-progressivism. Yet, unlike Wight and Butterfield, Rengger, while using theological language, chose not to ground his pessimism on a profession of faith, thus making his anti-Pelagianism perhaps less convincing.

The late anti-Pelagian Rengger is the target of Chris Brown's chapter as well. Brown detects a shift in Rengger's pluralist sensibility, from a more Rortyan/Oakeshottian scepticism that makes no commitment to a single vision of the world and leaves the possibility of reformist action open, to a darker, blanket condemnation of progressivism that smacks of dogmatism. For Brown, early Rengger was motivated by Rortyan anti-foundationalism and Oakeshottian pluralism viewing the role of international theory as that of a conduit channelling an edifying conversation between convives rather than a vehicle for the production of systematic and scientific, namely objective, knowledge about the international. But whereas early Renggerian scepticism did not dismiss the possibility of international reform, the Rengger of anti-Pelagian pessimism and of the war against teleocracy seems, for Brown, to fall victim to the very foundationalism he previously denounced. Brown's critique is, by his own admission, particularly harsh here, accusing Rengger of a 'sleight of hand' for his use of an obscure theological metaphor (Pelagianism) as a vehicle for the outright rejection of all attempts at international reform. Brown thinks that such a pessimism is unjustified and unfair to most reformers that tend to be motivated by no faith in human perfectibility but only by a pragmatic belief in piecemeal social change. Brown offers as evidence of the relative success of that ameliorative pragmatism, the relative decline over time, even if fragile, of mass violence associated with war and civil conflict, accompanied by a decline in other forms of global social and economic injustice such as poverty, malnutrition, racism, and homophobia. The final example he offers of Rengger's alleged slip into dogmatic pessimism is what he views as the latter's one-sided reading of the just war tradition as a tradition of restraint. Brown claims that the just war tradition is a lot more ambiguous on the question of the use of force and that Rengger's reluctance to remain receptive to that ambiguity closed down avenues of conversation contrary to the true spirit of Renggerian pluralism.

Michael C. Williams' chapter traces Rengger's relevance for the study of a current event that seems to have escaped the attention of contemporary IR theorists, the rise of the global reactionary Right. Williams argues that Rengger was uniquely equipped to help us understand this event exactly because of his familiarity with the kind of political theory that 'deals in darkness'. Williams discusses some of Rengger's work on anti-Pelagian thinkers, like John Gray, Judith Shklar, and Bernard Williams, to understand the complex, paradoxical mixture of anti-liberal ethno-culturalism and technological elitism that characterizes the new anti-globalization Right in America and Europe today. One could hardly argue that any of the anti-Pelagians that Rengger examines in his work could share the New Right's vision, but the critique of capitalism and the globalization of market values is part of what Rengger would recognize as traditional conservative concerns.[56] Similarly, Rengger's critique of the culture of human rights and the increasing abstraction of global legal regimes captures some of the resentment that marks the New Right's revolt against global liberal managerialism. Important though it may be to note the overlap between the radical conservative and the 'dystopic' liberal critiques of liberal progressivism and utopianism, Rengger's anti-Pelagianism rather serves as a corrective to both excessive liberalism and radical conservatism. Here, however, Williams raises reasonable doubts regarding the capacity of Rengger's 'civil' conservatism to counter the forces of radical conservatism that flout older conservative values. Rengger's call for a return to an aesthetic conservatism of civil conversations in pluralist contexts appears impotent, akin to a swan-song of traditional conservatism, compared to the aggressive discursive and aesthetic strategies of the New Right on social media and its allergy to conversation. Rengger's conservative vision is valuable, concedes Williams, but may prove a 'weak rejoinder' to the New Right 'Jacobins'.

Anthony F. Lang, Jr's chapter focuses on Rengger's treatment of the idea of rules and rule following. He describes Rengger as a reluctant rule follower, meaning that while he entertained a healthy respect for rules and rule-based

---

[56] See Ian Hall and Nicholas Rengger, 'The Right that failed? The ambiguities of conservative thought and the dilemmas of conservative practice in international affairs', *International Affairs* 81, 1 (2005), pp. 69–82.

behaviour, Rengger was a critic of what Judith Shklar called legalism, the blind adherence to the legal frameworks governing international conduct. Lang singles out Rengger's critique of the just war tradition and especially of its state-centric revival in the 20th century into what we now call just war theory. As part of his general attack on teleocratic forms of politics that, in Oakeshottian terms, treat political community as an enterprise association, Rengger would lament the contemporary distortion of just war thinking, twisting a tradition that was about restraining war into an instrument for the justification of the use of force in the service of political ends. And yet, Rengger did not deny that the just war tradition was governed by a set of rules, only that these rules should be grounded exclusively on the positivist international legal order that sustains the primacy of the nation-state and its morality. As Lang points out, the general point Rengger wants to make is not that rules don't apply to politics, but that rule following requires casuistic judgement, especially in the complex world we live in. Rengger, however, reminded us that in ancient and medieval forms of political theory judgement was applied in a shared cultural, political, and ethical framework within which making judgements made sense. The latter is no longer possible in the modern context, a situation which threatens to cripple every effort to apply practical judgement in contemporary affairs. Here, for Lang, Rengger sets the bar unnecessarily too high. Nevertheless, Lang still believes that early Rengger's emphasis on practical judgement can help us navigate novel and complex terrains such as the new rules surrounding cyberwarfare. Indeed, for Lang, Rengger's thought may inspire ways of rethinking rule following as the application of virtue-based contextual judgement in technologically challenging environments where the diversity of intersecting agents and interests revalidates the requirement of civility in world politics.

Rengger's aversion to legalism and the abuse of the just war tradition in the service of ideological goals and power-hungry politicians wins the attention of Caroline Kennedy-Pipe's chapter, too. Her chapter, however, looks not only at Rengger's ambivalence towards the just war tradition but also at his wider treatment of the question of war, and more specifically, the actuality of war. Perhaps with a hint of nostalgia, Rengger agreed with Michael Ignatieff and Christopher Coker that part of what was the problem with modern just war theory had to do with the depersonalization of the conduct of war and the rise of technologies of mechanized killing, like drone warfare, that has removed the heroic element, or the human element of risk-taking, from the battlefield. Rengger may have been abhorred by this development, but Kennedy-Pipe is surprised that someone with such an interest in the human face of war had no time for the brutal business that war is. For Kennedy-Pipe, Rengger exemplified an awkwardness towards discussing the destructiveness of war and the consequence the conduct of war may have on the prospects of peace. In an intriguing argument that has never been made before about

Rengger, she puts forward the claim that Rengger's later critique of the just war tradition may be derived from a latent pacifist sensibility that finds no moral justification for the use of force in a state-centric world. Such an assessment may actually throw some light on Chris Brown's earlier objections to Rengger's refusal to admit any occasion where the use of force may be justified. Perhaps the only practically relevant option left in a world where judgement is compromised by state-captured morality is pacifism. It also lends credit to Ian Hall's observation that Rengger shared more than one may think with Martin Wight who also had an ambivalent relationship with pacifism throughout his life.

In the final chapter, Valerie Morkevičius examines Rengger's take on just war by foregrounding Rengger's insight that the just war tradition is not necessarily about 'just war' nor about devising a 'theory' of it, but about the necessity of applying justice even in extreme contexts, like war, where our common humanity is challenged. Just war thinking, for Rengger, is then nothing but a species of practical morality, an application of judgement in search for contextual justice or, better, for the prevention of injustice. Looking at just war thinking as a moral practice invites us to appreciate the classics of the just war tradition who refused to accord apriori moral primacy to the state and its interests in their judgement on right authority and right intention. Rengger's scepticism, however, did not ascribe any special status to international institutions or 'the international community' either, since to his mind both tended to be expressions of a teleocratically oriented world order promoting 'common purposes' and claiming the authority to use violence in the service of those purposes. As Morkevičius observes, Rengger's fondness for the Augustinian roots of the classical just war tradition also stems from the epistemological humility that lay at its core which combined scepticism for one's own position with openness to the truth of others in a culturally diverse world. Morkevičius looks favourably at Rengger's critique of the progressive secularization, legalization, and liberalization of the just war tradition since the 18th century as well as at Rengger's condemnation of the stretching of the tradition to encompass preventive war or an expansive definition of the legitimate use of force for humanitarian reasons. Rengger's realism, pluralism, and epistemological scepticism are appreciated for recommending a healthy distance both from the truisms of our time and from the tendency to dramatize the uniqueness of the challenges we are facing, always eager, like Esau, to exchange our birthright for a bowl of soup, so to speak.

PART I

Anti-Pelagianism and the Civil Condition in World Politics

2

Revisiting Rengger's Anti-Pelagianism

Noël O'Sullivan and Sophia Dingli[1]

Introduction

According to Nicholas Rengger, the study of modern political theory and international relations (IR) is divided between two conflicting views. He terms the more optimistic 'Pelagian' and the more sceptical 'anti-Pelagian'. It will be suggested that although Rengger succeeds in clarifying the assumptions underlying Pelagianism, he is less successful in identifying a coherent form of non-realist anti-Pelagianism. In this chapter we will examine in particular the version of non-realist anti-Pelagianism he claimed to find in Oakeshott. Since Oakeshott has been accused of an idealist methodology which yields a model of civil association open to the charge of being itself Pelagian, Rengger's reliance on him exposes Rengger's own anti-Pelagian project to the charge of succumbing to the 'faint but bewitching glow of ideal theory'[2] of which he accuses Rawls and other modern idealists and rationalists. Rengger's project, we conclude, might have been more coherent if he had instead linked it to a theory of prudence and the contemporary debate about the political. First, however, we begin with a discussion of Rengger's chosen terminology.

---

[1] A short section of this chapter has been previously published in the following article: Sophia Dingli, 'Conceptualising peace and its preconditions: the anti-Pelagian imagination and the critical turn in peace theory', *Journal of International Political Theory* 17, 3 (2021), pp. 468–87.

[2] Nicholas Rengger, *The Anti-Pelagian Imagination in Political Theory and International Relations: Dealing in Darkness* (London and New York: Routledge, 2017), p. 3.

The Pelagian and anti-Pelagian imagination in political and international theory

During the last two centuries, Rengger observes, 'the chief highways of European political thought have been dominated by traffic following directions marked by words such as progress, science and reason'. During the present century, he continues, 'Alongside such familiar vehicles as liberalism, socialism, Marxism and the like we might now add various forms of critical theory, various forms of environmentalism and perhaps especially cosmopolitanism.' Perhaps the best-known manifestation of the Enlightenment rationalist heritage to which Rengger points in contemporary Anglophone political philosophy is 'ideal theory' represented above all by John Rawls and his followers.[3]

Despite the disasters of the 20th century, Rengger notes, even IR theorizing has succumbed during the past 50 years to the 'bewitching glow' of idealist theorizing, in the form of a 'broadly progressive' orthodoxy 'focused on notions such as rights, law, governance, justice and so on'. According to Rengger IR progressivism is manifested in cosmopolitan approaches which see transnational institutions as vehicles for rebuilding the global order as well as in liberal internationalism and radical approaches. Despite their differences, these approaches, he argues, 'are all concerned to emphasize that, problematic and recalcitrant though the world might be, our fate is up to us to determine'.[4] It is the latter conviction – that our fate is entirely in our own hands – that is the core of what Rengger terms the Pelagian view of political theory and IR.

The 'Pelagian' characterization of such approaches takes its name from the British monk Pelagius who in the 5th century AD denied Augustine's doctrine of original sin which claimed that salvation could only come through the grace of God. Instead, Pelagius held that human beings were intrinsically good and capable of self-perfection.[5] Rengger contends that from the 17th century onwards political thought at large can be seen as a secularized version of the Pelagian heresy, manifested in attempts to 'rationalize' institutions in a way which would solve once and for all perennial political problems such as poverty, inequality, conflict, and war. The three main characteristics of Pelagian political and international theories, according to Rengger, are an understanding of human nature and institutions as perfectible; a teleological conception of the end of politics as a secularized version of salvation – a utopia, that is, which it is within

---

[3] Rengger, *The Anti-Pelagian Imagination*, pp. 1, 3.
[4] Rengger, *The Anti-Pelagian Imagination*, p. 3.
[5] Rengger, *The Anti-Pelagian Imagination*, p. 4.

human power to bring into existence; and a conception of political theory as providing a map with which to achieve it (for a slightly different reading, see Schick in this volume).

What then is Rengger's alternative to Pelagianism? He summarized his position in a dense concluding paragraph of the epilogue to *The Anti-Pelagian Imagination in Political Theory and International Relations* in 2017, in which he wrote that a modern anti-Pelagian:

> will acknowledge, with the realist, the intractability of the practical world, but refuse the realist's accommodation to the logic of that world, and rather seek to understand it from the outside, as it were. Such an individual might also accept, with many who seek to reform the world, that sometimes reform will occur and that sometimes it should be welcomed, but they would also refuse the claim that such reform either would be or should be necessarily permanent, and that somehow the world of human conduct will itself change. And, again, they will stand outside the logic of the world. And that, perhaps, is the point with which we might close. The world of international relations will look very different when viewed through the lens of the anti-Pelagian imagination: not because many of the features of the world will be unfamiliar, but because the logic of how they are understood and what follows from that understanding will be very different. And, at bottom, the difference is a moral one; the sceptical anti-Pelagian imagination offers a world viewed from the perspective of a different scale of values. That is its opportunity – and its challenge.[6]

As Rengger fully acknowledged, this compressed summary of his position was deeply influenced by a number of different contemporary critics of Pelagianism, although he observed that: 'Modern anti-Pelagians agree only about what they oppose, not about what they propose.'[7] Notable among them he included such diverse thinkers as Chris Brown, William Connolly, John Gray, Carl Schmitt, Stephen Toulmin, Leo Strauss, Michael Oakeshott, Judith Shklar, George Santayana, and Jean Bethke Elshtain. Given the diversity and comprehensive nature of their viewpoints, the question naturally arises of how successfully Rengger managed to develop a distinct position of his own. In order to answer this, it is necessary to unpack the different strands of thought in the summary of his position just quoted.

---

[6] Rengger, *The Anti-Pelagian Imagination*, p. 168.
[7] Rengger, *The Anti-Pelagian Imagination*, pp. 4–5.

Sources of Rengger's non-realist anti-Pelagianism

The first strand is Rengger's insistence that his position differs greatly from various well-known versions of realism in being essentially ethical, rather than just a cynical insistence on the ubiquity of power and interest. He also insisted, however, that his ethical claim distinguished him not only from realism but also from the moralism that has characterized modern Western thought about politics since the Enlightenment. Whereas realist reductionism stresses the predominance of power and interests, moralism systematically subordinates politics to morality, with the disastrous result that Western democracies prone to moralism have responded to ideological disagreement by demonizing the opponent, thereby rendering non-belligerent diplomatic compromise impossible.

Rengger was very conscious that his rejection of moralism converged with Carl Schmitt's critique of the anti-political tendency of post-Enlightenment liberal theory and was at pains to distance himself in two crucial respects from the concept of the political which Schmitt opposed to moralism. In the first place, Rengger maintained, Schmitt's reduction of politics to the relation of friend and enemy in *The Concept of the Political* does no more than revive Clausewitz's simplistic definition of politics as war by other means. Schmitt's second error, Rengger observes, is his mistaken assumption that the rejection of liberal moralism entails the rejection of liberalism *in toto*. While Rengger acknowledges the validity of Schmitt's critique of much 19th-and-20th-century liberal thought, he observed that Schmitt was wrong to overlook the fact that liberalism 'is open to very different readings' from Schmitt's own.[8] Indeed, Rengger was particularly attracted to the anti-totalitarian and anti-utopian liberalism of thinkers like Judith Shklar and Bernard Williams. Their liberalism, which was based upon the remembrance of terrible human wrongs, did not evade the political nor fall back to simplistic thinking and illiberal practices. As Rengger's summary of his position quoted earlier indicates, he insists that the principal condition for a viable anti-Pelagian reformulation of contemporary political and international theory (liberal or otherwise) is that it must be developed from a standpoint 'outside the logic of the world'. But what exactly did this 'outside' perspective involve?

Rengger's answer leads to the second strand in his anti-Pelagian project, which is a distinction between political theory and political practice. Although theory may illuminate practice, Rengger holds, it can never *itself* become practice since theory and practice have different ends: while the theorist's goal is better understanding of political conduct, the practitioner's

---

8   Rengger, *The Anti-Pelagian Imagination*, p. 114.

is, at least ideally, more prudent doing.[9] Writing political theory with an eye on 'doing' does not improve but corrupts understanding by nurturing oversimplification and wishful thinking, or even a utopian desire to eliminate all the features of human life which give rise to politics.

Rengger's insistence on the gap between theory and practice was influenced in part by the work of Leo Strauss. He sympathized in particular with Strauss' claim that the great insight of ancient political thought, now forgotten in the modern period, was the impossibility of reason ever creating political consensus about the nature of justice, from which Strauss concluded that only a mixed constitution provides a viable type of political regime. At a deeper philosophical level, however, it was in the work of Michael Oakeshott that Rengger found the most cogent exploration of the relation between theory and practice.

According to Oakeshott, the aim of theorizing is purely intellectual: it is simply to see more clearly the limitations the world imposes upon practice, without any aspiration to guide it. In Oakeshott's own words, the aim of theorizing is:

> to distinguish the more permanent elements of the pattern of our politics, to accept them, not in the degree in which they are acceptable (for that becomes irrelevant) but in the degree in which they are unavoidable ... to find oneself a little less perplexed and a little more understanding of the unpleasing surface of politics.[10]

For Rengger, the appeal of Oakeshott's formulation of the theory/practice dichotomy is that it avoids not only both realism and moralism, on the one hand, but also, on the other, the spurious claim of so-called critical theory that all theorizing is suspect because it masks domination.[11] It may be noticed in passing that elsewhere in this volume Kate Schick has suggested that Oakeshott's modal distinction between theory and practice had a further appeal to Rengger, which is that it shielded Oakeshott and himself from confronting the sheer complexity of political reality. What is especially striking about this evasion of reality, Schick maintains, is that it appears at first sight to be inconsistent with Oakeshott's own pronouncements on political issues throughout his essays. She acknowledges, however, that the purpose of Oakeshott's interventions was to illustrate the nature of ideological (or 'rationalist', to use Oakeshott's own term) politics, rather than to prescribe

---

[9] Rengger, *The Anti-Pelagian Imagination*, p. 167.

[10] Michael Oakeshott, *The Politics of Faith and the Politics of Scepticism* (London: Yale University Press, 1996), p. 20.

[11] Rengger, *The Anti-Pelagian Imagination*, pp. 16, 166–7.

political policies. Schick argues, nevertheless, that Oakeshott's distinction between ideological clarification and political prescription is problematic. But despite her reservations, Schick admits that neither Oakeshott nor Rengger was primarily concerned to engage prescriptively in the political world. Although suggestive, Schick's critique of the theory/practice dichotomy made by Oakeshott and Rengger will therefore not be pursued in the present context.

The third strand in Rengger's anti-Pelagian project draws on the study of history in order to identify ineliminable tensions in the human condition. On Rengger's use of history, Caroline Kennedy-Pipe's sympathetic summary of his position is illuminating. Rengger, she writes:

> took particular issue with those such as John Mueller who believed that war had gone out of fashion, along with arcane rituals such as duelling or inhumane practices such as slavery. War had not, in Rengger's opinion, been 'unlearnt' ... Rengger also intellectually jousted with those scholars who believed that the 'thickness' of international law, [together with] a certain type of humanitarianism, and liberalism, could mitigate the essential darkness of international politics.[12]

Kennedy-Pipe's summary is apt, but Rengger's critics were quick to point out that his historical pessimism is a highly vulnerable basis for anti-Pelagianism since it cannot forestall the predictable response of a more radically inclined thinker like Richard Ned Lebow, who countered by remarking that:

> History teaches Rengger that fear-based worlds have always been the default condition of international relations. But the future need not resemble the past ... Policies tempered by the lessons of tragedy and history, and implemented by skilful leaders, do hold out the prospect of progress. The so-called lessons of history can ... [have] the unfortunate potential to make our expectations of a fear-based world self-fulfilling – just as naïve notions of escaping from them can make them even more fearful.[13]

Rengger's anti-Pelagian historical pessimism was on firmer ground, however, when he confined it to criticizing specific responses to particular historical events. A good instance is his response to Jean Bethke Elshtain's patriotic

---

[12] Caroline Kennedy-Pipe, 'Nicholas Rengger and two wars', *International Relations* 34, 4 (2020), pp. 621–6 (621).

[13] Richard Ned Lebow, *Coercion, Cooperation, and Ethics in International Relations* (Abingdon: Routledge, 2007), p. 410.

defence of the US war on terror in the aftermath of 9/11, in the course of which Elshtain claimed that the US, and only the US, had a moral mandate to reshape international affairs in a way which would end terror. Responding to Elshtain, Rengger wrote that:

> surely there is more than a touch of 'imperial grandiosity' in [Elshtain's] belief that the United States is the guarantor of human dignity in the contemporary world and that it is the special responsibility of the United States, because of both its political character and the temper of the times, to act as the 'indispensable nation'. 'We, the powerful', as she puts it, have first perhaps to examine the sources of our own power rather than merely assuming that it is 'ours' to deploy in the service of justice as we wish. As Augustine [of whom Elshtain is such a great admirer] recognized very well, part of the 'seductive lure' of 'imperial grandeur' is the belief that we can do great good with our great power, but the reality is likely to be that, as always, power corrupts.[14]

As Caroline Kennedy-Pipe remarks, by maintaining that Elshtain's defence of the American reaction raised major problems for scholars sympathetic to the just war tradition, Rengger articulated the concerns of those who believed that moralizing the war on terror in the aftermath of 9/11 had indeed 'taken too many pernicious turns', including the endorsement of torture, extraordinary rendition, and 'black sites'.[15]

Although it was suggested earlier that Rengger's defence of historical continuity as a foundation for anti-Pelagianism was inconclusive, an important feature of his conception of historicity not so far noticed remains to be considered. This is his critique of some especially literate fellow anti-Pelagians who sought, in a post-9/11 debate, to strengthen the historical perspective by linking it to the tragic vision. In order to put Rengger's intervention in this debate in perspective, it is necessary to consider briefly the prior framework for the debate about the tragic vision that had been created by scholars such as Timothy Reiss in *Tragedy and Truth*. 'The tragic', Reiss writes, 'is a dimension of real existence. … Tragedy belongs to literature and to theatre, the tragic belongs to life'.[16] Echoing Reiss, Richard Corrigan insisted that we must:

> make a distinction between 'tragedy,' which is a constantly changing dramatic form that makes manifest and communicates the experience

---

14 Rengger, *The Anti-Pelagian Imagination*, p. 128.
15 Kennedy-Pipe, 'Nicholas Rengger and two wars', p. 624.
16 Timothy J. Reiss, *Tragedy and Truth: Studies in the Development of a Renaissance and Neoclassical Discourse* (New Haven, CT: Yale University Press, 1980), p. 1.

of tragedy and the feelings it arouses, and the 'tragic,' which is a particular way of looking at experience that has persisted more or less unchanged in the Western world from the time of Homer to the present. When we talk about tragedy we are in the realm of aesthetics; when we discuss the nature of the tragic, we are in the realm of existence. In short, the difference between the two is the difference between art and life.[17]

The distinction between art and life made by Reiss and Corrigan is adopted by Rengger in a 2005 article in which he gave it additional support by quoting Oakeshott's review of Morgenthau's *Scientific Man vs. Power Politics*, where Morgenthau attempted to defend a realist onslaught on what he termed 'liberal rationalism' by applying the tragic vision to politics.[18] Although generally sympathetic to Morgenthau's anti-rationalism, Oakeshott wrote that human life:

> is not tragic, either in part or in whole: tragedy belongs to art, not to life. And further, the situation [Morgenthau] describes – the imperfectability of man – is not tragic, nor even a predicament, unless and until it is contrasted with a human nature susceptible to a perfection which is, in fact, foreign to its character.[19]

It was in opposition to thinkers like Oakeshott, whose scepticism about applying tragedy or even 'the tragic' view of existence to politics Rengger invoked, that Richard Ned Lebow sought to defend Morgenthau's view of the political applicability of the tragic vision by arguing that the merit of Morgenthau was that he shared with Thucydides:

> [a] tragic understanding of politics reflected in their belief that order was fragile, that human efforts to control, or even reshape, their physical and social environments were far more uncertain in their consequences than most leaders and intellectuals recognized, and that hubris – in the form of an exaggerated sense of authority and competence – only made matters worse.[20]

---

[17] Richard W. Corrigan, *Tragedy: Vision and Form* (London: Harper & Row, 1981), p. 8.

[18] Hans J. Morgenthau, *Scientific Man versus Power Politics* (Chicago: Chicago University Press, 1946).

[19] Michael Oakeshott, *Religion, Politics and the Moral Life*, edited by Timothy Fuller, (New Haven, CT: Yale University Press, 1993), pp. 107–08.

[20] Richard Ned Lebow, *The Tragic Vision of Politics: Ethics, Interests and Orders* (Cambridge: Cambridge University Press, 2003), p. x.

Lebow subsequently reinforced his message by claiming that: 'Tragedy is inescapable, and efforts to circumvent it by power and intellect risk making it more likely.'[21] What is strange about Lebow's understanding of the tragic, however, is that he identifies it with Morgenthau's surprisingly rationalist claim that a theory of the tragic requires philosophers to find underlying universal truths in the study of history and then adapt them to contemporary circumstances.[22]

If we ignore Lebow's passing lapse into rationalism, what is of interest is that his commitment to the applicability of the tragic vision to politics has been expanded upon by such notable theorists of IR as Rengger's distinguished friend Chris Brown. In an article on "'Tragic choices" and contemporary international political theory', Brown maintained that the tragic is simply the awareness that 'human action sometimes, perhaps often, involves a choice between two radically incompatible but equally undesirable outcomes, that whatever we do in a given situation we will be, from one perspective, acting wrongly, which constitutes for many contemporary writers the essence of a tragic vision of the world'. The practical relevance of the tragic sense, Brown writes, is that it 'ought to cause us to act modestly, to be aware of our limitations and to be suspicious of grand narratives of salvation which pretend that there are no tragic choices to be made'. The modesty inculcated by tragic awareness, in turn, encourages sensitivity in writing about the difficulties attaching to the ideals of humanitarian intervention, the key question being 'whether the genuinely tragic nature of these situations is recognised in the [humanitarian] discourse. The answer, I think, is generally "no"'.[23]

Confronted by the opposition of thinkers like Morgenthau, Lebow, and Brown, then, Rengger's hope of finding decisive support for his rejection of the applicability of the tragic vision to politics by invoking Oakeshott proves as overly optimistic as his quest for an historical foundation for anti-Pelagianism. Before moving on, however, it is instructive to note that Rengger's contribution to the debate neglected two arguments which might have served his purpose by enabling him to advance a positive alternative to attempts to apply the tragic vision to politics. The first is that the familiar virtues of prudence, humility, careful study, responsibility, and patriotism would do the same work as the tragic vision in encouraging politicians to make more modest and realistic decisions, as well as helping political scientists to avoid universalist insensitivity to concrete contexts,

[21] Richard Ned Lebow, 'Tragedy, politics and political science', *International Relations* 19, 3 (2005), pp. 329–36 (330).
[22] Lebow, *The Tragic Vision of Politics*, p. 242.
[23] Chris Brown, 'Tragedy, "tragic choices" and contemporary international political theory', *International Relations* 21, 1 (2007a), pp. 5–13 (5–6, 11, 9).

without the need to invoke tragedy at all. The second objection to defenders of the tragic vision neglected by Rengger is the possibility of appealing instead to its sister muse, the comic vision – an omission all the more surprising because Rengger does not appear to have noticed how potentially sympathetic Oakeshott appeared to be to the comic vision when he observed that: 'Humour is the attitude which a full realization of mortality induces, and which is the only answer to mortality. Humour [is] the maturity of sentiment.'[24]

Oakeshott's sympathy for the comic vision was shared by, for example, James Feibelman, who noted that the connection between comedy and tragedy is often 'so close as to render them hardly distinguishable' since both require a conflict, as well as recognition of it. Feibelman also points out that Bergson, among others, maintains that comedy is closer to 'real life' than tragedy. But if that is so, then it is surely plausible to argue that comedy might be better placed than tragedy to produce the kind of anti-Pelagianism Rengger admires by combating hubris, inducing modesty, and nurturing a general sense of our limitations. The comic vision, that is, might be precisely the best source of the kind of 'revaluation of values' for which Rengger called in the summary of his anti-Pelagian position quoted earlier. The possibility of a 'revaluation of values' by the comic vision is indeed explicitly suggested by Feibelman when he emphasizes the 'corrosive effect' of humour in eating away 'the solemnity of accepted valuation, and thus [calling] for a revaluation of values'.[25]

In fairness to Rengger, it must be added that there is one point where he touches briefly on the place of the comic vision in Oakeshott's thought. This occurs when Rengger comments sympathetically on Oakeshott's retelling of the story of the Tower of Babel in *On History*. The *manner* of Oakeshott's retelling of that tale, Rengger remarks, is as central as his anti-rationalist interpretation of it. 'What for Morgenthau would have been a tragic tale,' Rengger observes, 'becomes, in Oakeshott's hands, almost a comedy or, if not a comedy, then a story of human wilfulness with many comic overtones'.[26] Quite why Rengger does not pursue this suggestive thought is difficult to say. Perhaps the answer is that he regards the comic vision as too trivial for the grand purpose of discussing IR. If that is so, they thereby risk making the elementary mistake of understanding by comedy 'the funny' or 'the laughable'.[27]

---

[24] Michael Oakeshott, *Notebooks, 1922–86*, edited by Luke O'Sullivan, (Exeter: Imprint Academic, 2014), p. 249.

[25] James Feibleman, (1962) *In Praise of Comedy: A Study of its Theory and Practice*, (New York: Russell & Russell, 1962), pp. 202, 201, 182.

[26] Rengger, *The Anti-Pelagian Imagination*, p. 165.

[27] Feibleman, *In Praise of Comedy*, p. 168.

It was not only anti-Pelagian defenders of the tragic vision whose intellectual assistance Rengger declined to incorporate into his project, however. He also seized upon the fact that some anti-Pelagians inadvertently retain an apolitical perspective which leads them to conclusions inconsistent with their anti-Pelagian premises. A pertinent example of such inconsistency is a 'dystopic liberal' like Bernard Williams who, while rejecting 'moralism'[28] and defending the modest goal of negative liberty, argued for the necessity of adopting pre-political ethical conditions for political legitimacy in the form of adherence to human rights.[29] Another example of anti-Pelagian incoherence is provided by Hedley Bull. Despite his admiration for Bull, Rengger identified an ambiguity in Bull's early writings between scepticism and perfectionism which rendered Bull's later work increasingly incoherent as he gradually embraced moral universalism while never abandoning his early scepticism.[30]

Inconsistency, however, is not the only criticism Rengger made of some would-be fellow anti-Pelagian thinkers. The fourth strand in his synthesis concerned the necessity of avoiding the tendency of some anti-Pelagian thinkers to be too extreme, thereby becoming self-destructive. One form of self-destruction occurred, Rengger believed, when anti-Pelagianism tended 'to become the mirror image of what it opposes'. This unintentional mirroring arises either from excessive pessimism about human nature, or from 'nostalgia for a better-ordered past'.[31] Rengger's targets here are thinkers like John Gray, Judith Shklar, Leo Strauss, and – once again – Hans Morgenthau. In John Gray's case, excessive pessimism, and consequent political oversimplification, takes the form of Gray's overemphasis on the prevalence of apocalyptic religion in contemporary political thinking. Rengger charges that Gray's account is overly pessimistic, refusing to recognize the variety of religious and particularly Christian thought and the debt owed to it by the realism Gray favours.

In a different form, excessive pessimism characterizes Leo Strauss' insistence that failure to appreciate the inability of reason to provide a universal consensus on justice must inevitably issue in authoritarian rule. In like vein, as has already been seen, Rengger argues that thinkers such as Morgenthau who call the human condition 'tragic', or else 'dystopic', as do Shklar and her fellow defenders of what she terms the 'liberalism of fear', fail to understand that what they berate are in fact very ordinary (and ineliminable)

---

[28] Whereby pre-political, moral imperatives either provide limits to political action or direct it. See: Bernard Williams, *In the Beginning was the Deed: Realism and Moralism in Political Argument* (Princeton, NJ: Princeton University Press, 2005), Ch. 1.

[29] Rengger, *The Anti-Pelagian Imagination*, pp. 68–9.

[30] Rengger, *The Anti-Pelagian Imagination*, pp. 19–34.

[31] Rengger, *The Anti-Pelagian Imagination*, pp. 5, 166–7.

features of the human condition.[32] The various forms of excessive pessimism castigated by Rengger in some of contemporary anti-Pelagian thinkers, in other words, blind them to the familiar fact that human beings are both greedy and charitable, both avaricious and merciful, both nasty and nice.

There is, however, a second form of extremism which vitiates the thought of other would-be anti-Pelagians. This second form characterizes anti-Pelagians who indulge 'nostalgia for a better-ordered past'. Among them, de Maistre perhaps deserves pride of place. The defect of this second from of extremism, Rengger observes, consists of perfectionist tendencies that condemn anti-Pelagians who indulge it to a reactionary form of political theorizing which mirrors the very kind of rationalistic Pelagian prescriptivism they castigate.[33]

Turning to the fifth and final strand of thought in Rengger's search for a foundation for a non-realist anti-Pelagian position, it is at once his most ambitious and indeed the most problematic. It consists of his attempt to conscript Oakeshott as a fellow 'non-realist' anti-Pelagian by not only invoking Oakeshott's distinction between theory and practice, already noticed, but invoking, more generally, what Rengger terms a 'sensibility'[34] he finds at the heart of Oakeshott's thought and regards as the core of an anti-Pelagian alternative to realism. Rengger identifies four intimately related aspects of Oakeshott's sensibility.

The first is scepticism, the ultimate root of which Rengger traces to Oakeshott's Idealist denial that reason can provide a theoretically privileged vantage-point from which to judge moral and political experience. For Oakeshott, Rengger rightly remarks, no such vantage-point can exist because 'we cannot penetrate behind "understanding" to something [unconditionally] "real"; the world is – and can only be – a world of understandings, and cannot be anything else'.[35] These understandings are of course diverse. Among them Oakeshott distinguishes what he terms five 'modes of experience' as autonomous or irreducible ways of understanding 'reality', viz. the practical, the historical, the scientific, the aesthetic, and the philosophical. Although these modes have no interconnection, merely lying side by side, so to speak, and being incapable of challenging each other's irreducible independence, the great folly of Western rationalist thinkers has always been to reject the different modalities and to confuse, in particular, the practical, scientific, and philosophical modes of experience in the hope of providing a wholly objective approach to politics and ethics. 'Perhaps it is in the sphere of

---

[32] Rengger, *The Anti-Pelagian Imagination*, pp. 162–8, 76–7.
[33] Rengger, *The Anti-Pelagian Imagination*, pp. 166–7.
[34] Rengger, *The Anti-Pelagian Imagination*, p. 164.
[35] Rengger, *The Anti-Pelagian Imagination*, p. 164.

international relations', Oakeshott observes, 'that the project of a science of politics has made itself most clear ... From Grotius to the United Nations a continuous attempt has been made ... to elaborate the principles of a science of peace'.[36]

Only if we accept Oakeshott's insistence on the distinctive 'modality' of all understanding, Rengger writes, 'can we be content to be what we are, understanding the inevitably fragmentary character of our experiences and the tensions and dissonances of human life and conduct'.[37] He also agrees with Oakeshott that:

> because politics (and international politics) are realms of human conduct where the voice of science is merely inappropriate ... the voices that we need to chiefly understand in politics ... and in international politics ... are those of history and philosophy. Any attempt to understand international politics and ... interpret it must therefore start with them.[38]

By way of further emphasizing how alien to Oakeshott the application of a rationalist or scientific approach is to the practical mode of experience, Rengger notes approvingly that Oakeshott's historical sense includes a 'permanent interest in myth', of which his retelling of the story of the Tower of Babel referred to earlier is an apt illustration.[39]

While the relevance of Oakeshott's political scepticism to a non-realist anti-Pelagianism is indisputable, the relevance of Rengger's interpretation of the second and third aspects of his 'sensibility' is less so. The second is Oakeshott's sympathy for the religious outlook, which involves a distinction between the 'religious' and the 'worldly' man that rests on a conception of religion almost the reverse of ordinary usage. 'The religious man', Oakeshott writes, 'seeks freedom ... from all embarrassment alike of regret for the past and calculation on the future ... *memento vivere* is the sole precept of religion and the religious man'. His commitment to the present, Oakeshott continues, means that only the religious man is truly worldly. The 'world' which actually exists, however, is mistakenly committed to:

> an immortality found in some far distant perfection of the race ... [because] in the world's view, human life is an insignificant episode, brief as a dream; it is only the hoarded achievements of men which are

---

[36] Oakeshott, *Religion, Politics and the Moral Life*, p. 103.
[37] Rengger, *The Anti-Pelagian Imagination*, p. 165.
[38] Rengger, *The Anti-Pelagian Imagination*, p. 167.
[39] Rengger, *The Anti-Pelagian Imagination*, p. 167.

real and substantial ... but [for the religious man] the only immortality which fascinates him is a present immortality; so far as is possible he lives as an immortal.[40]

Precisely why Rengger considers this somewhat idiosyncratic form of religious sensibility relevant to anti-Pelagianism becomes clear when he maintains that, for Oakeshott, it precludes 'the attempt to surrender self for something else: the future, the party, the race, or whatever'. It rejects, in other words, ideological fanaticism. More generally, it is from this that 'flow most of Oakeshott's characteristic positions in political philosophy: his emphasis on individuality, his acceptance of pluralism and diversity, his account of civil association as the form of political association best suited to individuals understood as he understands them, and his account also of the threats to civil association'.[41] This interpretation of Oakeshott, however, is doubtful at best. In so far as Oakeshott's 'characteristic positions in political philosophy' have a primary source, this is surely the conception of the good as a self-chosen life explored at length in the first part of On Human Conduct.[42] Oakeshott's idiosyncratic characterization of the religious man is only an incidental aspect of his overall commitment to a self-chosen life as alone compatible with human dignity rather than the source of his political thought at large.

The relevance of the third aspect of Oakeshott's 'sensibility', admired by Rengger, to anti-Pelagianism is no less problematic. This is an aesthetic view which is indeed characteristic not only of Oakeshott's interpretation of the religious man but of life in general. This aesthetic perspective, as Rengger rightly notes, not only echoes Walter Pater[43] but also reflects Oakeshott's high esteem for Augustine and Montaigne, both of whom shared it, albeit in somewhat different idioms. It is not at all clear, however, why an aesthetic perspective should have anti-Pelagian rather than Pelagian political implications. Schiller's 1793 Letters on the Aesthetic Education of Man, for example, prefigured the German Romantic movement by advancing the essentially Pelagian or perfectionist thesis that only an aesthetic education of the populace could end self-division and create the wholeness of life necessary for political life in the good society.

---

[40] Oakeshott, Religion, p. 37.
[41] Rengger, The Anti-Pelagian Imagination, p. 166.
[42] Michael Oakeshott, On Human Conduct.
[43] Pater was perhaps the most important figure in the early articulation of the aesthetic movement which argued that we must experience life in the aesthetic mode, searching for intense experience and beauty rather than prioritizing socio-political considerations related to the 'good' prevalent in the practical mode of experience.

Rengger's Oakeshottian anti-Pelagianism and Fred Dallmayr's reading of Oakeshott

If Rengger's interpretation of Oakeshott, and by extension his anti-Pelagianism, is sometimes questionable, it is to his credit that he comprehensively rejected Fred Dallmayr's interpretation of the practical outcome of Oakeshott's sensibility as the political ideal of a global conversation of humankind transcending all national, ethnic, and cultural frontiers. In his comments on Dallmayr's interpretation, Rengger's own anti-Pelagianism and its relation to Oakeshott's work, is thrown into sharp relief.

Drawing in particular on Oakeshott's essay 'The voice of poetry in the conversation of mankind',[44] Dallmayr maintained that Oakeshott proposed in that essay to replace the dominant rationalist discourse inspired by science and utility with:

A different, more flexible and encompassing paradigm of discursive human interaction which he labels 'conversation' ... Above all, conversational encounter is not 'an enterprise designed to yield an extrinsic profit, a contest where a winner gets a prize'; rather, it is 'an unrehearsed intellectual adventure'. This conversational paradigm, Oakeshott proposes, is 'the appropriate image of human intercourse' because 'it recognizes the qualities, the diversities, and the proper relationships of human utterances'.

In an age of globalization, Dallmayr continues, 'Oakeshott's proposal gains a new and unprecedented significance' which is that 'it becomes urgently important to extend [Oakeshott's] paradigm beyond the domestic arena: that is, to structure not only intra-societal interactions in non-domineering and non-manipulative ways, but to explore the prospects of a similarly non-coercive global discourse conducted across national and civilisational boundaries'.[45]

Why, exactly, does Rengger reject Dallmayr's interpretation of Oakeshott's conversational metaphor? He gives four convincing reasons, each of which identifies an important misunderstanding of Oakeshott by Dallmayr. The first is Dallmayr's assumption that the term conversation as Oakeshott uses it in the 'Voice of poetry' has any political bearing. In fact, Rengger emphasizes, Oakeshott's concern with conversation in that essay is purely aesthetic, by

---

[44] Michael Oakeshott, 'The voice of poetry in the conversation of mankind', in *Rationalism in Politics and Other Essays* (Indianapolis: Liberty Press, 1962/1991), pp. 488–542.

[45] Fred Dallmayr, 'Conversation across boundaries: political theory and global diversity', *Millennium: Journal of International Studies* 30, 2 (2001), pp. 331–47 (331).

which Oakeshott means that it is motivated purely by the desire and ability to experience mutual delight in following wherever the conversation happens to lead, without any extraneous practical concern. Conversation in this aesthetic mode only arises, Oakeshott explains, when:

> thoughts of different species take wing and play round one another, responding to each other's movements and provoking one another to fresh exertions ... There is no symposiarch or arbiter; not even a doorkeeper to examine credentials ... voices which speak in conversation do not compose a hierarchy ... it is an unrehearsed intellectual adventure ... with conversation as with gambling, its significance lies neither in winning nor in losing, but in wagering.[46]

Dallmayr's second mistake is his assumption that conversation in Oakeshott's aesthetic sense can take place between different civilizations, whereas Oakeshott himself believes it is possible only between a few individuals – ideally, Oakeshott suggested on another occasion, between no more than four, whom he emphasized would belong to the same civilization.[47] These individuals, Oakeshott stressed, would inevitably be exceptional beings since: 'The intellectual life of the majority of men and women is cankered by a passion for indiscriminate knowledge.' Only those escape this canker who set themselves 'to consider and master their own experience', which is the principal condition for contributing to a conversation.[48] It is this rare achievement, Rengger rightly emphasizes, which inspired Oakeshott's well-known distinction between the barbarian and the civilized man. It is the ability to participate in conversation, Oakeshott wrote, 'and not the ability to reason cogently, to make discoveries about the world, or to contrive a better world, which distinguishes the human being from the animal and the civilized man from the barbarian'.[49]

With this distinction in mind, Rengger cannot resist a barbed reference to Huntington's portrayal of a 'clash of civilizations', which would have been 'viewed with amused scepticism by Oakeshott, since it would have been an assumption of the latter that the understanding of civilisation on which it is predicated is hopelessly confused; the opposite of civilisation is barbarism, not another civilisation'.[50]

---

[46] Oakeshott, 'The voice of poetry', pp. 489–90.
[47] Oakeshott, *Notebooks*, p. 308.
[48] Oakeshott, *Notebooks*, p. 147.
[49] Oakeshott, 'The voice of poetry', p. 490.
[50] Nicholas Rengger, 'The boundaries of conversation: a response to Dallmayr', *Millennium: Journal of International Studies* 30, 2 (2001), pp. 357–64 (360).

Dallmayr's third mistake is his assumption that Oakeshott's reference to different 'voices' in a conversation refers to the voices of specific individuals or cultures. In fact, Rengger points out, the 'voices' to which Oakeshott refers are neither personal nor cultural ones but are, rather, the different understandings of reality provided by what he terms different 'modes of experience'. Between these modes, Oakeshott maintains, there can be no direct communication of any kind, no order of precedence as between them, and certainly no possibility of guiding political practice by any of them. The modes can, as it were, only listen to the different views of reality each offers, and then go their separate intellectual ways.

The fourth mistake Rengger identifies is Dallmayr's attempt to deepen the political relevance of Oakeshott's concept of conversation by linking it to Oakeshott's esteem for friendship in a way which would provide a contemporary version of Aristotle's ideal of civic friendship. As Rengger observes, however, Dallmayr's neo-Aristotelian twist to Oakeshott neglects the fact that Aristotle's civic form of friendship 'contains elements of functionality and utilitarianism', whereas for Oakeshott 'friendship is personal intimacy of a very particular kind. So, I am not sure,' Rengger concludes, 'how it would be possible to combine, as Dallmayr suggests, elements of Oakeshott's treatment [of friendship] with Aristotelian reflections on civic friendship'.[51]

Limitations of Oakeshott's (and Rengger's) thought

Though Rengger's reading of Oakeshott avoids the misunderstandings entailed in Dallmayr's reading, the extent to which Oakeshott's work can act as a foundation for the construction of a non-realist anti-Pelagianism at the domestic and international levels is questionable. Although Rengger is always suggestive and sometimes brilliant, his heavy reliance on Oakeshott presents several major problems. The first is that what he appeals to is a 'sensibility' he claims to find at the heart of Oakeshott's philosophy and political theory. Perhaps he is right. The problem, however, is that one may take or leave a sensibility just as one pleases. The sensibility may of course be a highly refined one, as it obviously is in Oakeshott's case, but this does not alter the fact that a sensibility is not, in itself, an argument of any kind. It therefore cannot provide a reasonable basis for Rengger's anti-Pelagianism.

There is, however, a second problem, which is that a very different interpretation of Oakeshott's sensibility has been advanced by thinkers like Hanna Pitkin and Robert Berki.[52] For Pitkin, the essence of Oakeshott's

---

[51] Rengger, 'The boundaries of conversation', p. 361.
[52] Hannah F. Pitkin, 'The roots of conservatism: Michael Oakeshott and the denial of politics', in L.A. Coser and I. Howe (eds), *The New Conservatives: A Critique from the Left*

sensibility is that it is profoundly unpolitical and cannot, therefore, be invoked in support of a politically relevant anti-Pelagianism. Although Pitkin's critique was confined to essays on politics by Oakeshott prior to his magnum opus, *On Human Conduct*, it is unlikely that this work would have led her to modify her position. Oakeshott, she maintains:

> is, in the last analysis, one of those political theorists who, like Plato, are so deeply concerned about the nature of power, interest, conflict, that they develop a theory in which those problems are eliminated rather than solved, a theory essentially unpolitical. It is not ... that Oakeshott is naively unaware of problems of conflict and power; on the contrary, like Plato, he is so much aware and afraid of them that he cannot conceive of any way in which mere human beings could hope to control them.[53]

This may seem an unjust criticism in view of Oakeshott's subsequent acknowledgement in *On Human Conduct* of the role of power and interest in his analysis of the 'enterprise association' governments he regarded as increasingly dominant in the modern West. Rengger made precisely this point when he remarked that Oakeshott's treatment of the history of the modern European state in the third part of *On Human Conduct* 'shows that he saw just how central interests and power were to the character of the modern state'.[54] Pitkin's reply would presumably be that Oakeshott's own favoured political model was civil association, of which she would in all likelihood say that this model merely confirmed her view that, for Oakeshott, politics is an essentially 'idyllic' activity that only:

> takes place near the surface of ... life, making needed minor adjustments as conditions change ... There is no real connection required between politics and community; politics is peripheral to the communal, significant life of the society ... Those who govern never need to exercise much power, for the small and partial actions they take are scarcely noticed by the governed; they are the gyroscope that keeps the ship of state on an even keel. The citizens, in turn, are content to be governed, for they have what they need and feel no reason to question their way of life.[55]

(New York: Quadrangle, 1973), pp. 243–88; Robert N. Berki, 'Oakeshott's concept of civil association: notes for a critical analysis', *Political Studies* 29, 4 (1981), pp. 570–85.

[53] Pitkin, 'The roots of conservatism', p. 285.
[54] Rengger, 'The boundaries of conversation', p. 360.
[55] Pitkin, 'The roots of conservatism', p. 259.

Even if the charge of being 'unpolitical' levelled by Pitkin against Oakeshott's sensibility is dismissed as ill-conceived, a still more serious charge levelled by Robert Berki strikes at the very heart of Rengger's attempt to construct a non-realist anti-Pelagianism based on his interpretation of Oakeshott's sensibility. According to Berki, this sensibility is itself ultimately Pelagian. Focusing on Oakeshott's ideal of civil association, Berki finds at the heart of it two contradictory elements. One is Oakeshott's presentation of civil association as a purely moral, non-substantive relationship in which coercion has no place. The other is his presentation of civil association as a relationship which protects freedom by enforcing the rule of law. The crucial function of protection by civil association, however, means the need for institutional provision of law enforcement, which goes beyond morality. Law enforcement means, in Berki's words, 'not the lyric music and poetry of morality [but too] such hard, mundane goings on as fines, imprisonments, arrests, search-warrants, police-batons, solitary cells, riot emergencies, hangings'.[56]

Civil association, then, is not, and cannot be, a purely moral association but is characterized by conflict and law-breaking of various kinds. Oakeshott's failure to recognize this in his idealist method of constructing civil society as a purely moral order, however, yields an essentially one-sided abstraction, from which the morally impure elements intrinsic to political reality are systematically removed. Ironically, Berki concludes, this means that Oakeshott's morally purified and substantively contentless model of civil association replicates the ideal communist society of Marx. In Berki's own words, 'Marx's communism is nothing but the abstract ideal of civil association expressed in terms of an historical utopia. Oakeshott's concept of civil association is nothing but a formulation of the *essential* core of the ideal of communism expressed in the alternative idiom of political philosophy.'[57] More generally, Oakeshott's idealist method for constructing civil association not only leaves it indistinguishable from Marxism but from utopian thought at large. As Berki puts it, 'the content of Oakeshott's concept [of civil association] does not meaningfully distinguish it from the "ideal" vision of utopian thought [in general]'.[58] In justice to Oakeshott, and also to Berki himself, however, it must be added that Berki is at pains to emphasize that he is:

not criticizing Oakeshott for *what* he says or explains or justifies. I am critical of *how* he develops and presents his arguments ... I am interested in him as an *idealist* political thinker. My contention is that

---

[56] Berki, 'Oakeshott's concept of civil association', p. 575.
[57] Berki, 'Oakeshott's concept of civil association', p. 582, emphasis in original.
[58] Berki, 'Oakeshott's concept of civil association', p. 570.

the substantive notion of 'civility', as adumbrated thought not fully defined by Oakeshott, is a valid and valuable concept which deserves to be further developed ... But I also argue that 'civil association' as a concept [is subject to criticism] on account of the idealist one-sidedness that it contains [in Oakeshott's presentation of it].[59]

As Berki indicates, then, the philosophical idealism inherent in the Oakeshottian 'sensibility' to which Rengger appeals means that it cannot provide a solid foundation for his non-realist anti-Pelagianism. At best, Rengger's Oakeshottian commitment leaves him open to the charge of evading the political, and at worst of injecting a utopian core into his thought. In a word, Rengger himself appears to succumb to 'the faint but bewitching glow of ideal theory' of which, it was seen at the outset, he accused John Rawls and his followers.

Towards a more viable anti-Pelagian position

This does not, however, mean that Rengger's life work was in vain. If we drop the Pelagian/anti-Pelagian terminology around which his thought revolved, it may be seen instead as a series of illuminating contributions to a topic which was foremost in ancient political theory but has all but disappeared from the modern agenda in the post-Kantian era. This is the nature of practical wisdom or *phronesis*, which is the virtue of prudence. In this perspective Rengger's work complements that of other scholars like Chris Brown, as is evident in Brown's (2010) remarkable collection of essays entitled *Practical Judgement in International Relations Theory*.[60] Rengger's work also complements, among others, Alasdair McIntyre's neo-Aristotelian quest for a phronetic social science uncontaminated by positivist and rationalist influences. However, it is perhaps Douglas J. Den Uyl's study of *The Virtue of Prudence* that brings out most succinctly the full extent of the problem of prudence which underlies much of Rengger's thought without quite surfacing. As Den Uyl remarks, 'prudence, perhaps more than any other virtue, illustrates an underlying debate over the foundations of ethics that has seldom seen the light of day'.[61] The reason why the debate seldom occurs is an extraordinary development in Western ethical thought. This is that prudence, which was the supreme virtue in Western thought until roughly

[59] Berki, 'Oakeshott's concept of civil association', p. 580, emphasis in original.
[60] Chris Brown, *Practical Judgement in International Political Theory: Selected Essays* (Abingdon: Routledge, 2012).
[61] Douglas Den Uyl, *The Virtue of Prudence* (London: Peter Lang Publishing Inc, 1991), p. 10.

the end of the 17th century, now refers primarily to self-interested utility maximization, and is therefore no longer a virtue at all. How is it possible, Den Uyl asks, 'for something to go from being the supreme virtue to being barely a virtue at all?'[62]

Although the answer is complex, Den Uyl maintains that an important part of it is that 'classical' or pre-modern ethical thought generally had a teleological view of ethics, in which the purpose of ethics was to provide guidance on the end or *telos* of individual self-perfection. In the modern world, however, teleology has for the most part been abandoned, and ethics was therefore no longer thought of as offering a guide to conduct. This does not mean, Den Uyl adds, that it was generally doubted that morality exists, even though sceptical voices of that kind were sometimes heard. It was, rather, that the real question now became the 'meta-ethical' one of what sort of theory, or framework, 'was best suited for explaining the phenomena of moral experience. In this respect, ethics had no purpose. It was a given of everyday experience that was amenable to theoretical experience'.[63] It is against this background change that the self of everyday life came to be thought of as a collection of instincts, feelings, or duties for which it no longer made sense to seek an overall *telos*, over the pursuit of which the cardinal virtue of prudence presided.

In order to provide a slightly more complete sketch of the aspects of the history of prudence relevant at present, it must be added that neither classical nor modern theory provided a specifically *political* theory of prudence. For Aristotle, Den Uyl observes, the proper use of the term 'prudence' (or *phronesis*) 'was with respect to the practical wisdom needed by individuals for achieving their own particular form of self-perfection. Other uses, such as the political, were derivative'.[64] In the modern world, likewise, the term prudence has no direct political application since the primary concern of the state is with protecting rights deemed to have a universal applicability.

It is then against the background of this hiatus – the lack, that is, of a specifically political theory of prudence – that Rengger's search for a coherent non-realist anti-Pelagian theory must be viewed. In order to develop such a concept of prudence, however, it would have been necessary for Rengger to extend his project yet further, to the concept of the political itself. In the latter connection, Rengger's insistence on the ethical nature of his own position, in opposition to versions of realism which rejected an ethical foundation, would also have required him to confront the concept of legitimacy either dismissed by realism, or reduced by it to calculations of rational interest.

---

[62] Den Uyl, *The Virtue of Prudence*, p. 1.
[63] Den Uyl, *The Virtue of Prudence*, p. 6.
[64] Den Uyl, *The Virtue of Prudence*, p. 238.

Rengger might perhaps have found a bridge, albeit a somewhat philosophically flimsy one, between the concepts of prudence, politics, and legitimacy in David Hume's observation that:

> Political writers have established it as a maxim, that, in contriving any system of government, and fixing the several checks and controls of the constitution, every man ought to be supposed a *knave*, and to have no other end, in all his actions, than private interest ... [Otherwise] we ought to look for nothing but faction, disorder, and tyranny from ... government.[65]

The novelty of Hume's way of linking prudence and politics is worth emphasizing: his contention is that practical wisdom depends, not on elaborate philosophical theorizing about human nature and society, but purely on the pretence (that is, practical presupposition) necessary in order to avoid folly. In this respect Hume is in the company of Aesop, several of whose fables have as their theme the avoidance of folly as the basis of practical wisdom. One of the best known is about the chickens who trust the fox. The end of Aesop's story is sad, with blood and feathers everywhere; but the moral is that the chickens have only their own folly to blame.

If Rengger had sought a philosophical alternative to Hume's appeal to pretence as the basis of prudence in politics, then the more recent work of Stuart Hampshire on the presuppositions of an ethically based concept of the political would have been relevant.[66] The principal precondition for this, Hampshire maintains, is the prudent mutual recognition of each other by all participants – both individuals and/or groups – as willing to settle their disagreements by non-violent methods.[67] Such recognition is not only prudent but is indeed constitutive of the ethical basis of political relationships, which entails acceptance (albeit conditional) of adversarial thinking. If adversaries are simply not recognized, and their opinions not appreciated from their own point of view, even if only to be rejected, then there is no political relationship. In such cases of non-recognition, with the concomitant non-recognition of institutional procedures for negotiating and accommodating different opinions, what remains is domination.[68] Even when

---

[65] David Hume, *Of the Independence of Parliament*, available at: http://press-pubs.uchicago.edu/founders/documents/v1ch11s4.html, emphasis in original.

[66] Stuart Hampshire, *Innocence and Experience* (London: Penguin, 1996), p. 150.

[67] This argument of course echoes political theories of agonism like those formulated by Chantal Mouffe and Bonie Honig. See: Chantal Mouffe, *The Return of the Political* (London: Verso, 1993); Bonnie Honig, *Political Theory and the Displacement of the Political* (London: Cornell University Press, 1993).

[68] Hampshire, *Innocence and Experience*, p. 155.

political recognition occurs, however, it does not promise a final resolution, and certainly not that conflict as such will disappear since, as Hampshire put it in his Tanner lectures, 'there will never be a harmony in the soul or in the city'.[69] It is failure to recognize this that entails a slide into the Pelagian optimism that Rengger so eloquently castigated. The very nature of the political, then, is what – in Rengger's terminology – Pelagianism fails to acknowledge.

Finally, it is necessary to refer briefly to Rengger's need to theorize more explicitly the concept of legitimacy implicit in his insistence on the ethical basis of his position. Legitimacy, as Oakeshott observes, demands more than the expression of a subjective moral attitude: it entails recognition of the authority of a state (or other institution) acknowledged to be capable of engendering obligation on the part of those within its sphere of competence.[70] Legitimacy in this sense is implicit in the concept of the political itself, in so far as the political presupposes mutually acknowledged procedures for resolving conflicts in a peaceful spirit of compromise. Since participants are not, however, *obliged* to acknowledge the authority of procedures that obligate them, violent conflict is constantly possible. In practice, there are many purely contingent reasons why a political order might (or might not) be considered broadly legitimate – reasons, that is, other than fear of coercion.[71] Even when such reasons exist, however, the ethical basis of the political order may remain extremely fragile, especially at the international level. Even if it acquires a certain stability, the ethical basis of a polity's legitimacy is never final but is always subject to constantly changing conditions of conflict and unequal power relations.[72]

Conclusion

As we illustrate earlier, Rengger's exploration of anti-Pelagian thought in political and international theory is admirable for its breadth and acuity regarding the limitations of some of the most important contemporary anti-Pelagian thinkers. His engagement with Oakeshott is instructive particularly in the context of international theory, where Oakeshott's work is often misconstrued and simplistically transmorphed into yet another type of middle-of-the-road Pelagianism. However, we contend that Rengger's

---

[69] Stuart Hampshire, 'Justice is conflict: the soul and the city', *Tanner Lectures on Human Values* 19 (1998), pp. 148–71 (149).

[70] Oakeshott, *On Human Conduct*.

[71] John Horton, 'Realism, liberal moralism and a political theory of modus vivendi', *European Journal of Political Theory* 9, 4 (2010), pp. 431–48 (443).

[72] Matt Sleat, 'Realism, liberalism and non-ideal theory or, are there two ways to do realistic political theory?', *Political Studies* 64, 1 (2016), pp. 27–41.

non-realist anti-Pelagianism, with its high indebtedness to Oakeshott, leaves something to be desired. Our brief reflections on prudence, on the political and on legitimacy, however, are no more than tentative, their sole purpose being to suggest how Rengger's admirable quest for a non-realist anti-Pelagianism might have been extended, had he been granted time to develop his critique more. The loss of Nick Rengger will long be felt by those fortunate to have known him and debated with him.

3

Poetics and Politics: Rengger, Weber, and the *Virtuosi* of Religion

John-Harmen Valk

Introduction

Rarely does the published work of Nicholas Rengger directly engage the thought of Max Weber, a rather interesting lacuna given the centrality of Weber to the international political themes and thinkers with which Rengger engaged over the course of his career and in response to which he sought to carve out his own unique stance. Weber features in the title of Rengger's unpublished 2001 inaugural lecture at the University of St Andrews, and a book manuscript on which Rengger was working at the time of his death was to explore the significance of Weber's 'Politics as a vocation' lecture with respect to several present-day dilemmas of ethics and politics.[1] It is only in *International Relations, Political Theory and the Problem of Order* that Rengger indicates at any length the great significance that he sees Weber's thought holding for international political theory, and yet even this discussion is rather limited.[2]

---

[1]   The title of Rengger's inaugural lecture is 'Kant, Weber and Dr. Pangloss: world politics between progress and tragedy'. A tentative title for the book manuscript communicated to the author was *Global Politics as a Vocation*, a brief synopsis of which can be found in the Notes on Contributors to Daniel R. Brunstetter and Cian O'Driscoll, eds, *Just War Thinkers: From Cicero to the 21ˢᵗ Century* (Abingdon, UK: Routledge, 2018).

[2]   Nicholas J. Rengger, *International Relations, Political Theory and the Problem of Order: Beyond International Relations Theory?* (London; New York: Routledge, 2000a), pp. 9, 44, 60, 62, 204.

This chapter therefore explores Rengger's notion of the modern anti-Pelagian imagination – a notion that figured prominently in his later work – with respect to Weber's thought. It traces affinities between Rengger and Weber in their diagnoses of how rationalization and the concomitant loss of an ethic of brotherliness characterize the modern disenchantment of the world. Rengger's wish to sustain an ethic of brotherliness meets its limits, however, in so much as his delineation of the relationship between theory and practice militates against the desire to root lives within networks of living concern. The chapter thus explores Rengger's distinction between theory and practice, poetics and politics, in light of Weber's discussions of the *virtuosi* of religion which feature prominently in Weber's writings on the sociology of religion, but which also play a central, albeit more recessed, role in his discussion of ethics and politics as outlined in his 'Politics as a vocation' lecture.[3] The chapter problematizes Rengger's insistence on a staunch distinction between theory and practice, and poetics and politics more specifically, arguing that there is a need to recognize the important influence of the poetic, world-disclosive force of the lives of exemplary figures like Weber's *virtuosi* of religion upon politics so as to sustain the sort of politics of limits and the centrality of mercy and charity that Rengger himself so values.

The chapter begins with two sections discussing themes that Rengger shares with Weber – a critique of rationalization and a problematization of the loss of an ethic of brotherliness. In order to unpack the latter theme in Rengger's thought, it explores his discussion of the philosopher Charles Taylor's rendering of Ivan Illich's account of the parable of the Good Samaritan. A subsequent section flags the dilemma that confronts Rengger's desire to situate mercy and charity at the heart of human existence and which arises from his delineation – itself revealed to be embroiled in significant ambiguities – of theory and practice. The chapter then turns, in the following section, to Weber's emphasis on the *virtuosi* of religion, supplemented with insights from Paul Ricoeur, Talal Asad, and Charles Taylor, in order to suggest an alternative understanding of the relation between poetics and politics that might sustain the priority to mercy and charity that Rengger himself desires. This alternative understanding, the chapter notes in closing, might resonate to a certain degree with what the chapter previously highlighted as a weaker reading of Rengger's theory and practice distinction.

---

[3] Max Weber, 'Politics as a vocation', in H.H. Gerth and C. Wright Mills (eds and trans), *From Max Weber: Essays in Sociology* (New York: Oxford University Press, 1946).

Weber and Rengger: rationalization

The modern anti-Pelagian imagination towards which Rengger motions shares with Weber a criticism of what Weber famously termed the modern disenchantment of the world. The modern disenchantment of the world, according to Weber, arises with:

> the knowledge or belief that if one but wished one *could* learn it at any time. Hence, it means that principally there are no mysterious incalculable forces that come into play, but rather that one can, in principle, master all things by calculation. This means that the world is disenchanted. One need no longer have recourse to magical means in order to master or implore the spirits, as did the savage, for whom such mysterious powers existed. Technical means and calculations perform the service.[4]

Modern disenchantment entails the loss of belief in mysterious forces at play in the world. Yet, modern disenchantment is not merely a stripping away of belief, according to Weber; what at heart characterizes disenchantment is a shift in belief, a shift from the belief in mysterious forces to the belief that all problems are in principle solvable by the application of human reason. The process of modern disenchantment is thus better understood as a dual vector of disenchantment and of re-enchantment in the form of rationalization. The disenchantment of the belief in mysterious forces gives way to a re-enchantment in the form of a belief that all problems are in principle solvable. Hans Morgenthau, who draws significantly from Weber, provides an apt articulation of the emergence of this vector of rationalization that marks the modern disenchantment of the world when he states:

> The Age of Science has completely lost this awareness of unresolvable discord, contradictions, and conflicts which are inherent in the nature of things and which human reason is powerless to solve. For this age the problems which confront the human mind, and the conflicts which disturb and destroy human existence, belong of necessity to one of two categories: those which are already being solved by reason and those which are going to be solved in a not too distant future.[5]

---

4   Max Weber, 'Science as a vocation', in H.H. Gerth and C. Wright Mills (eds and trans), *From Max Weber: Essays in Sociology* (New York: Oxford University Press, 1946), p. 139, emphasis in original.

5   Hans J. Morgenthau, *Scientific Man vs Power Politics* (London: Latimer House, 1947), p. 175.

Weber rejects the modern faith in the inexhaustible application of human reason. This is the case, for one, because the rationalization of the world has led to the differentiation of distinct spheres of action – economic, political, aesthetic, erotic, and intellectual, for example – each of which are oriented towards ultimate and incommensurable values.[6] Science is simply incapable of adjudicating between these ultimate values, implying that human calculation cannot ultimately master the modern disenchanted world. The clash of value spheres forces a choice between ultimate values that transcends the capacity of technical rationality. Far from being wholly secularized, the modern disenchanted world is, like the ancient one, a 'polytheistic' world.[7]

Second, Weber rejects rationalization because of the dangers to which it gives rise. It 'dethrone[s] this polytheism in favor of the "one thing that is needful"'.[8] This attitude is particularly problematic in the political realm, Weber notes, where it quickly transforms into a chiliasm preaching the merits of 'the use of force for the *last* violent deed'.[9] Weber here speaks specifically of revolutionary socialism, but the point might be applied more broadly, as Morgenthau does, when he speaks of the liberalism of Woodrow Wilson who argued that: 'The war for national unification and for "making the world safe for democracy" is then indeed … the "culminating and final war for human liberty", the "last war", the "war to end war"'.[10] The impetus to override the 'polytheism' of the differentiated value spheres spurred on by a rationalistic faith in the propensity of human reason for mastery leads not to the end of conflict but breeds it further.

Taking his cue from Michael Oakeshott, Rengger draws attention to this vector in a similar manner and affixes to it the title of rationalism. For the rationalist, states Rengger, the conduct of practical affairs is at heart a matter of solving problems, the mere management of crises through the application of reason. Rationalist politics is perfectionist in that the rationalist understands there to be no political problem to which there is not in principle a rational solution, and which is by extension thus the perfect solution; lacking in this perspective is the notion of a resolution which is merely the best given the circumstances. Rationalist politics is also a politics of uniformity. The rationalist may acknowledge that there is not a universal solution capable of addressing all of the ills of political society. However, on the rationalist

---

6 Max Weber, 'Religious rejections of the world and their directions', in H.H. Gerth and C. Wright Mills (eds and trans), *From Max Weber: Essays in Sociology* (New York: Oxford University Press, 1946), pp. 331–57.
7 Weber, 'Science as a vocation', pp. 147–8.
8 Ibid., pp. 148–9.
9 Max Weber, 'Politics as a vocation', p. 122, emphasis in original.
10 Morgenthau, *Scientific Man*, p. 51.

perspective, the solution for any particular ill is always and everywhere applicable for all like ills.

According to Rengger, this rationalist politics exhibits several pitfalls. For one, rationalism rests on a priority to technical knowledge, a form of knowledge understood to comprise a set of rules that can be learned and applied in practice. This technical knowledge contrasts with a practical knowledge which is learned only in its use and which thus cannot be explicitly articulated in rules. Rationalism is problematic also because of its presentism. It encourages a particular form of thinking fixated upon solving the crises of the moment, the result of which is the squeezing out of other modes of thinking such as the historical. The ensuing danger, warns Rengger, is that 'we are likely to become prisoners of the assumptions of the moment, some of which may well have created the problems in the first place'.[11] Rationalism thus closes off other ways of understanding that might emerge in the process of approaching the past on its own terms rather than from the perspective of the present's felt need. Seeking distance from the present is precisely one way of addressing present problems, for it affords the possibility of seeing how others identified and addressed their own problems. Recognition of present problems can arise precisely from the pursuit of other forms of understanding which are not problem-driven.[12]

Rationalism is problematic, moreover, because of its blindness to the realities of the human condition. The problem with rationalism is that it attempts 'to make human beings something other than what, in fact, they are'.[13] In this respect, Rengger agrees with Morgenthau's assertion that the problem with rationalism is that it thinks that the *animus dominandi*, the

---

[11] Nicholas J. Rengger, 'Political theory and international relations: promised land or exit from Eden?', *International Affairs* 76, 4 (October 2000), pp. 755–70 (769–70).

[12] Rengger, 'Political theory and international relations', pp. 765–70. It should be noted that Rengger's discussion of rationalism's weakness does not here exhibit the contours of the stauncher theory/practice distinction characteristic of his later work, discussed later. Rengger does here allude to distinct modes or voices, and he also flags the risk of the 'Platonic temptation' that lures the philosopher into thinking they can help in the real world of politics. However, the discussion remains at the level of a warning rather than of a more assertive claim that theory cannot become practice. On this more assertive claim, see Nicholas J. Rengger, 'Epilogue: tragedy or scepticism?', in *The Anti-Pelagian Imagination in Political Theory and International Relations: Dealing in Darkness* (Abingdon, UK: Routledge, 2017), p. 167. The issue discussed in the following paragraph is presumably one factor leading to the shift in Rengger's understanding of the theory/practice distinction, along with a solidification of the lines between voices discussed later. The downplaying of attention to practical knowledge is presumably another. On the latter see Nicholas J. Rengger, 'Practical judgement: Inconsistent – or incoherent?', in Mathias Albert and Anthony F. Lang, Jr (eds), *The Politics of International Theory: Reflections on the Work of Chris Brown* (Basingstoke, UK: Palgrave Macmillan, 2019b), pp. 55–68.

[13] Rengger, 'Epilogue', p. 165.

insatiable lust for power that supersedes even the limits of human selfishness, can be excised and that the conflicts that arise from it can be solved.[14] Otherwise stated, rationalism has always operated with the assumption 'that there was a shortcut to heaven, and that heaven would and could be built on Earth'.[15] But this, according to Rengger, is only to accentuate the ills faced in the political realm. Quoting a couplet referenced by Oakeshott, Rengger highlights the problems with rationalism: 'Those who in fields Elysian would dwell / Do but extend the boundaries of Hell'.[16] Indeed, it is this warning about the reduction of politics to problems and the thought that such problems lend themselves to the perfect solution that underpins Rengger's critique of modern just war theory. Such rationalist reasoning, in Rengger's view, leads not to a reduction in the use of force as its self-justificatory claim would suggest, but rather leads to a '*deepening* of the uncivil condition that international politics already resembles'.[17] Evident in this statement are parallels with Weber's warning about the last violent deed.

Weber and Rengger: brotherliness

Rengger's discussion of the modern anti-Pelagian imagination also shares with Weber the sense that, beyond rationalization as a central aspect of the modern disenchantment of the world, there is another key dimension which might be understood as the inverse side of the same coin. This is the concomitant loss of an ethic of brotherliness. Weber traces the decline of an ethic of brotherliness from kinship societies through salvation religions to modern society. Kinship societies, notes Weber, are structured around an ethic of brotherly reciprocity, but this brotherliness is marked by a primacy to natural blood ties and marital ties understood to hold a certain power deserving of respect. There is thus an evident in–group/out–group character to this ethic of brotherliness along kinship lines. Salvation religion shatters kinship ties by devaluing blood and marital ties in favour of ties to fellow members of the religious community; in so doing, it transfers and extends the ethic of brotherliness from familial ties to the religious community. In place of familial ties, the suffering common to all believers serves as the basis for brotherly relations. The significance of this move, for Weber, is that the

---

[14] Ibid., pp. 162–3.

[15] Nicholas Rengger, 'Bull: a double vision?', in *The Anti-Pelagian Imagination in Political Theory and International Relations: Dealing in Darkness* (London and New York: Routledge, 2017), p. 25.

[16] Michael Oakeshott, 'The Tower of Babel', in *On History and Other Essays* (Oxford: Basil Blackwell, 1983), p. 194, as cited in Rengger, 'Epilogue', p. 168.

[17] Nicholas J. Rengger, *Just War and International Order: The Uncivil Condition in World Politics* (Cambridge: Cambridge University Press, 2013a), p. 162, emphasis in original.

ethic of brotherliness becomes potentially universal: 'its ethical demand has always lain in the direction of a universalist brotherhood, which goes beyond all barriers of societal associations, often including that of one's own faith'.[18] As this ethic of brotherliness is absolutized, the demand for brotherliness extends from neighbour to humanity, and even to one's enemy.[19]

The rationalization indicative of the modern disenchantment of the world, however, signifies a loss of such an ethic of brotherliness. The logics of the value spheres subvert any relation of brotherliness. In the economic sphere, the logic of supply and demand determines an object's worth, and the market economy actively discourages intervention so as to prevent any distortion to the logic of supply and demand. As a result, the manner of exchange is divorced from the individual will of participants who, out of a sense of ethical obligation to kinsfolk or to the lesser-off, might adjust prices accordingly. The logic of the market has no space for brotherliness, and the impersonal forces of the market thus turn around to master humanity.[20] A similar development occurs in the political sphere, which according to Weber pertains to 'the distribution, maintenance, or transfer of power'.[21] In so much as the function of the state is ultimately to manage the external and internal distribution of power,[22] the political sphere is itself divorced from the concrete instances of personal relations. This is the case either because the striving to share power or to change the distribution of power entails the domination of persons and thus the reduction of persons to things, or because bureaucratic management follows rational rules of the maintenance of order rather than following any regard for the person.[23] In both the case of the modern rationalized economy and the rationalized state apparatus, what is lost with the depersonalization of modes of conduct is brotherly engagement, that is, the loss of love or *caritas*.[24]

It is a similar sense of the loss of an ethic of brotherliness that also troubles Rengger about the modern disenchantment of the world. Indeed, on several occasions, Rengger refers to Oakeshott's statement that 'no rationalistic justice (with its project of approximating people to things) and no possible degree of human prosperity can ever remove mercy and charity from their

---

[18] Weber, 'Religious rejections', p. 330.
[19] Ibid., pp. 329–30.
[20] Ibid., pp. 331–3. See also Max Weber, *Economy and Society: An Outline of Interpretive Sociology*, Vols. 1–2, edited by Guenther Roth and Claus Wittich (Berkeley, CA: University of California Press, 1978), p. 636.
[21] Weber, 'Politics as a vocation', p. 78.
[22] Weber, 'Religious rejections', p. 334.
[23] Weber, 'Politics as a vocation', p. 78; 'Religious rejections', pp. 333–4; *Economy and Society*, p. 975.
[24] Weber, 'Religious rejections', p. 334; *Economy and Society*, p. 1188.

place of first importance in the relations of human being'.[25] However much Rengger never really dwells on the point, he here provides a glimpse of the importance of relations of brotherliness to his thought and the direct link that he, like Weber, sees between rationalist politics and the loss of an ethic of brotherliness. In fact, it is the sense of brotherliness exemplified in the virtues of mercy and charity that sits at the heart of his anti-Pelagian sensibility. That the virtues of mercy and charity are the very reason for such an anti-Pelagian imagination is evident in Rengger's statement near the end of *Just War and International Order* about the need for:

> an Augustinian recognition of the limits of our knowledge and a humility towards our capacity to alter the conditions of our existence – an 'anti-Pelagian' recognition if you will – and [a humility] that accommodates us to the continuing importance of charity and mercy and the possibilities that exist for us to make spaces for these and related virtues in our world.[26]

To contest rationalistic politics is, for Rengger as for Weber, to attempt to redress a loss of the brotherliness of direct relations.

Rengger's review of Charles Taylor's *A Secular Age* provides a further picture of the place of this sense of an ethic of brotherliness in Rengger's thought. It is striking that of the 'over 874 pages of hugely erudite and often quite stunning virtuoso argumentation' that comprise the book, Rengger chooses to comment only on Taylor's engagement with Ivan Illich's reading of the parable of the Good Samaritan. What intrigues Rengger about Taylor's account of Illich's reading is the manner in which it brings to light 'the astonishingly radical claims' which have been hidden by the very familiarity of the parable.[27] The parable is given in response to the question 'Who is my neighbour?'. According to the parable, a traveller is robbed, beaten, and left to die. Both a priest and a Levite, who are important figures in that Jewish society, pass by the dying man. But, a Samaritan, a reviled outsider, stops, binds the dying man's wounds, and

---

[25] Michael Oakeshott, 'Scientific politics', in *Religion, Politics and the Moral Life*, edited by Timothy Fuller (New Haven, CT: Yale University Press, 2011), p. 108, as cited in Nicholas J. Rengger, 'Tragedy or scepticism? Defending the anti-Pelagian mind in world politics', *International Relations* 19, 3 (2005a), pp. 321–8 (326). See also Rengger, 'Epilogue', p. 163; Ian Hall and Nicholas Rengger, 'The Right that failed? The ambiguities of conservative thought and the dilemmas of conservative practice in international affairs', *International Affairs* 81, 1 (January 2005), pp. 69–82 (81).

[26] Rengger, *Just War*, p. 175.

[27] Nicholas J. Rengger, 'On theology and international relations: world politics beyond the empty sky', *International Relations* 27, 2 (2013b), pp. 141–57 (145).

brings him to an inn to recover. Taylor, Rengger notes, highlights the typical, modern reading of the parable according to which the answer to the question 'Who is my neighbour?' is understood to be not those who belong to one's specific group or nation but rather any human being. All human beings are to be, without discrimination, the recipients of one's assistance. This reading conveys a lesson in a specific direction. It fixates on a movement out of the parochial, out of the particularity of belonging, and it translates that movement to a universal register of moral rules which dictate how one should behave. On this reading, the parable represents one of the sources from which springs the universalist moral consciousness of modernity.

Taylor notes that for Illich, however, such a reading entirely misses the heart of the parable. The point of the parable is not to convey a new set of moral rules that are universally applicable, but rather to disclose a new way of being. It is indeed the case that the parable depicts a Samaritan who shatters the regnant notions of belonging, of insider and outsider. But, he does not do so out of any sense of moral duty; rather, he does so out of a sense of being called by the dying man himself. In this sense, the parable does not motion towards universality, whatsoever, if universality is understood as a sort of categorical grouping classifiable according to its sharing a common property such as being members of a specific nation-state or being bearers of rights. Rather, the parable initiates a new network of *agape* – the love of God for humanity – that extends outwards and links 'particular, enfleshed people to each other'.[28] This sort of network resembles kinship networks in that it consists of brotherly relations rather than a shared category. Yet, it also splits from kinship networks in that this new network is not bound by an existing 'we'; it creates links across the insider/outsider distinction in favour of a mutual togetherness based not on kinship ties but on *agape*. Rengger summarizes this reading by stating that: 'One might put it like this: the point of Illich's argument is to emphasise the *particularity* of the Samaritan – the point of the general [modern] way of reading it is to emphasise his *universality*'.[29]

Now, the problem for Illich and Taylor, and indeed for Rengger, is that, in the very desire to sustain the spirit of this network, an effort is undertaken to institutionalize the personal relations by the introduction of rules and the division of responsibilities. This normalization of the network gives rise in turn to modern bureaucracies and their rationality and rules that pertain to impersonal categories of people. It thus initiates

---

[28] Charles Taylor, *A Secular Age* (Cambridge, MA: Belknap Press of Harvard University Press, 2007), p. 739, as cited in Rengger, 'On theology', p. 146.

[29] Rengger, 'On theology', p. 146, emphasis in original.

a 'fetishism of rules and norms'. More troubling, implies Rengger in quoting Taylor, is that:

> A world ordered by this system of rules, disciplines, organizations can only see contingency as an obstacle, even an enemy and a threat. The ideal is to master it, to extend the web of control so that contingency is reduced to a minimum. What role, for example, does (or could) contingency play in contemporary analytical international ethics, for example. By contrast contingency is an *essential* feature of the [Samaritan] story as an answer to the question that prompted it. Who is my neighbour? The one you happen across, stumble across, who is wounded there in the road.[30]

The subsequent danger of this banishment of contingency, notes Rengger, again drawing from Taylor, is that codes are not innocent. Codes establish themselves as a response to deep metaphysical needs, and indeed codes are not altogether eliminable. But, they quickly become fetishized, and they can even feed into a sense of moral superiority and also serve as the basis from which to characterize other groups as evil and inhuman. This sensed superiority justifies battles against 'axes of evil and networks of terror' until suddenly 'we discover to our surprise and horror that we are reproducing the evil we defined ourselves against'.[31]

In his brief review, Rengger suggests that Taylor's characterization of Illich on the Good Samaritan raises two points of relevance for international relations. For one, he suggests that it raises questions about dominant approaches to international ethics with their focus on global distributive justice and the related institutionalization of distributive structures. Rules are not avoidable, he notes, but it is important to think about rules within the context of the critique of norm fetishism that Taylor and Illich bring to light. Second, he notes that Taylor's allusion to the war on terror as the end result of rationalization and indicative of the loss of an ethic of brotherliness 'is too direct to need much commentary'.[32] In both instances one can see the centrality of mercy and charity to Rengger's thought. A rush towards institutionalizing mechanisms of distributive justice can lead to a loss of brotherliness in that it depersonalizes relations between enfleshed individuals. The loss of a certain humility regarding the limits to knowledge and capacity likewise banishes mercy and charity in the push to impose universal norms and codes on unwitting and different populations.

---

[30] Taylor, *Secular Age*, p. 742, as cited in Rengger, 'On theology', p. 146, emphasis in original.

[31] Taylor, *Secular Age*, p. 743, as cited in Rengger 'On theology', p. 147.

[32] Rengger, 'On theology', p. 147.

Rengger: theory and practice

Now, Taylor concludes his discussion of Illich with a point that Rengger does not mention. On the question of how to resist the perils of code fetishism, Taylor states: 'We should find the centre of our spiritual lives beyond the code, deeper than the code, in networks of living concern, which are not to be sacrificed to the code, which must even from time to time subvert it.'[33] Rengger would here presumably agree, albeit with the caveat that, as Rengger notes and Taylor himself acknowledges: 'This message comes out of a certain theology, [but] it could be heard with profit by everybody.'[34]

To root lives in networks of living concern beyond the code means certainly, for Rengger, to give primacy of place to an ethic of brotherliness, to the virtues of mercy and charity, and to create spaces in which those virtues can be practised. But, it means also, and more fundamentally, to adopt a sensibility that would be distinct from Taylor as well as from Weber. As Rengger states:

> Oakeshott's injunction to remember charity and mercy is his oblique way of saying that the best ways of dealing with the dissonances of the world depend upon us accepting human life and its vicissitudes as it is and they are, neither trying to wish them out of existence, as Pelagians do, nor overly romanticise them, as some other anti-Pelagians do by talking of the 'tragic' character of existence.[35]

To prioritize mercy and charity is to operate from a certain scepticism which accepts human beings and human action as 'simply what they are', without attempting to rid existence of its imperfections and without lamenting those imperfections as tragic.[36] It is to adopt the habitude of what Oakeshott calls the 'religious man'. The 'religious man', on this view, lives the present as though it were eternity. In contrast to the 'worldly man' who fixates on the perceived immortality of some distant future, the religious man lives for the moment free 'from all embarrassment alike of regret for the past and calculation on the future'.[37] This articulation of the habitude of the 'religious man' shares much with the description that Oakeshott gives to poetry; for, as poetic activity delights in that which has appeared, so too

---

33 Taylor, *Secular Age*, p. 743.
34 Ibid., p. 743, as cited in Rengger, 'On theology', p. 147.
35 Rengger, 'Tragedy or scepticism?', p. 327.
36 Rengger, 'Epilogue', p. 164.
37 Michael Oakeshott, 'Religion and the world', in *Religion, Politics and the Moral Life*, edited by Timothy Fuller (New Haven, CT: Yale University Press, 2011), p. 37, as cited in Rengger, 'Epilogue', p. 165.

does the 'religious man' delight in the world as it is. The two blend into each other when Oakeshott states that: 'To listen to the voice of poetry is to enjoy, not a victory, but a momentary release, a brief enchantment'.[38] At the interpersonal level this 'religious man' is one who delights in the exchange of conversation with fellow convives without the felt need to end somewhere or accomplish something.[39] There is thus a direct link between this scepticism and an ethic of brotherliness of direct, personal relations and the wariness of rules and codes which can hinder the flourishing of such interpersonal exchange.

From the standpoint of Rengger's sensibility, however, there is a major issue confronting this endeavour to root lives within networks of living concern deeper than moral rules and code fetishism, that is, in Rengger's terms, deeper than rationalism. For the alternative sensibility to which Rengger motions is one that is poetic; and, on his own insistence it cannot pass over into practice. The world of the poetic and the world of practice cannot be elided.[40] In this respect the poetic is one voice among others – including also, importantly, history and philosophy – that falls under the umbrella of theory.[41] And theory, Rengger adamantly asserts, cannot '*become* "practice"; to become, of itself, an engagement in the world or give rise to such an engagement'.[42]

Rengger is unfortunately rather elusive on his reasoning for why it is the case that theory cannot cross over into practice, and poetics into politics more specifically, providing only sporadic inferences as to the specific dimensions of Oakeshott's philosophy upon which he bases the claim. One presumably key reason is the central tenet of Oakeshott's philosophy that human experience is marked by a number of distinct modes which simply cannot be run together. Thus, Rengger insists that the voice of science, unlike history and philosophy, is inappropriate to an understanding of the realm of politics.[43] Likewise, he claims that the:

> point of political theory is to consider a whole gamut of possible ways of understanding and interpreting the world in which we live,

---

[38] Michael Oakeshott, 'The voice of poetry in the conversation of mankind', in *Rationalism in Politics and Other Essays* (London: Methuen & Co, 1962), p. 247; see also Nicholas J. Rengger, 'The boundaries of conversation: a response to Dallmayr', *Millennium: Journal of International Studies* 30, 2 (2001a), pp. 357–64 (363).

[39] Rengger, *Just War*, p. 174.

[40] Rengger, 'Epilogue', p. 165.

[41] Rengger, 'Boundaries of conversation', pp. 362–3; 'Political theory and international relations', p. 770.

[42] Rengger, 'Epilogue', p. 167, emphasis in original.

[43] Ibid., pp. 164–5, 167.

its history, the values (many and diverse) which constitute it and the possibilities of conflict and co-operation within it and how we should understand and interpret them.[44]

The historical voice is, for Rengger, crucial amid the effort to explore the diversity of ways of understanding the world and its history. Yet, what distinguishes the historical voice – the exploration of thinkers and traditions from previous eras – is its distancing from the problems and mindsets of the contemporary world so as to better understand how those in a different age both framed and responded to their own problems. To adopt the historical voice, asserts Rengger:

> is most emphatically not to be 'problem-driven' or 'problem-solving' in our approach, because it is to understand that very often we recognize our 'problems' as such only on our way to other kinds of understanding, and it is the pursuit of such understanding that is the appropriate disposition of political theory.[45]

The philosophical voice, marked by its pursuit of a matter internal to the endeavour, in the task of theory is 'to follow the argument wherever it goes and to be as honest as one can be about one's assumptions, presuppositions and conclusions'.[46] Both at the level of history and at the level of philosophy, then, there is a distinct mode of experience and a distinct voice that separates the process of theoretical reflection from the world of practice.

Rengger provides even less indication as to why the poetic voice specifically might be understood to be modally distinct from the world of practice.[47] Perhaps it is the case because, as Oakeshott specifies in his essay 'The voice of poetry', the realm of poetry pertains to delight whereas the realm of practice pertains to the desire for pleasure through manipulation and exploitation;[48] in this respect poetry becoming practice would cease to be poetry because desire so construed is fundamentally at odds with delight. And yet, this supposition is complicated by Oakeshott's own admission that friendship and love, while still pertaining to the realm of practice rather than the realm of poetry, are 'ambiguously practical' because they are, like delight, concerned with

---

[44] Nicholas Rengger, 'Progress: Kant, Mendelssohn and the very idea', in *The Anti-Pelagian Imagination in Political Theory and International Relations: Dealing in Darkness* (London and New York: Routledge, 2017), p. 16.

[45] Rengger, 'Political theory and international relations', p. 770.

[46] Rengger, 'Kant, Mendelssohn', p. 16.

[47] Rengger, 'Epilogue', p. 165.

[48] Oakeshott, 'Voice of poetry', pp. 207, 217.

'whatever it turns out to be'.[49] It is complicated also because of Oakeshott's admission that: 'Having an ear for the voice of poetry is to be disposed to choose delight rather than pleasure or virtue or knowledge, a disposition which will reflect itself in practical life in an affection for its intimations of poetry.'[50] Such a statement seems then to infer a certain crossover between the worlds of the poetic and of practice.

Given this closer relation between the world of the poetic and the world of practice, presumably another key reason for Rengger's insistence that theory cannot become practice, one separate from the modal distinction point, flows from his agreement with Oakeshott that human beings and human actions are simply what they are.[51] Rengger quotes Oakeshott's response to Hans Morgenthau that highlights this perspective on human existence: 'the situation [Morgenthau] describes – the imperfectability of man – is not tragic, nor even a predicament, unless and until it is contrasted with a human nature susceptible to a perfection which is, in fact, foreign to its character'.[52] The problem with Morgenthau, according to Oakeshott and Rengger, is that he romanticizes the human condition because his very way of depicting the situation takes on the hues of tragedy by resting upon a notion of the perfectibility of human nature. Counter to the optimism of liberal progressivism, Morgenthau diagnoses the imperfectability of human nature; he contests the Kantian notion of a transformation of the will. And yet, Morgenthau's reason for lament at this situation arises only because he still compares it with its opposite – human perfectibility. Now, whereas earlier the distinction between theory and practice pertained to the distinction between voices – the historical, the philosophical, the poetic, and all collectively contrasted, as theory, with the practical as itself a voice – here the distinction seems to contrast the real world (of practice), which in this case is not a voice, and understandings of the world (the world of theory). Both the rationalistic reformer and the tragic vision of a Morgenthau problematically operate within the logic of a world according to which understandings of the world – the perfectibility of humanity – are the measure of the world's true character.

Yet, to render Morgenthau's perspective as a problematically romantic aestheticization of the world sits seemingly uneasily with Oakeshott's idealism from which Rengger draws, according to which it is not possible to access the world as it really is shorn of the understandings that make it up.[53] For, it would seem that, according to this rendering

---

[49] Ibid., p. 244.
[50] Ibid., p. 247.
[51] Rengger, 'Epilogue', p. 164.
[52] Oakeshott, 'Scientific politics', p. 108, as cited in Rengger, 'Epilogue', p. 163.
[53] Ibid., p. 164.

of Morgenthau, the diagnosis of the human condition can be made in the first instance – human beings simply are what they are – and only secondarily superimposed with a normative stance of response – a certain 'bohemian nihilism'.[54] Rengger seems to imply as much when he speaks of how the world from the perspective of an anti-Pelagian imagination will look different, not because many of its features will be distinct, but 'because the logic of how they are understood and what follows from that understanding will be very different … the sceptical anti-Pelagian imagination offers a world viewed from the perspective of a different scale of values'.[55] Rengger here implies the existence of an underlying reality replete with its inherent features, the response to which hinges upon the logic of the sensibility adopted. It seems all the more apparent in Rengger's acknowledgement that Oakeshott does think that theory, whether in its historical, philosophical, or poetic voices, can serve to fend off the 'corruption of our consciousnesses', by which Oakeshott means that they can better reveal the nature of the world and help in resisting being rhetorically seduced by 'ambiguous statements and irrelevant argument' that would falsely portray the world in a different way.[56] And yet, however much these voices might afford a better view of the world, Rengger still insists that they cannot become practice. This is the case not only because of the modal distinction – to clarify a view of the world is not to approach the world as to be manipulated – but also because they cannot 'help build a better world' both because the world is intractable and because the intractability of the world pushes attempts to master it into measures that are folly and often worse than the problem.[57]

In light of the ambiguities in Rengger's discussion of the distinction between theory and practice, poetics and politics, one manner by which to read his position might be a weaker one, namely that poetry, as world-disclosive, cleaves more to traditional knowledge attained only in use and thus cannot be formulated into an explicit set of rules.[58] Accordingly, poetry cannot become a direct engagement in the world in the sense of providing a roadmap forward; it can provide at best a sort of inchoate 'know-how' or orientation in the world. This would seem to align more closely with Rengger's emphasis on the need to sustain the content of an ethic and the need for adverbial rather than substantive procedures to guide political

---

54 Rengger once employed the term 'bohemian nihilism', in conversation with the author, to characterize his sensibility. Disparate statements in his written work also suggest such a label. See Rengger, *Just War*, p. 30; 'Epilogue', p. 168.
55 Rengger, 'Epilogue', p. 168.
56 Ibid., p. 167; 'Boundaries of conversation', p. 362.
57 Rengger, 'Epilogue', pp. 167–8; 'On theology', pp. 146–7.
58 Rengger, 'Political theory and international relations', p. 766.

conduct, that is, procedures that guide the manner of conduct rather than the destination of that conduct.[59] It would also fit better with Rengger's insistence that we should indeed celebrate the *persona* of the 'religious man' and that it is this sort of *persona* to which we should aspire if we do not wish our politics to decline into an uncivil condition,[60] this because the aspiration after a *persona* implies the poetically-inspired entraining of a *habitus*.[61] Indeed this weaker reading would seem to capture better the inclination of Rengger's earlier work where he emphasizes the importance of practical judgement and also a threefold understanding of political theory,[62] an understanding that includes not only the historical exploration of how it is that a society has arrived at where it is, but also the important task of asking 'what we should seek to build – what associations, what institutions, what identities – to live our lives better, to minimize our failures and our fears, and increase our chances of, as Socrates would have put it, living *well*'.[63] It is this task that Rengger more closely links with practice, stated explicitly and in rather distinct contrast to his later work: 'There are, of course, many ways of theorizing, but it seems to me that one of the central assumptions we should make is that the type of "theory" we need the most is in fact one which is rooted in practice.'[64] Indeed, here exhibited is a closer alignment with the neo-Aristotelianism of Stephen Toulmin from whom Rengger takes a greater distance in one of his last publications, a piece in which he explicitly returns to the theme of practical judgement that marked some of his early work, but now in a manner much more closely aligned with an Oakeshottian insistence on the distinction between theory and practice.[65] However much one might draw out a weaker reading of Rengger's sensibility, therefore, it is overshadowed, certainly in his later writings, by his insistence on a staunch separation between theory and practice, poetics and politics. Moreover, this weaker reading is one that, while he may leave it open even in his later work in so much as he still holds to the possibility of fleeting reform, however rare,[66] he spends little time defending or elaborating. A certain way out of the impasse

---

[59] Rengger, *Just War*, pp. 170–1.

[60] Ibid., p. 176.

[61] The emphasis on habit in Rengger's first book represents another instance of a weaker reading of his stance. See Nicholas J. Rengger, *Political Theory, Modernity and Postmodernity* (Oxford: Blackwell, 1995a).

[62] Rengger, *Political Theory, Modernity and Postmodernity*; *International Relations, Political Theory and the Problem of Order*.

[63] Rengger, *International Relations, Political Theory and the Problem of Order*, p. 201, emphasis in original.

[64] Ibid., p. 202.

[65] Rengger, 'Practical judgement'.

[66] Rengger, 'Epilogue', p. 168.

Rengger's ambiguity presents to any attempt to root lives in networks of living concern thus meets its limits.

Weber supplemented: an alternative

A turn back to Weber can locate a point from which to start thinking about a more nuanced notion of the relation between theory and practice, poetics and politics, and one which makes possible the rooting of lives in networks of living concern framed by an ethic of brotherliness. Weber's outlook is undoubtedly one marked by tragedy, if not outright despair. While one might wish to demur from the tragic and despairing tone, what is still important in Weber's sensibility is the evident desire or longing for the ethic of brotherliness which he recognizes to be vanishing with the onslaught of rationalization. This sense of desire is not the desire of which Oakeshott speaks when he characterizes the practical realm as the pursuit of pleasure through manipulation and exploitation. This is a desire and longing more akin to the poetic delight of which Oakeshott speaks, a delight in the joys of living well together. That this is a desire for living well together is evident in the examples of brotherliness that Weber holds up. He refers, for example, to St Francis of Assisi as a *virtuoso* of religion who takes on the mendicant life not in order to use others as a means towards sustaining his own needs and pleasures, but rather so as to live in brotherly relations with fellow human beings and also with the physical world, this by welcoming their receptive generosity as a transformative gift. Such *virtuosi* like Assisi succeed in living a life that is 'not of this world' while still working very much in the world, and this without succumbing, Weber notes, to the political means of violence.[67] It is also evident in the fact that Weber commends those unfit for the pursuit of politics to instead take up brotherliness in personal relations as a more admirable response than succumbing to bitterness or capitulating to regnant powers.[68] It is evident too when he speaks of being moved by youth groups motivated towards genuine acts of brotherliness.[69] In all these cases, Weber's desire and longing is for the delight of living well together with others in relations of brotherliness not governed by the impersonalization of power.

Now, however much Weber evinces a desire for this brotherliness, he equally insists that politics is not the realm in which it is to be practised. It is in this respect that he insists that an ethic of ultimate ends, and in particular that of brotherly love, is at odds with an ethic of responsibility. The responsible politician must act without appeal to any such final grounds proffered by

---

[67] Weber, 'Politics as a vocation', p. 126; 'Religious rejections', p. 332.
[68] Weber, 'Politics as a vocation', p. 128.
[69] Weber, 'Science as a vocation', p. 155.

the ethic of ultimate ends. Yet, Weber does still reconcile the two such that an ethic of ultimate ends is not altogether absent. The politician who truly lives out the vocation of politics, for Weber, is the heroic individual who, in the face of the meaninglessness of the world, nevertheless acts according to ethical limits. The true politician, for Weber, is precisely a Nietzschean hero who creates value through pure force of the will, but not in such a manner that would represent an unhinged will to power that flagrantly runs roughshod over all those in its wake. The true politician in a disenchanted world is that individual who in creating values precisely creates limits. In this respect, sense can be made of Weber's insistence that an ethic of responsibility does not preclude an ethic of ultimate ends; indeed, he insists that it is the heroic individual who holds the two together, albeit always in tension, in the appropriate manner. The politician who declares: 'Here I stand' makes a statement of ethical justification – of value creation – as to why they refuse both to equate a perspectival notion of ultimate ends with the character of reality and to impose that notion upon those under their authority at all costs. This claim is not a claim to absolute principle, but a claim to the refusal of insisting upon absolute principle; it is a self-justificatory claim for not insisting on following the course of the absolute, irrespective of the consequences.

David Owen and Tracy Strong's attention to Weber's notion of maturity is helpful in understanding how Weber sees the possibility of a certain rapprochement between an ethic of conviction and an ethic of responsibility.[70] The mature human being for Weber, they suggest, is one who, in the face of the inevitable tension between one's values and the context of one's life, acts in a manner whereby one takes 'both the conditions and terms of one's own life and values upon oneself and make[s] them one's own'.[71] Maturity is therefore to reject as a crutch the conviction that one's stance holds transcendental warrant which can thus enable a refusal to face up to the realities of one's context and the consequences that will result from one's actions. To take one's position in the world upon oneself as does the mature human being is, for Weber, according to Owen and Strong, an act 'that is taken in a kind of void'.[72] There is no guarantee that the position is the appropriate one – it is legitimated only by the impressiveness of the freely chosen commitment of the one who takes the stand[73] – and yet one takes responsibility for assuming it. This sense of maturity, state Owen and Strong, finds its roots in Kant's discussion of Enlightenment as the casting

---

[70] David Owen and Tracy B. Strong, 'Introduction', in David Owen and Tracy B. Strong (eds) and Rodney Livingstone (trans), Max Weber, *The Vocation Lectures* (Indianapolis: Hackett Publishing Company, 2004), pp. xl–xlv.

[71] Ibid., p. xlii.

[72] Ibid., p. xlv.

[73] Ibid., pp. xiii, xlv.

off of the tutelage of tradition,[74] but it represents a radicalization of this line of critical inquiry in a Nietzschean vein in so much as it refuses even the security of the transcendental structures of reason as a source of meaning.[75]

The Nietzschean voluntarism inherent in Weber's sense of the mature politician is undoubtedly central to his emphasis on an ethics of responsibility, but Owen and Strong's rendering of this stance as in a void misses important nuances to Weber's standpoint. Owen and Strong note that a vocation for Weber is both active and passive. It is passive, they note, in so much as one gives oneself to that which calls. Yet, Owen and Strong accentuate the moment of decision which, importantly for maturity, makes of the call one's own. Moreover, they suggest that this decision in favour of acknowledging the call is undertaken 'without reference to any grounding or act other than the freely chosen commitment of individuals to their own particular fates'.[76] Any link between a call and the response to it, therefore, lies wholly upon the side of the active, mature individual who makes the call their own. But, this rendering fails to adequately foreground the dimension of feeling, of being moved, that even Owen and Strong at moments recognize in Weber's thought. That which groundlessly legitimates the mature politician, they suggest, is nothing more than the very impressiveness of their actions which represent a manifestation of what is authentically human. The operative place of impressiveness would imply, therefore, that there is a dimension of desire at play which, in turn, both suggests that the dimension of passivity is more extensive and that it calls into question the notion of decision undertaken in a void. In Weber's radicalized Kantianism, a movement of desire oriented by the dignity and nobility of the mature *persona* motivates the bringing together of an ethic of conviction and ethic of responsibility in an appropriate and authentic way, just as for Kant, as Taylor notes, the dignity and nobility of rational agency commands respect and moves him.[77]

Beyond the moment of passivity and desire in Owen and Strong's own rendering of Weber on maturity, moreover, Owen and Strong miss altogether the language of being moved that Weber employs also with respect to those who take up an ethic of brotherliness in the realm of personal relations. Indeed, Weber himself does not fully acknowledge the implications of his admiration for the *virtuosi* of religion when he discusses the reconciliation of the ethic of ultimate ends with the ethic of responsibility. Weber misses how the very inclination to an ethic of limits is mediated by the worlds of

---

[74] Ibid., p. xliin n68.

[75] Ibid., pp. xiv–xix.

[76] Ibid., p. xiii.

[77] Charles Taylor, 'Iris Murdoch and moral philosophy', in *Dilemmas and Connections: Selected Essays* (Cambridge, MA: Belknap Press of Harvard University Press, 2011), p. 11.

brotherliness poetically disclosed by exemplary figures like the *virtuosi* of religion who capture his imagination, spur his desire, and thus motivate his action for a politics of limits. As Paul Ricoeur notes, striking about Weber's discussion of politics as a vocation is the great respect that he holds for the ethic of brotherliness and which he locates in various individuals and traditions.[78] It is precisely because of the very absolute ethic that Weber reads in the Sermon on the Mount, for example, that Weber sees a dilemma calling for responsible judgement.[79] The inspiration of this absolute ethic in its gesture towards alternative relations of brotherliness spurs one to take upon oneself the responsibility for one's actions, and in so doing to guard also against the danger inherent in the responsible use of force which is the slide into a ruthless *machtpolitik*.[80] Hence the ethic of responsibility is not a mere exertion of will, but rather the practical judgement of a will motivated by desire for the ethic of brotherliness perceived in poetically disclosed worlds that capture its imagination.

The nobility of the maturity of the responsible politician highlighted by Owen and Strong presupposes the dignity of the *persona* who exemplifies an ethic of brotherliness in personal relations. The choice of Weber's mature politician is mediated historically and religiously by way of the lives of exemplary figures like the *virtuosi* of religion. One might go even further, as does Talal Asad, to suggest that this mediation occurs not simply via the worlds poetically disclosed by such figures, but also, and perhaps more importantly, by way of a *habitus* constituted through embodied traditions shaped by the exemplary figures that have gone before. The 'Here I Stand' is not an expression of will that creates value in the face of a void where all choices lie on the table; rather, it is the expression of the feeling that one has no other choice given the sort of person that one is.[81] Authenticity is here not a cultivation of an 'aesthetics of the self', but the outgrowth of a learned

---

[78] Paul Ricoeur, 'Éthique et politique', in *Lectures 1, Autour du politique* (Paris: Éditions du Seuil, 1991), p. 238. For an insightful account of Ricoeur's reading of Weber, one which has helped in the crystallization of thoughts drawing from Ricoeur in this paragraph, see Ernst Wolff, *Political Responsibility for a Globalised World: After Levinas' Humanism* (Bielefeld, Germany: Transcript, 2011), pp. 228–33.

[79] It would be important not to understand this absolute ethic in the form of command. For, it arises precisely in the form of a world poetically disclosed that speaks to the imagination and constitutes desire. A poetically disclosed world calls for interpretive judgement rather than blind obedience.

[80] Paul Ricoeur, 'The tasks of the political educator', in David Stewart and Joseph Bien (eds), *Political and Social Essays* (Athens, OH: Ohio University Press, 1974), p. 288.

[81] Talal Asad, 'Free speech, blasphemy, and secular criticism', in Talal Asad, Wendy Brown, Judith Butler, and Saba Mahmood, *Is Critique Secular? Blasphemy, Injury and Free Speech*, The Townsend Papers in the Humanities, No. 2 (Berkeley, CA: Townsend Center for the Humanities, University of California, 2009), pp. 20–63 (45–6, 62n42).

body that has cultivated appropriate capacities and aptitudes such that it acts within a world the contours of which are already marked by a certain ethical shape.[82] While a desire-driven *habitus* of this sort complicates any sense of autonomous self-fashioning, it also does not represent a blind obedience. For, aptly performed action 'requires not only *repeating* past models but also *originality* in applying them in appropriate/new circumstances'.[83] On this view, then, the 'Here I Stand' is not the distancing from desire that Owen and Strong claim,[84] but rather the result of a historically- and religiously mediated cultivation of certain desires – in Weber's case, the desire constituted by an exemplary ethic of brotherliness – over others – the desire spurring pursuit of a *machtpolitik*.

The merit of this Ricoeurian and Asadian addendum to Weber is that it shows how Weber's language of being moved by the *virtuosi* of religion, however much overshadowed by his insistence upon an ethic of responsibility as expression of will, highlights the manner by which the poetic enters the practical, political realm. The lives of exemplary figures poetically render worlds that speak to the imagination and constitute desire, and by so doing entrain a habitude, an *ethos*, that predisposes action in particular directions. As Taylor notes, not only do the lives of exemplary figures fine-tune a sense of what it means to live well, they also move others.[85] In moving others, their poetic rendering entails a sort of half-step to becoming practice, for it steers action down certain avenues.

Rengger revisited

Rengger's account, however admirable his emphasis on mercy and charity, unfortunately lacks such a link between poetics and politics, between theory and practice, evident in this supplementation to Weber. As such, Rengger's account risks providing no indication of how the limited reform that he insists is possible might be brought about, that is, how lives might be rooted in networks of living concern. A weak reading of Rengger's insistence on the distinction between theory and practice might be just such a place that could benefit from this account of the worlds poetically disclosed by the actions of exemplary figures like those *virtuosi* of religion whom Weber mentions. This weak reading would need to be tilted towards Rengger's emphasis in

---

[82] Talal Asad, *Secular Translations: Nation-State, Modern Self, and Calculative Reason* (New York: Columbia University Press, 2018), pp. 74–5.
[83] Talal Asad, 'Thinking about religion, belief, and politics', in Robert A. Orsi (ed), *The Cambridge Companion to Religious Studies* (Cambridge: Cambridge University Press, 2012), pp. 36–57 (42), emphasis in original.
[84] Owen and Strong, 'Introduction', p. xliv.
[85] Taylor, 'Iris Murdoch', p. 12.

his early work on a political theory driven by the question of what would need to be built in order to increase the chances of living well. So too would it need to pursue Rengger's indication that if one were actually to speak of the carry-over of theory into practice, then one would need 'to consider the things on which at least the political world of practice most obviously relies – rhetoric, motivation and how to change it, the psychology and ethics of conversion',[86] and in particular to consider how any argument would need to take the form of an imaginative exercise outlining an alternative vision that shows why one should see the world in a distinct light.[87] It would also need to consider Rengger's statement that:

> We might finally agree with [Stephen R.L.] Clark and Plato that it is the job of 'poets' – a group that includes philosophers and perhaps even political scientists – to give voices to the wind. In doing so, perhaps Political Science and International Relations – and even elements of politics and international relations – might be changed out of all recognition.[88]

For it is in such an assertion that Rengger seems to grasp Taylor's point about the poetic force of the *virtuosi* of religion, namely that they can raise others to a vertically higher plane from where a particular dilemma might be seen differently such that new possibilities might be entertained.[89] Such poetic force makes reform, however fleeting, possible because it lessens the intractability of a world in which people are purportedly simply what they are. It certainly does not furnish any code or blueprint, which both Taylor and Rengger, in any case, see as papering over both moral dilemmas and the issue of moral motivation while also eviscerating charity.[90] But, it does imply that, by constituting the capacity for practical judgement, the poetic can instill a recognition of the value of mercy and charity and effect a half-step towards creating the space within which such virtues might be exercised.

---

[86] Rengger, 'Kant, Mendelssohn', pp. 16–17.

[87] Rengger, *Political Theory, Modernity and Postmodernity*, pp. 169–70; 'Politics and international relations', in Mervyn Davies, Oliver D. Crisp, Gavin D'Costa, and Peter Hampson (eds), *Christianity and the Disciplines: The Transformation of the Disciplines*, (London: Bloomsbury, 2012b), pp. 167–82; 'Post-secularism: metaphysical not political?', in *The Anti-Pelagian Imagination in Political Theory and International Relations: Dealing in Darkness* (London and New York: Routledge, 2017), p. 152.

[88] Rengger, 'Politics and international relations', p. 180.

[89] Charles Taylor, 'Perils of moralism', in *Dilemmas and Connections: Selected Essays* (Cambridge, MA: Belknap Press of Harvard University Press, 2011), pp. 349–50.

[90] Taylor, 'Perils moralism', p. 365.

4

'Keep Your Mind in Hell, and Despair Not': Gillian Rose's Anti-Pelagianism

Kate Schick[1]

Those who in fields Elysian would dwell
Do but extend the boundaries of Hell.

Michael Oakeshott[2]

Keep your mind in hell, and despair not.

Staretz Silouan, 1866–1938[3]

Nicholas Rengger introduced me to the British philosopher Gillian Rose in 2004, and in so doing opened a door to a way of thinking and an ethos that continues to capture my imagination nearly two decades on. It is fitting that I return to Rose in this chapter honouring Rengger's work on anti-Pelagianism, as I have no doubt that part of what attracted me to Rose's thought was her resolute refusal of the Pelagian heresy of seeking a 'short cut to heaven'[4] twinned with a rejection of the politics of tragedy. My years studying with Rengger imbued in me a profound mistrust of theories that

[1] I am grateful to Emily Beausoleil, Jenny Ombler, Vassilios Paipais, Ben Thirkell-White, and Claire Timperley for their invaluable comments and suggestions.
[2] Michael Oakeshott, 'The tower of Babel', in Michael Oakeshott, *On History and Other Essays* (Indianapolis: Liberty Fund, 1999), p. 210.
[3] Epigraph to Gillian Rose, *Love's Work: A Reckoning with Life*, 1st American edition (New York: Schocken Books, 1995).
[4] Michael Oakeshott, *Rationalism in Politics and Other Essays* (Indianapolis: Liberty Fund, 2010), p. 465.

refuse to 'deal in darkness';[5] Rose's work emphatically does, enjoining us to 'keep [our] mind[s] in hell' but–crucially–to 'despair not'.[6]

This chapter has two parts. In Part One, I briefly sketch modern anti-Pelagianism, drawing primarily on Rengger's collected essays on the *Anti-Pelagian Imagination: Dealing in Darkness*.[7] I highlight four elements of Rengger's anti-Pelagianism: a sceptical relation to knowledge; a disconnect between theory and practice; a refusal of tragic visions of politics; and a particular orientation to 'the world'. In Part Two, I argue that Rose's speculative philosophy can rightly be understood as anti-Pelagian – she, too, refuses Pelagian heresies that would 'mend diremption in heaven or on earth';[8] instead, she cultivates equivocation in relation to knowledge and exchanges blueprints for action for *aporia*, or pathlessness. Like Rengger, Rose also refuses the temptation of tragedy in response to the 'darkness' of modern politics. However, I argue that Rose's work commits more fully to the project of dealing in darkness. While Rengger (following Oakeshott) cultivates a certain distance from the world, exemplified by his meditations on the relationship between theory and practice,[9] Rose calls us to a dogged and risk-filled engagement (and re-engagement) with everyday practical politics.

Modern anti-Pelagianism

In early Christianity, the Pelagian heresy refers to the idea promulgated by Pelagius, *contra* Augustine, that human beings are essentially good and can work unaided towards salvation. Following Michael Oakeshott, Rengger argues that modern political thought is dominated by a sensibility that we might term 'Pelagian', which believes 'problematic and recalcitrant though the world might be, our fate is up to us to determine. Our salvation lies, as it always has done, in our own hands'.[10] The vast majority of (Pelagian) political and IR theorists assume positive moral and political progress can be achieved by manipulating the political order via 'notions such as rights, law, governance, justice and so on'.[11] This assumption underpins approaches of

---

5   Michael Oakeshott, 'Introduction to Leviathan', in *Hobbes on Civil Association* (Indianapolis: Liberty Fund, 1960), p. 6; Nicholas Rengger, *The Anti-Pelagian Imagination in Political Theory and International Relations: Dealing in Darkness* (London and New York: Routledge, 2017), p. 2.

6   Rose, *Love's Work*.

7   Rengger, *The Anti-Pelagian Imagination*.

8   Gillian Rose, *The Broken Middle: Out of Our Ancient Society* (Oxford: Blackwell, 1992), p. xv.

9   Rengger, *The Anti-Pelagian Imagination*, pp. 167–8.

10   Ibid., p. 3.

11   Ibid., p. 3.

varying orientation – liberalism, Marxism, socialism, some forms of critical theory – and, perhaps especially, cosmopolitanism: 'the vehicle of choice, one might say, for those aiming to reach the "Promised Land" of human progress in the twentieth century'.[12] In Oakeshott's words, Pelagian thought proposes a 'short cut to heaven',[13] an image he illustrates via the Babel myth, whereby the builders of the immense tower can be understood as 'scientists' willfully attempting to reach heaven via their own efforts despite this being 'an impossibility'.[14] The deeply held belief that progress is possible – even inevitable – buttresses a commitment to perfecting the political order. It is this mark of perfectibility that is so central to Pelagian thought.

There is another set of responses to the darkness of global politics, however, which Rengger terms 'modern anti-Pelagian'. These cover a variety of approaches; '[m]odern anti-Pelagians agree only about what they oppose, not about what they propose'.[15] Rengger employs the term anti-Pelagian because:

> It is a term that escapes all the usual (and often rather tired) divisions that tend to bedevil contemporary political thought at whatever level, 'left/right', 'conservative/radical', 'realist/liberal' and so on; it allows me to focus on the sceptical, anti-perfectionist, non–utopian assumptions that *inform* theoretical reflection on human activities (including politics) without being *reducible* to any particular 'theory' (or even a group of 'theories').[16]

Anti-Pelagianism opposes the idea that humanity can 'save itself' through the accumulation of (scientific) knowledge that can then be wielded to better mould the political order. It opposes strong assumptions of moral progress, ideal theory, future-orientation, 'the building of ever more sophisticated castles in the air'.[17] It stands in radically different relation to knowledge and to action, choosing scepticism over certainty and seeing theory as 'world disclosing' rather than 'action coordinating'.[18]

A central plank of modern anti-Pelagian thought is a thoroughgoing scepticism of attempts to 'fix' understandings of the world and prescribe solutions for its ills. It opposes the committed pursuit of certain knowledge

---

[12] Ibid., p. 1.
[13] Ibid., p. 107; Oakeshott, 'The tower of Babel', pp. 179–210.
[14] Rengger, *The Anti-Pelagian Imagination*, p. 165; Oakeshott, *Rationalism in Politics and Other Essays*, p. 465.
[15] Rengger, *The Anti-Pelagian Imagination*, p. 5.
[16] Ibid., p. 4, emphasis in original.
[17] Ibid., p. 3.
[18] Ibid., p. 83.

in preference for a very different relation to knowledge. In a discussion of William Connolly's anti-Pelagianism, Rengger unpacks the notion of scepticism, highlighting the room for ambiguity that it creates:

> the most obvious term one might use [to describe Connolly's attitude to the modern (or late modern) sensibility] is scepticism: scepticism, that is to say, towards the ambitions that require the assertion of *the* truth or *the* method of discovering it, that require fixed identities, sole allegiances, clear hierarchies and a resistance of the idea of ambiguity.[19]

A sceptical relation to knowledge leaves space for not knowing, for uncertainty, for ambiguity; it rejects the 'scientific' desire for epistemic certainty and for the precise wielding of certain knowledge for particular ends.

The profoundly different relation to *knowledge* is twinned in anti-Pelagian thought with a profoundly different relation to *action*. For mainstream rationalist (or Pelagian) approaches, theory is taken as a guide for action. Ethical theories are often devised at a distance from practical politics but are intended to serve as a guide for political action. In this way, they 'do a great deal of work in contemporary political life',[20] 'providing a foundation from which to launch particular political moves or strategies'.[21] However, anti-Pelagian thought disrupts this close relationship between theory and practice, calling into question the commitment to ethical theory as primarily 'action coordinating' and arguing for the importance of theory that is, instead, primarily 'world disclosing'.[22] Indeed, Rengger argues that 'there are reasons for supposing that ethical theory is *better* understood as world disclosing than action coordinating'.[23] He continues:

> the kind of understanding [Oakeshott] thinks we can have of the world does enable us to see more clearly the character of that world and thus resist false attempts to portray the world in a different light. What it cannot do, however – and what I am suggesting he is right to suggest it cannot do – is to *become* 'practice'; to become, of itself, an engagement in the world or give rise to such an engagement ... what I am here

---

[19] Ibid., p. 92, emphasis in original.

[20] Madeleine Fagan, *Ethics and Politics after Poststructuralism* (Edinburgh: Edinburgh University Press, 2013), p. 1.

[21] Fagan, *Ethics and Politics*, p. 2.

[22] Rengger, *The Anti-Pelagian Imagination*, pp. 83–4; Stephen K. White, *Political Theory and Postmodernism* (Cambridge, England; New York: Cambridge University Press, 1991), pp. 25–7.

[23] Rengger, *The Anti-Pelagian Imagination*, p. 84, emphasis in original.

calling the anti-Pelagian sensibility runs counter to one of the most general assumptions made about scholarship in international relations (and indeed elsewhere in the social and political science) – that it can have a direct and positive impact on the world of practice, that it can help to build a better world.[24]

For Rengger, theory 'simply is what it is' – it 'does not offer "guidance" of any sort at all'.[25] Rather than offering specific guidelines for action, 'the root of ethics is ethos – a manner of being'.[26] The *ethos* of an anti-Pelagian imagination can be understood as a form of *Sittlichkeit*, drawing us towards ethical life.[27]

Rengger's disruption of the modern assumption that theory ought to act as a guide for practical action stems in no small part from his reading of, and adherence to, Oakeshott's distinction between modes of experience.[28] In his famous essay, 'The voice of poetry in the conversation of mankind', Oakeshott distinguishes between different modes of experience, or 'voices', which encompass different modes of speaking and comprise a wider conversation in which none of the voices takes precedence. These voices include history, science, practice, and aesthetics. Oakeshott maintains, however, that '[i]n recent centuries the conversation, both in public and within ourselves, has become boring because it has been engrossed by two voices, the voice of practical activity and the voice of "science": to know and to contrive are our pre-eminent occupations'.[29] This Western obsession with the practical and the scientific is, for Oakeshott, not only boring, but also deeply problematic:

> for a conversation to be appropriated by one or two voices is an insidious vice because in the passage of time it takes on the appearance of a virtue. All utterance should be relevant; but relevance in conversation is determined by the course of the conversation itself, it owes nothing to an external standard. Consequently an established monopoly will not only make it difficult for another voice to be heard, but it will

---

[24] Ibid., p. 167, emphasis in original.

[25] Ibid., p. 16. Indeed, Rengger points out the dangers of turning to theory for guidance, saying that theoretical reflection 'can, and usually does, have a *terrible* influence' on practice (Ibid., p. 16, emphasis in original). He continues by contending that '[t]he problem is the kind of knowledge that is assumed – universalistic, not particularistic, general, not local' (Ibid., p. 16).

[26] Ibid., p. 84, emphasis in original.

[27] Ibid., p. 84.

[28] Michael Oakeshott, *Experience and Its Modes* (Cambridge University Press, 2015); Oakeshott, *Rationalism in Politics and Other Essays*.

[29] Oakeshott, *Rationalism in Politics and Other Essays*, p. 493.

also make it seem proper that it should not be heard; it is convicted in advance of irrelevance.[30]

The appropriation of the (Euro)modern conversation by the voices of science and of practical activity has become so normalized that it has edged out other voices, deeming them irrelevant in the context of a conversation fixated in large part on knowing and doing.

In his reflections on Oakeshott's metaphor of the conversation, Rengger maintains that although Oakeshott does not believe that we can 'escape practice', he does think it is possible 'to corral it'[31] and thus to allow other modes of speaking – of history, philosophy, poetry – to be given voice. Rengger argues that '[i]t is because philosophical voices – and historical ones – are *not practical* that gives them their distinctive role and character. If one subsumes philosophy or ... history into the idiom of practice, then one has violated the character of the conversation'.[32] However, modern political thought has overwhelmingly become subsumed into this idiom, adhering to what Oakeshott terms 'the politics of faith'[33] – that is, the mode of speaking of the majority of political and IR theory is underpinned by a faith in perfectionism, a belief that we can reach heaven via our own efforts. As such, Rengger argues, they fall into the Pelagian heresy that we can pursue salvation unaided. Resisting the 'politics of faith' is difficult: Rengger observes that its 'deeply sedimented assumptions' are at the heart of modern political theory and that trying to 'overcome this logic ... will require rethinking, even unthinking, many of the beliefs and assumptions that have shaped the way we think about ourselves'.[34] *Anti-Pelagian* voices disrupt many of these assumptions and, as such, are important interlocutors for Rengger as he seeks to make space for a more multi-vocal conversation.

What unites modern anti-Pelagians, then, is an opposition to and disruption of dominant assumptions about knowledge and action and the relation between the two. Anti-Pelagians oppose knowable 'hyperrationalist' theory of a particular orientation: 'seduced by the lure of thinking that it can "help"'[35] by serving as a direct guide for political practice. The

---

[30] Ibid., pp. 493–4.
[31] Nicholas Rengger, 'The boundaries of conversation: a response to Dallmayr', *Millennium: Journal of International Studies* 30, 2 (2001a), p. 363.
[32] Rengger, 'The boundaries of conversation', p. 362, emphasis added.
[33] Timothy Fuller, ed, *Michael Oakeshott: The Politics of Faith and the Politics of Scepticism* (New Haven, CT: Yale University Press, 2009); Rengger, 'The boundaries of conversation', p. 363.
[34] Rengger, 'The boundaries of conversation' pp. 363–4.
[35] Nicholas Rengger, 'Political theory and international relations: promised land or exit from Eden?', *International Affairs* 76, 4 (2000), p. 769.

future-oriented, utopian orientation of Pelagian thought is anathema for anti-Pelagians, who insist that we attend to the here-and-now, that we be willing to 'deal in darkness'.[36]

Anti-Pelagianism is a broad church, however, and although its adherents are united in what they oppose, they differ in their response to the darkness to which they insist we attend. For political realists such as Hans Morgenthau, and for contemporary thinkers who revive that tradition, human life is best understood as tragic and it is the inability to face the inherent tragedy of political life that is at the root of the 'disease' of liberal thought.[37] For Rengger, following Oakeshott, however, this is a deeply problematic view that risks becoming a 'mirror image' of the progressive narratives that anti-Pelagians reject, and this is where political realism departs from the anti-Pelagian imagination.[38] Where narratives of progress rest on a belief that they can usher in a better future – to 'dwell in fields Elysian' – narratives of tragedy depend on a 'nostalgia for a better ordered past'.[39] Rengger insists that 'human life is not "tragic", it is just life … one should see political life not as a "dystopia", but just as political life in all of its varieties and messiness'.[40]

A second point of departure for political realism from a modern anti-Pelagian imagination is that 'it still makes "the world" the standard',[41] accepting the logic of the dominant world order and working within the constraints of that (state-centric, capitalist, individualist) world. Although it sees clearly the impossibility of securing heaven on earth, its tragic vision nonetheless operates within the bounds of existing structures. For Rengger, realism in IR remains 'a child of the world; to be sure, a chastened child, one aware of the problems and pitfalls that lie in store for the world's children, but a child of the world for all that'.[42] A more thoroughgoing anti-Pelagianism, for Rengger, would 'stand *outside* the logic of [the] world':[43]

---

[36] Rengger, *The Anti-Pelagian Imagination*, p. 2; Michael Oakeshott, 'Introduction to Leviathan', in *Hobbes on Civil Association* (Indianapolis: Liberty Fund, 1960), p. 6.

[37] Hans Morgenthau, *Scientific Man Versus Power Politics* (Chicago: University of Chicago Press, 1946), p. 6. See also discussions in, for example, Tony Erskine and Richard Ned Lebow, *Tragedy and International Relations* (Palgrave Macmillan: 2012); Christoph Frei, *Hans J. Morgenthau: An Intellectual Biography* (Louisiana State University Press: 2001); Richard Ned Lebow, *The Tragic Vision of Politics: Ethics, Interests, and Orders* (Cambridge University Press, New York: 2003); William E. Scheuerman, 'Was Morgenthau a realist? Revisiting Scientific Man Vs. Power Politics', *Constellations* 14 (2007), pp. 506–30; Michael C. Williams, *The Realist Tradition and the Limits of International Relations* (Cambridge University Press: 2005).

[38] Rengger, *The Anti-Pelagian Imagination*, p. 166.

[39] Ibid., p. 166.

[40] Ibid., p. 76.

[41] Ibid., p. 166.

[42] Ibid., p. 166.

[43] Rengger, 'Political theory and international relations', p. 168, emphasis added.

A modern anti-Pelagian will acknowledge, with the realist, the intractability of the practical world, but refuse the realist's accommodation to the logic of that world, and rather seek to understand it from the outside, as it were. Such an individual might also accept, with many who seek to reform the world, that sometimes reform will occur and that sometimes it should be welcomed, but they would also refuse the claim that such reform either would be or should be necessarily permanent and that somehow the world of human conduct will itself change. And, again, they will stand outside the logic of his world. And that, perhaps, is the point with which we might close. The world of international relations will look very different when viewed through the lens of the anti-Pelagian imagination: not because many of the features of the world will be unfamiliar, but because the logic of how they are understood and what follows from that understanding will be very different.[44]

For Rengger, realist thought parts ways with the anti-Pelagian imagination – or ethos – when it insists on understanding and engaging the world on its own terms. Standing *outside* the logic of the world, for Rengger, is one of the hallmarks of anti-Pelagian thinkers – a refusal to take the world as given as they engage in the task of world-disclosure.

Rose's anti-Pelagianism

On the face of it, perhaps, Gillian Rose's radical Hegelianism has little in common with Oakeshottian conservatism. However, as Rengger argues, the conception of anti-Pelagianism is compelling in part because it helps us to think across the usual (somewhat tired) divisions between left and right, radical and conservative. Rengger relished the provocation of his stance in rejecting progressive politics for a resolute anti-Pelagianism; this provocation, in turn, opened me to the possibilities that inhere in thinking otherwise. Part of what made Rengger a wonderful co-reader of Rose was that their thought met in their anti-Pelagianism, in their refusal of utopian visions and tragic resignation.[45] Rose's thought sits *between* tragedy and utopia.[46] She emphatically refuses utopian short cuts to heaven, be they via the rationalist wielding of certain knowledge or messianic visions of a world made new. She also refuses to perceive the darkness of modern politics as tragic, insisting

---

[44] Rengger, *The Anti-Pelagian Imagination*, p. 168.
[45] Rengger supervised my PhD thesis at the University of St Andrews from 2004 to 2008.
[46] Kate Schick, *Gillian Rose: A Good Enough Justice* (Edinburgh: Edinburgh University Press, 2012), pp. 105–25.

that to invoke the notion of tragedy is too often to abrogate responsibility and foreclose political action. Rose argues that both these positions take *easy paths*, refusing the uncertain and risky work that characterizes engagement with 'the city in which we all live'.[47] In what follows, I briefly sketch Rose's refusal of utopian hope and tragic pessimism, before turning to her radical Hegelian orientation towards knowing and acting as 'fallible and precarious, but risk-able'[48] – an orientation that, I argue, is resolutely anti-Pelagian. I finish by reflecting on the ways in which Rose and Rengger's thought diverges and argue that Rose's relation to 'the world' more resolutely 'deals in darkness'. I maintain that although Rose's speculative theory refuses to be captured by the *logic* of the world, it does not stand *outside* the world; instead, it engages doggedly with everyday practical politics in pursuit of a 'good enough justice'.[49] As such, Rose's work commits more fully to the project of world disclosure, seeing the journey of coming to know as one that requires knowers themselves to be vulnerable and open to risk.

Utopia and tragedy as euporia

Like Rengger, Rose emphatically refuses utopian shortcuts to heaven. The idea of utopia, coined by Thomas More in 1516, has, at its core, a play-on-words that signals its inherent ambiguity. Depending on the Greek prefix used, it can mean 'good place' (εὐ) or 'non-place' (οὐ) – referencing a place of perfection or happiness on the one hand or a place that does not (yet) exist on the other.[50] A Rosean philosophy rejects utopias of both kinds, noting that to 'dwell in fields Elysian'[51] is to bypass the difficult work of the political in the here and now by focusing on a future perfection or idyllic past.

As discussed earlier, modern Pelagian thinking invokes utopias of the first kind – 'good place' – and is marked by a fundamental belief in the perfectibility of the world, adhering strongly to the Pelagian heresy of being able to achieve salvation unaided. These progressive approaches are deeply rooted in Enlightenment visions of progress, focusing on universal notions such as 'rights, law, governance, justice' as paths to moral progress.[52] They have a particular relation to knowledge, gathering 'useful knowledge'[53] that can be used to explain both what has happened and what should be done.

47 Gillian Rose, *Mourning Becomes the Law: Philosophy and Representation* (Cambridge: Cambridge University Press, 1996), p. 34.
48 Rose, *Mourning Becomes the Law*, p. 13.
49 Gillian Rose, *Love's Work*, p. 116.
50 Miguel Abensour, 'Persistent utopia', *Constellations* 15, 3 (2008), p. 407.
51 Oakeshott, 'The Tower of Babel', p. 210.
52 Rengger, *The Anti-Pelagian Imagination*, p. 3.
53 Raymond Geuss, *Outside Ethics* (Princeton, NJ: Princeton University Press, 2005), p. 3.

This knowledge is confident and certain; those who wield it see it as the 'key to human salvation'.[54] However, Rose rejects the hubris of progressive rationalism's claim to 'absolute and universal authority' and its concomitant sweeping of 'all particularity and peculiarity from its path'.[55] This confident path – that understands both 'what is' and 'what ought to be done'[56] – is *euporia*, the easy way. The combination of confident epistemology and confident moral judgement leaves little room for vulnerability in the pursuit of universal good and fails to acknowledge that 'all moral judgement is unsafe'.[57]

Utopias of the second kind (referencing a 'non place') are marked by the absence of a positive vision of a 'good place' that might be worked towards and achieved; instead, they act as a counterpoint to the bleakness of modern global politics by marking a 'stubborn impulse toward freedom and justice' despite this bleakness.[58] Radical leftist thinkers who embrace this version of utopia advocate a politics of the *impossible*, holding fast to a vision of a world made new in the face of ongoing domination and oppression. These visions vary: Walter Benjamin invokes the memory of an ideal age,[59] Jacques Derrida references a future-to-come outside teleological history,[60] and Slavoj Žižek insists that we '*hold this utopian place of the global alternative open*, even if it remains empty, living on borrowed time, awaiting the content to fill it'.[61] What unites these thinkers, though, is a refusal to fill out their utopian visions or to posit reformist steps that might be taken towards a knowable goal. Their relation to knowledge is radically different from progressive liberal thinkers – in the place of confident certainty is radical uncertainty;

---

54 Gillian Rose, *Paradiso* (Menard Press, 1999), p. 25.

55 Rose, *Love's Work*, p. 128.

56 Geuss, *Outside Ethics*, p. 3. Geuss (2005) refers to the query 'What ought we to do?' as the 'central ethical question'. The response generates 'some set of universal laws or rules or principles; in particular, a set of universal laws on which "we" would all agree (under some further specified circumstance)', p. 3.

57 Kimberley Hutchings, 'A place of greater safety? Securing judgement in international ethics', in Amanda Russell Beattie and Kate Schick (eds), *The Vulnerable Subject: Beyond Rationalism in International Relations* (Basingstoke: Palgrave Macmillan, 2013), p. 26; see also Kate Schick, 'Gillian Rose and vulnerable judgement', in Amanda Russell Beattie and Kate Schick (eds) *The Vulnerable Subject: Beyond Rationalism in International Relations* (London: Palgrave Macmillan UK, 2013), pp. 43–61.

58 Abensour, 'Persistent utopia', p. 407.

59 Walter Benjamin, *Illuminations* (New York: Schocken Books, 2007).

60 Jacques Derrida, *Specters of Marx: The State of the Debt, the Work of Mourning, and the New International* (New York: Routledge, 1994), p. 18; Owen Ware, 'Dialectic of the past/ Disjuncture of the future: Derrida and Benjamin on the concept of messianism', *Journal for Cultural and Religious Theory* 5, 2 (2004), pp. 99–114.

61 Judith Butler et al., *Contingency, Hegemony, Universality: Contemporary Dialogues on the Left* (Verso, 2000), p. 325, emphasis in original.

in the place of certain hope is 'hope in a blank utopia'.[62] However, Rose sets her face against this version of utopia, too, arguing that the content-less promise invoked by these visions of utopia distracts from engagement with the here-and-now and invites a 'counsel of hopelessness' in the guise of messianic hope.[63]

Rose, then, refuses utopian visions of either kind – perfectionist or messianic – arguing that they displace attention from lived social and political realities and invite a deeply problematic relation to reason.[64] However, like Rengger, she also refuses the invocation of tragedy in response to the gap between the desire for progress towards the good and the reality of ongoing domination and oppression. A Rosean sensibility has much in common with political realism's annihilating critique of rationalist political theory, expressed particularly powerfully by Hans Morgenthau. Rose shares Morgenthau's critique of liberal rationalism's belief in 'the power of science to solve all problems and, more particularly, all political problems which confront man in the modern age',[65] rejecting the disembedded and disembodied gathering of 'more facts' to solve political problems.[66] She also shares Morgenthau's critique of robust moral progress towards the good. However, where Morgenthau perceives the imperfectability of humanity as deeply tragic, and necessitating a conservative politics of the possible,[67] Rose emphatically refuses resignation. As I argue later, Rose insists that we unflinchingly confront *what is* and doggedly engage in the difficult task of coming to understand the varied actualities'of modern life, as well as take the risk of acting politically in response. The epigraph to her philosophical memoir, *Love's Work*, urges us to 'keep your mind in hell, and despair not'.[68]

---

[62] Dominick LaCapra, *Writing History, Writing Trauma*, Parallax (Baltimore: Johns Hopkins University Press, 2001), p. 152.

[63] Rose, *Mourning Becomes the Law*, p. 70. See also Schick, *Gillian Rose*, pp. 119–22.

[64] In the case of moral rationalism's 'good place' utopias, reason is too often instrumentalized for particular, predetermined ends, becoming profoundly impoverished. In the case of radical 'non place' utopias, reason is too often demonized for being exclusionary and oppressive and thus becomes 'despairing rationalism without reason', Rose, *Paradiso*, p. 28. See the discussion in Kate Schick, ' "The tree is really rooted in the sky": Beside difficulty in Gillian Rose's political theory', in Joshua B Davis (ed), *Misrecognitions: Gillian Rose and the Task of Political Theology* (Cascade Books, 2018), pp. 87–106.

[65] Hans Morgenthau, *Scientific Man Versus Power Politics* (Chicago: University of Chicago Press, 1946), p. vi.

[66] Morgenthau, *Scientific Man Versus Power Politics*, p. 215.

[67] Morgenthau laments: '[s]uspended between his spiritual destiny which he cannot fulfill and his animal nature in which he cannot remain, [man] is forever contemned to experience the longings of his mind, and his actual condition as his personal, eminently human tragedy'. Morgenthau, *Scientific Man Versus Power Politics*, p. 221.

[68] Gillian Rose, *Love's Work*, epigraph, attributed to Staretz Silouan, 1866–1938.

The injunction to keep your mind in hell asks us to start by examining the contours of misrecognition that shape our social and political worlds, working towards a deeper understanding of the structures and norms that sustain oppressive practices. However, Rose enjoins us to 'despair not' in response to continued abuses of power and privilege, maintaining that to despair is to abscond responsibility. Instead, she invites us to do the political work of coming to understand and mourn losses and to take the risk of acting politically in pursuit of a 'good enough justice'.

Towards an aporetic anti-Pelagianism

Rose's anti-Pelagian refusal of utopian and tragic visions of politics refuses the seduction of *euporia*, of easy paths that preclude engagement with the here and now. Rose's emphatic refusal of these approaches – rationalist, messianic, or despairing – stems from her radical Hegelianism, which has a profoundly different orientation to knowing and acting. Like other anti-Pelagian thinkers, Rose refuses the future-orientation of modern Pelagianism that directs us away from the contours of our actually existing world in preference for sketching a better future. Instead, Rose starts with an examination of *what is*, arguing that our task as social and political theorists is to begin with the work of tracing the contours of the worlds in which we live. Her present-focused examination of actuality is difficult theory, refusing grand(iose) theories' simple visions in preference for subtler philosophies that she describes as 'grey in grey':

> This subtle array, this grey in grey, would turn hubris not into humility but into motile configuration. Grey in grey warns against philosophy's pride of *Sollen*, against any proscription or prescription, any imposition of ideals, imaginary communities or 'progressive narrations'. Instead, the 'idealizations' of philosophy would acknowledge and recognize actuality and not force or fantasize it.[69]

Rose's relation to knowing starts from where we are, rather than where we ought to be, turning away from the pride of prescription towards an ongoing journey towards comprehension characterized by 'motile configuration'.

As discussed earlier, one of the central planks of anti-Pelagian thought is its opposition to the dogged pursuit of epistemic certainty in preference for ambiguity and scepticism. Rose's relationship to knowing is decidedly anti-Pelagian, inviting uncertainty and equivocation in the place of certainty. For Rose, following Hegel, the journey of 'coming to know' is ongoing and

---

[69] Rose, *The Broken Middle*, p. xi.

precarious: it is a journey of recognition, which implies an initial cognition that is partial or mistaken in some way needing to be re-cognized, or known again.[70] In this way, recognition works against ignorance, asking us to examine that which we think we know ('the familiar or well known') and to be willing to know again, as we work towards a fuller understanding of the world in which we live.[71] Rose asserts that 'wisdom works with equivocation',[72] rejecting the valorization of epistemic certainty in acknowledgement of the *ongoing* endeavour of coming to know. This aporetic or struggle-filled path leads us on a journey in which we will inevitably make mistakes and need to know again – to re-cognize – as we negotiate our worlds. Rose's embrace of equivocation includes a profoundly countercultural willingness to '[be] in uncertainties'.[73]

Part of knowing equivocally, for Rose, is knowing *relationally* and *vulnerably*. Rose points to the relational (Hegelian) dimensions of coming to know via our encounters with others rather than primarily through the accumulation of rational facts and data. She argues that it is a mistake to think of ourselves as 'isolated [selves] separate from community and corporation'.[74] Instead, we are relational and vulnerable subjects who are always in the process of becoming through our encounters with others. As for Hegel, for Rose:

> the moment of mutual recognition involves a 'speculative' realisation on the part of the ego that its identity already contains within it aspects of the other and that its being is really a relational, inter-dependent existence, a form of social being (*Gemeinwesen*) – the 'I that is We and We that is I'.[75]

The dance of mutual recognition, on this reading, involves the gradual transformation of our understanding of ourselves and of others; we come to understand that we are not isolated or atomized beings but relational and vulnerable. The journey towards recognition also invites equivocation; it renders our understanding of selves and others less self-certain as we

---

[70] Gillian Rose, *Hegel Contra Sociology* (London: Atlantic Highlands; N.J: Athlone; Humanities Press, 1981), p. 71.

[71] Rose, *Hegel Contra Sociology*, p. 71.

[72] Rose, *Mourning Becomes the Law*, p. 2.

[73] Rose, *Paradiso*, p. 31.

[74] Ibid., p. 26; see also Judith Butler, *Giving an Account of Oneself* (Fordham University Press, 2005).

[75] Tarik Kochi, 'Being, nothing, becoming', in Matthew Stone, Illan rua Wall, and Costas Douzinas (eds), *New Critical Legal Thinking* (Birkbeck Law Press, 2012), p. 137; see also Georg W. Hegel, *Phenomenology of Spirit* (Oxford: Clarendon Press, 1977), p. 110.

gradually come to understand the complex and many-layered contours of (mis)recognition that have shaped us.

Rose twins her anti-Pelagian relation to knowing – her refusal of the hyperrationalist pursuit of 'more facts'[76] to yield certain knowledge – with an anti-Pelagian relation to action. As discussed earlier, anti-Pelagian thought disrupts the relationship between theory and praxis, calling into question the unproblematic vision of political theory as 'action coordinating'.[77] The assumption that ethical theory could have a 'direct and positive impact on the world of practice'[78] is rejected by Rose as *euporia*, the easy way, in preference for *aporia*, or pathlessness. The aporetic way is 'without a predetermined path'[79] and requires us to be willing to sit with unknowing.

For Rose, theory does not *become practice* in the way that Pelagian scholarship assumes. However, although Rose maintains that theory does not offer positive guidance for 'what ought to be done' in relation to social and political ills, it is by no means divorced from praxis. Instead, Rose embraces an equivocal relation to action as well as knowledge: she insists that we risk acting politically, but that we do so aware that we will inevitably fail and need to act again. For Rose, political risk-taking is 'being at a loss yet exploring various routes, different ways towards the "good enough justice", which recognizes the intrinsic and the contingent limitations in its exercise'.[80] Once again, Rose eschews the counsel of perfection, of pristine guidelines for action, in favour of starting from where we are and taking the risk of working towards a situated justice. She sees failure as an inevitable part of this journey of risk-filled engagement, whereby failure does not entail reproach or devastation, but is learned from and seen as a productive part of an engaged political life.

Possibilities/provocation

Rose's thought resonates with Rengger's characterization of anti-Pelagianism on multiple levels: it emphatically refuses utopian and tragic visions of politics and its orientation to knowledge and action are radically countercultural. However, it also diverges from Rengger's thought, highlighting again the point he makes about anti-Pelagian thinkers being united by what they *oppose*, not what they *propose*. Rose's deeply relational way of knowing, for example, differs markedly from Rengger's Oakeshottian anti-Pelagianism,

---

[76] Morgenthau, *Scientific Man Versus Power Politics*, p. 215.
[77] Rengger, *The Anti-Pelagian Imagination*, pp. 83–4.
[78] Rengger, 'Political theory and international relations:?', p. 167.
[79] Rose, *The Broken Middle*, p. 201.
[80] Rose, *Love's Work*, p. 116.

as does her emphasis on aporetic political engagement. In closing, I bring together these differences by noting that Rose's orientation to 'the world', while still anti-Pelagian, differs markedly from Rengger's Oakeshottian orientation. I argue that the dogged commitment to engage in everyday practical politics that characterizes Rose's speculative philosophy commits more fully to the project of world disclosure, reflecting the entangled quality of being in the world as we come to know it (however equivocally).

In the final paragraph of *The Anti-Pelagian Imagination*, Rengger argues that modern anti-Pelagians 'stand outside the logic of [the] world',[81] in contrast to realists whose thought is captured by the world's logic and who are unable (or unwilling) to escape it. For Rengger, standing outside the logic of the world implies a principled refusal to be captured by dominant visions of the world, whether these be progressive visions that claim to know the world and be able to change it (in particular, rationalist, ways), or tragic visions that claim to know the world but be tragically powerless to effect change. Thus far, Rose's thought is in accord with Rengger's anti-Pelagianism. However, there is a *distancing* implied by Rengger's Oakeshottian theorizing that is not present in Rose's thought, and it is here that I think Rose and Rengger part ways. This difference is apparent both at the level of theory and of praxis, which I discuss in turn.

Rengger's meditations on our relation to the world stem from his reading of Oakeshott's distinction between 'religious' and 'worldly' attitudes. Oakeshott remarks that 'what really distinguishes the worldly man is ... his belief in the reality and permanence of the present order of things'.[82] A worldly attitude accepts 'an intrinsic moral order'[83] from which unfolds a settled notion of what it means to be secure or successful and one that continues, unchallenged, into the future. In contrast, a 'religious' attitude 'seeks freedom ... from all embarrassment alike of regret for the past and calculation on the future ... *memento vivere* is the sole precept of religion'.[84] For Rengger, (Pelagian) modern thought – and, to a lesser extent, some forms of anti-Pelagianism – remains 'worldly': obsessed with the future and with 'standards that can allow us to make judgements that convey the certainties we need'.[85] They are captured by the world's logic and incapable of thinking otherwise. The anti-Pelagianism that Rengger advocates, however, refuses the future-orientation of Pelagian thought, instead, engaging with

---

[81] Rengger, *The Anti-Pelagian Imagination*, p. 168.
[82] Michael Oakeshott, 'Religion and the world', in *Religion, Politics, and the Moral Life* (New Haven, CT: Yale University Press, 1993); Rengger, *The Anti-Pelagian Imagination*, p. 94.
[83] Rengger, *The Anti-Pelagian Imagination*, p. 94.
[84] Oakeshott, 'Religion and the world', p. 37; Rengger, 'Political theory and international relations', p. 165.
[85] Rengger, *The Anti-Pelagian Imagination*, p. 95.

life in the present. He cites Oakeshott's reflections on the religious attitude, noting that '[t]he religious man will inherit nothing he cannot possess by actual insight ... nor will the future be allowed to lay its withering hand on the present ... the religious man ... sees all things in the light of his own mind, and desires to possess nothing save by present insight'.[86] This 'religiosity' – a paradoxical insistence on life lived in the present – is at the heart of Rengger's anti-Pelagianism.

Rose's refusal of Pelagian thought also insists on attention to the present; however, her Hegelian call to start from 'where we are' has a very different quality from Rengger's anti-Pelagianism. Although Rose's speculative theory refuses to be captured by the logic of the world, she insists that we attend closely to the logic of the world and trouble it. Rengger's claim that 'human life is not "tragic", it is *just life*'[87] implies an acceptance of life – however messy – that differs from Rose's aporetic engagement. Rose's world-disclosing theory insists that we start by examining the contours of our actually existing world(s), in a deeply Hegelian commitment to coming-to-know. However, this task of world disclosure, for Rose, is not done from a distance. Although we can resist capture by the logic of the world, as ethical theorists and political actors *we do not stand outside the world*; on the contrary we must understand ourselves as 'agent, enraged, and invested'.[88] Thus, when theorizing, we do not stand outside the world but inside it, starting from where we are, not where we ought to be.[89] Furthermore, *we bring ourselves to this task*, asking how we shape our worlds. The task of ethical theory, on this reading, is an engaged task – we do not, as Kimberly Hutchings put it, undertake it at little risk to our sense of selves; instead, '[international ethical and political theorists] put themselves, as well as those of whom they speak, on the line in the ethical judgements that they make'.[90] In bringing ourselves to this task, we do not do it alone – we do not 'see all things in the light of [our] own mind[s]'[91] – but in relationship, examining our relatedness to

---

[86] Oakeshott, 'Religion and the world', pp. 33, 38; Rengger, *The Anti-Pelagian Imagination*, p. 94.

[87] Rengger, *The Anti-Pelagian Imagination*, p. 76, emphasis added. See also Vassilios Paipais' recollection of Rengger's oft-made remark, which he would make with a shrug: 'life is, and always has been, simply life, nothing more or less than that, and there is nothing to bemoan in this'. Vassilios Paipais, 'Between faith and scepticism: Nicholas Rengger's reflections on the "hybridity" of modernity', *International Relations*, 2020, p. 631.

[88] Rose, *Mourning Becomes the Law*, p. 62.

[89] As already noted, Rengger's Oakeshottian theory insists on living in the present, untrammeled by the past or the future (see Oakeshott's meditations on a 'religious' perspective). However, Rengger's emphasis on living in the present has a very different quality to Rose's emphasis on the present, as I discuss later.

[90] Hutchings, 'A place of greater safety?', p. 39.

[91] Oakeshott, 'Religion and the world', p. 38; Rengger, *The Anti-Pelagian Imagination*, p. 94.

others and to ourselves and our embeddedness in histories and structures. Rengger, too, insists on an embedded understanding of our political lives, noting that our political preferences are 'rooted in our histories' and often 'partial, compromised or divided'.[92] However, Rengger's scepticism is more removed and less vulnerable than Rose's equivocation. Where Rose brings her worlds together,[93] Rengger adopts Oakeshott's central tenet of 'the modal distinctiveness of the different worlds of human experience',[94] where the world of practice and the world of the poetic operate only 'in oblique relation'.[95] As already discussed, Rengger insists that the richness of the philosophical voices' contributions to wider conversations stems from the fact that they are *not practical* – they help us to better understand the world in which we live but operate in separate and distinctive register to practical politics and cannot 'become practice'.

Rose's speculative praxis, too, refuses to be captured by the logic of the world. Like Rengger, she does not believe that theory can 'become practice', in a direct sense, acting as a blueprint for action that would usher in 'fields Elysian'. However, Rose is deeply committed to ethico-political action and this commitment is inextricably entwined with her philosophical orientation. As discussed earlier, alongside a commitment to an aporetic path that would come to better understand social and political actualities, sits a commitment to political risk-taking. This risky political engagement does not sit outside the world; on the contrary, it doggedly engages with everyday practical politics. This active political engagement:

> *comes to learn* that will, action, reflection and passivity have consequences for others and for oneself which may not be anticipated and can never be completely anticipated; which *comes to learn* its unintended complicity in the use and abuse of power; and hence to redraw, *again and again*, the measures, the bonding and boundaries between me and me, subject and subjectivity, singular and individual, non-conscious and unconscious. This is *activity beyond activity* ... The *work* of these experiences bears the meaning of meaning – the relinquishing *and taking up again* of activity which requires the fullest acknowledgement of active complicity.[96]

---

[92] Rengger, *The Anti-Pelagian Imagination*, p. 77.

[93] In an interview with Radio host Andy O'Mahoney, Rose maintained: 'In order to write philosophy or be a philosopher, you've got to bring together your emotional and your intellectual life. If you keep them separate, you'll be a bad philosopher'. Vincent W. Lloyd, 'Interview with Gillian Rose', *Theory, Culture and Society* 25, 7–8 (2008): p. 212.

[94] Rengger, *The Anti-Pelagian Imagination*, p. 165.

[95] Ibid., p. 119.

[96] Rose, *Mourning Becomes the Law*, p. 122, emphases in original.

For Rose, then, political engagement does not take place at a distance from oneself or others; action and reflection are deeply entwined, and we learn about ourselves (and our 'complicity in the use and abuse of power') and others as we act.

Standing outside the logic of the world, for both Rose and Rengger, is part of an ethos that for both thinkers is shot through with joy.[97] Perhaps this joy stems, in part at least, from an openness to surprises enabled by the rejection of (predictable) progressive politics. However, the joy that permeates their thought differs in quality. Joy, in Rengger's work, stems in part from a commitment to be content and to enjoy life despite its vicissitudes. He argues: '[o]nly if we can be content to be what we are, understanding the inevitably fragmentary character of our experiences and the tensions and dissonances of human life and conduct, may we properly enjoy ourselves and our lives'.[98] Once again, there is a distancing implied by Rengger's work that stems in part from his commitment to a disjuncture between theory and practice.

For Rose, in contrast, joy does not come from contentment, nor does it sit at a distance from the world of practice. Instead, joy stems from continuing to risk knowing and acting. A vulnerable and uncertain engagement with structures of power, 'whether disturbing or joyful ... is full of surprises'.[99] Indeed, for Rose, a faith-filled life 'lead[s] along the path of despair to the walkways of ripening olive trees'.[100] Where she is surprised by joy, love, and grace, she contends that it 'does not make me ecstatic, unreal, unworldly: it returns me to the vocation of the everyday – to [a] sense of quotidian justice'.[101] The ethos that Rose embraces – the pursuit of ethical life – is an ethos that stays in the fray, engaging with the everyday. Rose's insistence that we come to better understand our world and our place in it is twinned with a commitment to risk acting politically, not in confident expectation of positive political change, but in determined pursuit of a better justice – trying, failing, learning and trying again. The sometimes joyful and sometimes disturbing pursuit of ethical life insists that we 'deal in darkness', but that we do so not at the comfortable distance of Rengger's

---

[97] Indeed, I conjecture that the joyous aspects of Rose's work were in part what attracted Rengger to her thought – one of his comments during supervision sessions was that I needed to do more to capture this aspect of her thought.

[98] Rengger, *The Anti-Pelagian Imagination*, p. 165.

[99] Gillian Rose, *Judaism and Modernity: Philosophical Essays* (Oxford, UK; Cambridge, MA: B. Blackwell, 1993), p. 9.

[100] Rose, *Paradiso*, p. 38.

[101] Ibid., p. 21. For more on Rose and joy, see Schick, '"The tree is really rooted in the sky": Beside difficulty in Gillian Rose's political theory'.

anti-Pelagianism; instead, Rose implores us to bring our worlds together in a risky and entangled engagement with everyday life.

Conclusion

In this chapter, I have put Nicholas Rengger's work in conversation with Gillian Rose – an unlikely pairing at first glance. However, in reading Rose through Rengger, I have argued that both thinkers embrace an anti-Pelagian imagination that tarries with darkness: a sensibility that refuses both utopian fantasies of progress and tragic retreat into pessimism. Their uncompromising rejection of progressive and tragic narratives of global politics opens up the possibility of thinking otherwise. For Rose and Rengger, the disembedded and disembodied embrace of progressive politics is *euporia*, the easy way – an overly simplistic pursuit of a better world that refuses to 'deal in darkness'. However, by way of provocation, I have argued that although Rengger ostensibly deals in darkness, his commitment to world disclosure is constrained by the *distance* that his Oakeshottian adoption of modally distinct worlds implies. By refusing any but the most oblique contamination of the world of theory with the world of practice, Rengger fails to fully commit to the journey of coming to 'see more clearly the character of that world'.[102] I argue that Rose's aporetic and engaged ethos comes closer to coming-to-know the darkness that permeates global politics. She, too, disrupts an uncomplicated relation between theory and practice, but insists that we keep our minds in hell – that we continue to grapple with 'what is', that we stake ourselves as agents, enraged and invested – while despairing not.[103]

---

[102] Rengger, *The Anti-Pelagian Imagination*, p. 167.
[103] Rose, *Mourning Becomes the Law*, p. 62.

PART II

Challenging the
Anti-Pelagian Imagination

5

'A Dangerous Place to Be'?[1] Rengger, the English School, and International Disorder

Ian Hall

Introduction

Nicholas J. Rengger came to International Relations (IR) relatively late, by a circuitous route, and with unorthodox intellectual baggage. His PhD juggled aspects of Enlightenment political philosophy and approaches to the history of ideas.[2] Only afterwards, as a freshly minted political theorist, did he begin to address IR, as he searched for a niche in the unforgiving British higher education system of late 1980s. In various places, he encountered the 'English school of international relations' – or at least representatives of what was left of it – not so much in Bristol, perhaps, where he spent most of his early career prior to the move to St Andrews, but certainly in Aberystwyth, Leicester, and the London School of Economics (LSE), during stints as a

[1] The title refers to a notorious line in Rengger's *International Relations, Political Theory, and the Problem of Order* (London; New York: Routledge, 2000a) which reads: 'The problem, I suggest, with societal approaches like the English school and (at least modernist) constructivist views is that, as always, the middle of the road is just too dangerous a place to be' (p. 94). It also reflects Rengger's habitual overuse of question marks in titles. I am grateful to Vassilios Paipais for his invitation to contribute to his project, to Will Bain, Chris Brown, and Vassilios Paipais for helpful comments on earlier drafts, and to Mathew Davies for his timely mid-lockdown provision of one of Rengger's publications.

[2] N.J. Rengger, *Reason, Scepticism and Politics: Theory and Practice in the Enlightenment's Politics*, PhD Thesis, Durham University Library, 1987.

visiting fellow, and at BISA conferences. At that time, in those places, the English School's (ES) influence was still clear in curricula and concepts employed. Scholars who had known figures like Charles Manning, Martin Wight, and Hedley Bull still lectured, roamed corridors, or held forth in staff clubs and local pubs. They included people like Maurice Keens-Soper and Phillip Windsor, as well as younger scholars whose work was shaped by the tradition, like James Mayall and Hidemi Suganami. Convivial to a fault, Rengger's introduction to IR – and to the ES, in particular – was in no small part a result of conversations with all of these people and more.[3]

Rengger's approach to the field – especially to IR theory – was marked by these early experiences and by the texts to which they led him. He never became a card-carrying member of the ES, of course – he enjoyed buzzing about the field as a Socratic gadfly far too much for that. But the lop-sided dialogue that he started with the ES in the late 1980s continued, on and off, for the rest of his life, shaping the ways in which he framed and engaged with major issues in the field. And from the start, he found the historicist and interpretivist commitments of the early school congenial. He was manifestly impressed with Martin Wight's byzantine essays on the history of international theory.[4] He was also intrigued by the ways in which the early school handled the apparent tensions between the need for order in international relations (IR) and demands for justice. Above all, I think he was attracted to fact that the ES had, as the preface to *Diplomatic Investigations* famously put it, a 'pervading moral concern', but managed not to lapse into moralism or what he later called Pelagianism.[5]

At the same time, Rengger insisted that the ES's *via media* of what Wight called 'rationalism' – sitting between 'realism' and 'revolutionism' – was a

---

[3] The literature on the school is large and, in parts conflicting as to its tenets and membership, but see Barry Buzan *An Introduction to the English School of International Relations: The Societal Approach* (Cambridge: Polity, 2014); Tim Dunne, *Inventing International Society: A History of the English School* (Basingstoke: Macmillan, 1998); Andrew Linklater and Hidemi Suganami, *The English School of International Relations: A Contemporary Reassessment* (Cambridge: Cambridge University Press, 2007); and Brunello Vigezzi, *The British Committee on the Theory of International Politics (1954–1985): The Rediscovery of History* (Milano: Edizioni Unicopoli, 2005).

[4] See Martin Wight, *International Theory: The Three Traditions*, edited by Brian Porter and Gabriele Wight (Leicester: Leicester University Press, 1991); Martin Wight, *Four Seminal Thinkers in International Theory: Machiavelli, Grotius, Kant, and Mazzini*, edited by Gabriele Wight and Brian Porter (Oxford: Oxford University Press, 2005); and Martin Wight, 'Why is there no International Theory?' in Herbert Butterfield and Martin Wight, eds, *Diplomatic Investigations: Essays in the Theory of International Politics*, new edition (Oxford: Oxford University Press, (2019 [1966]), pp. 37–54.

[5] Herbert Butterfield and Martin Wight, 'Preface' to their edited *Diplomatic Investigations*, p. vii.

'dangerous place to be'. If you sat in the middle of the road, he repeatedly observed in conversation, and then in his book on political theory and international order, you were likely to get run over.[6] And there was a lot in the ES with which Rengger disagreed. Above all, he disliked its ethics, either in the original form developed by Wight and especially Bull, or in the quasi-cosmopolitan version promoted by the revived school after the end of the Cold War. But despite all those things, he kept returning to it as both an inspiration and a foil, and the reasons why he did that are worth exploring, because they cast light on his wider project, if I can call it that, in international political theory (IPT). So, to that end this chapter looks first at some of those exploratory essays in IR that Rengger published in the late 1980s and 1990s, many of which addressed, directly or indirectly, the ES or its core concerns. It then traces the evolution of his thinking on these concerns through his later work, leading up to his essays on Pelagianism. Before all that, I have to say a few words about the ES itself, to aid the interpretation of Rengger's treatment of its ideas.

Serpents and doves

Defining the ES is harder than it should be, partly because its later adherents are split on who did or should belong to it, and precisely for what it stands. It was given its (inaccurate) name by a critic – Roy Jones – who argued that it had come to dominate the British IR in the 1970s, as that field coalesced into a discipline.[7] Jones characterized what he called the ES as being committed to a version of philosophical idealism, holism, and historicism – to interpreting the causes and meaning of past phenomena in the context of the time and place in which they occurred.[8] He took it to be concerned with investigating a thing they called the 'society of states' and complained that its adherents did not clearly define it. He observed that the school opposed American social science and believed themselves to be taking a 'classical approach' but

---

[6] Rengger, *International Relations, Political Theory, and the Problem of Order.* I should note that I spent almost nine years at St Andrews, first as a MLitt student in Rengger's international theory seminar, just after he arrived at that university, then as one of his doctoral students, and finally as a colleague, so I heard this observation on many occasions.

[7] Many of the early English school were not English – Hedley Bull was an Australian who did become a British subject in the 1960s; Charles Manning was South African. The later school is much more diverse. On the coming together of a British discipline, see Ian Hall, *Dilemmas of Decline: British Intellectuals and World Politics, 1945–1975* (Berkeley and Los Angeles, CA: University of California Press, 2012), pp. 170–83.

[8] Here and throughout, I use the term 'historicism' to refer to the doctrine that social things must be understood and explained in the contingent context in which they occurred, which is taken to be unique and distinct from the present.

appeared also to cut themselves off from the canon of classic texts in political thought. Moreover, its members deprecated engagement with policy or any attempt to improve the world, which would be fine, Jones declared, if the ES was just a fringe group. The problem was that thanks to Charles Manning and Martin Wight at the LSE, above all, it now represented the mainstream approach, with followers spread throughout the country.[9]

Folklore has it that Jones' article caused considerable upset, but no formal response appeared for several years.[10] Perceptive studies of the work of Manning and Wight appeared, but the 'English school' moniker was not claimed by any set of adherents, nor was its approach defended against Jones' attack.[11] Indeed, the first answer to his challenge denied that there was an ES, on the grounds that philosophical differences between those Jones included in his analysis were too great to justify clumping them together in that way.[12] But by that point the idea of a school was increasingly accepted – and just as importantly, younger scholars were beginning to identify themselves with it or engage with its ideas.[13] Among them was Rengger, as we will see, who in 1988 published a piece in the LSE journal *Millennium* that explored the 'classical approach' and its limits.

It was not until the 1990s, however, that something like a standard account of what the ES was and what it stood for emerged, stimulated by the publication of Wight's 1950s lectures on international theory.[14] It was agreed that its early members were Manning and Wight at the LSE, as well as figures like Hedley Bull and Adam Watson associated with the British Committee on the Theory of International Politics, set up by the Cambridge historian Herbert Butterfield.[15] Its core concerns were taken to

---

[9]   Roy E. Jones, 'The English school of international relations: a case for closure', *Review of International Studies* 7, 1 (1981), pp. 1–13.

[10] By contrast, Michael Nicholson's dissection of Wight's work, which appeared alongside Jones' piece, quickly provoked a counterblast. See Michael Nicholson, 'The enigma of Martin Wight', *Review of International Studies* 7, 1 (1981), pp. 15–22 and Alan James, 'Michael Nicholson on Martin Wight: a mind passing in the night', *Review of International Studies* 8, 2 (1982), pp. 117–23.

[11] See Hidemi Suganami, 'The structure of institutionalism: an anatomy of British mainstream international relations', *International Relations* 7, 5 (1983), pp. 2363–81.

[12] Sheila Grader, 'The English school of international relations: evidence and evaluation', *Review of International Studies* 14, 1 (1988), pp. 29–44.

[13] Mark Hoffman, 'Critical theory and the inter-paradigm debate', *Millennium: Journal of International Studies* 16, 2 (1987), pp. 231–50.

[14] Martin Wight, *International Theory: The Three Traditions*, edited by Brian Porter and Gabriele Wight (Leicester: Leicester University Press, 1991). It should be noted that disagreement persists to this day as to the school's membership and theoretical commitments. See Mark Bevir and Ian Hall, 'The English school and the classical approach: between modernism and interpretivism', *Journal of International Political Theory* 16, 2 (2020), pp. 153–70.

[15] See Dunne, *Inventing International Society*.

be 'international society' or the 'society of states' and the rule- and norm-governed 'institutions' that constituted and regulated it.[16] Its adherents assumed the domain of international society was in some fundamental way distinct from domestic societies – its rules, norms, and institutions were of a different character, requiring specialist knowledge to understand them.[17] Its theoretical orientation was taken to be historical and normative, and broadly anti-positivist. And that made it an intriguing alternative to American social science and a potential platform for developing post-positivist agendas.[18]

Exactly how this should be done, however, soon split the ES's new followers. Some pushed for its insights to be integrated with mainstream theories, notably structural realism and regime theory.[19] This move involved setting aside the philosophical and normative commitments of the early school in favour of what its proponents argued was more rigorous conceptual development and analysis. Others argued that the contemporary school ought to defend and develop those commitments and use them to explore the rules and norms of contemporary international society.[20] Finally, the last group co-opted some of the early school's philosophical and normative orientations and pushed others aside, aiming to develop it both as a counterpoint to dominant theories in the United States and a vehicle for engaging in pressing debates in normative theory and political practice. This entailed shedding

---

[16] Barbara Roberson, ed, *International Society and the Development of International Relations Theory* (London: Pinter, 1998).

[17] This is a significant commitment, as it united the English school with the classical realists who 'invented' international theory in the US and sets them apart from behaviouralists who assert that all social action can be grasped with general theories. On the realists, see Nicolas Guilhot, ed, *The Invention of International Relations Theory: Realism, the Rockefeller Foundation, and the 1954 Conference on Theory* (New York: Columbia University Press, 2011) and on behaviouralism, see Mark Bevir and Ian Hall, 'International relations', in Mark Bevir (ed), *Modernism and the Social Sciences* (Cambridge: Cambridge University Press, 2017), pp. 130–54.

[18] See James Der Derian, ed, *International Theory: Critical Investigations* (Basingstoke: Macmillan, 1995); Tim Dunne, 'The social construction of international society', *European Journal of International Relations* 1, 3 (1995), pp. 367–89; and Roger Epp, 'The English school on the frontiers of international society: a hermeneutic recollection', *Review of International Studies* 24, 5 (1998), pp. 47–64.

[19] See Trevor Evans and Peter Wilson, 'Regime theory and the English school of international relations: a comparison', *Millennium: Journal of International Studies* 21, 3 (1992), pp. 329–51; Barry Buzan, 'From international system to international society: structural realism and regime theory meet the English school', *International Organization* 47, 3 (1993), pp. 327–52; and Richard Little, 'Neorealism and the English school: a methodological, ontological and theoretical reassessment', *European Journal of International Relations* 1, 1 (1995), pp. 9–34.

[20] See, for example, Robert H. Jackson, *The Global Covenant: Human Conduct in a World of States* (Oxford: Oxford University Press, 2000).

the conservativism of the first generation and embracing more progressive intellectual and political positions.[21]

Approaching the classics

Rengger took a considerable interest in the ES during this time, from the late 1980s, when a new generation of adherents was beginning to coalesce, until the late 1990s, by which point the school was well and truly re-established. During that decade or so, he published four essays on various aspects of ES theory.[22] His first piece probed its so-called 'classical approach', affirming some of Jones' key charges, namely that it was historicist and interpretivist, and pointing out that it was thus compatible with some approaches to political theory, including those of Richard Rorty and Quentin Skinner.[23] The second did something similar, arguing that the ES's conception of 'international society' could be construed and analyzed, in terms that political theorists would understand, as 'communitarian', opening up more avenues for dialogue.[24] The third was a bit different: essentially a sympathetic gloss on the ES's conceptions of culture and their relationships to international society and international order.[25] And the last argued that attempts to render the ES cosmopolitan via critical theory or constructivism – or an admixture of both – were unlikely to succeed, principally because international society was a society of states, and states were the principal obstacle to the realization of cosmopolitan ideals.[26]

---

[21] See Alexander J. Bellamy, 'Pragmatic solidarism and the dilemmas of humanitarian intervention', *Millennium: Journal of International Studies* 31, 3 (2002), pp. 473–97; or Nicholas J. Wheeler, 'Guardian angel or global gangster: a review of the ethical claims of international society', *Political Studies* 44, 1 (1996), pp. 123–35. For a helpful discussion of this turn, see also Chris Brown, 'Political thought, international relations theory and international political theory: an interpretation', *International Relations* 31, 3 (2017), pp. 227–40.

[22] For full disclosure, I should note that discussions that I had with Rengger about these differences within the school led me to write a review article on the topic: Ian Hall, 'Still the English patient? Closures and inventions in the English school', *International Affairs* 77, 4 (2001), pp. 931–42.

[23] N.J. Rengger, 'Serpents and doves in classical international theory', *Millennium: Journal of International Studies* 17, 2 (1988), pp. 215–25.

[24] N.J. Rengger, 'A city which sustains all things? Communitarianism and international society', *Millennium: Journal of International Studies* 21, 3 (1992b), pp. 353–69.

[25] Nicholas J. Rengger, 'Culture, society, and order in world politics', in John Baylis and Nicholas J. Rengger (eds), *Dilemmas of World Politics: International Issues in a Changing World* (Oxford: Oxford University Press, 1992a), pp. 85–103.

[26] Nicholas J. Rengger, 'On cosmopolitanism, constructivism and international society. Some reflections on British international studies at the fin de siècle', *Zeitschrift für Internationale Beziehungen* 3, H. 1 (1996b), pp. 183–99.

It must be said that each one of these essays was subversive, at least in part. All dug into the work of the early ES to interrogate the grounds on which scholars like Barry Buzan and Tim Dunne were – in different ways – attempting to construct a new version. Together they suggested that the ES was more conservative, intellectually and ideologically, than those scholars were perhaps willing to admit and less amenable to progressivist agendas. But the essays were not wholly destructive. Rengger found the international society tradition 'ethically profoundly confused at best and dangerous and harmful at worst', but it is also clear that he found some parts of the ES useful foils for his own theoretical project and others useful resources.[27]

Two issues concerned him in particular: Wight's strict separation of international theory from political theory, on the one hand, and on the other, the school's concept of international society. In 'Why is there no international theory?', first published in *International Relations* in 1960 and then reprinted in *Diplomatic Investigations*, Wight was famously categorical: 'international theory' is 'a tradition of speculation about relations between states' analogous to 'political theory', which is 'a tradition of speculation about the state'.[28] There is a great deal of the latter, he argued, but hardly any of the former, partly because most modern people seem to think that the international anarchy that emerged in Europe at the end of the medieval period will be transitory, and thus not worth worrying about, and partly because many are progressivists, unwilling properly or effectively to engage with the 'realm of recurrence and repetition' inherent in IR.[29] Even those that have thought deeply about IR have found it difficult, Wight concluded, because its challenges are 'constantly bursting the bounds of the language in which we try to handle it', involving as they do 'the ultimate experience of life and death, national existence and national extinction'.[30]

Rengger could well have simply dismissed or ignored these arguments and pressed on with his own project, which aimed at an IPT that erased the distinction Wight argued had to be drawn between the political and the international. Instead, he largely accepted them, while pressing on with that project. In part, he did so because he admired Wight's scholarship and – as we shall see – shared more than a little of his worldview. But in part too, he chose not to challenge Wight's arguments because he appreciated why they were made. Like the rest of the early ES – and indeed most post-war classical realists – Wight had asserted that IR formed a distinct domain of social activity

---

[27] Ibid., p. 189, n. 6.

[28] Wight, 'Why is there no international theory?', p. 37.

[29] Ibid., p. 46.

[30] Ibid., p. 53. See also Robert H. Jackson, 'Martin Wight, international theory and the good life', *Millennium: Journal of International Studies* 19, 2 (1990), pp. 261–72.

to defend it from the imperial claims of behaviouralism, then fashionable in American social science, in particular.[31] That approach held out the promise of a single unified social theory on a basis that Wight could not and would not affirm, and it was also progressivist, and therefore incapable, he thought, of grasping what needed to be grasped in IR.[32] Only 'historical literature' could do this, he thought – even 'political theory and law' struggled.[33]

Starting with Hedley Bull, this claim has unsettled many, including a number of scholars associated with the revived ES, but not Rengger.[34] In 'Serpents and doves', he pointed out that Wight's assertion that international theory might best be done as 'historical interpretation' left the door ajar for a certain kind of political theory, despite the earlier distinction he made between political and international theory. Its implicit historicism – its implicit assumption, in other words, that social phenomena are best understood and explained by reference to the historical context in which they occur – chimes with the work of Richard Rorty, Quentin Skinner, Michel Foucault, and others who argue that all theory is itself historically contingent: it arises in a particular place among a particular people for a particular purpose and according to a particular set of values.[35] The ES is compatible with a version of IPT, in other words, albeit one that shares its historicism. I will return to this claim in the next section.

The second issue raised by the school with which Rengger was concerned was its concept of the society of states or international society. Like Jones, he had doubts about the way in which the school – and, for that matter, most of the rest of IR – portrayed the sovereign state and placed it at the centre of their theories of international relations. Jones had argued that the state 'was far from given' and that in any case states do:

> not conform to one model of statehood: neither to one theory of
> the state nor to one kind of community (whether religious, ethnic

---

[31] Tim Dunne and Ian Hall, 'Introduction to the new edition', in Herbert Butterfield and Martin Wight (eds), *Diplomatic Investigations: Essays in the Theory of International Politics*, new edition (Oxford: Oxford University Press, 2019), pp. 1–5.

[32] On these issues, see Ian Hall, *The International Thought of Martin Wight* (New York: Palgrave, 2006).

[33] Wight, 'Why is there no international theory?', p. 53.

[34] Bull explicitly rejected Wight's equation, arguing that it was important to appreciate the 'singularity' of events, but that appreciation should not dissuade us from the pursuit of 'empirical generalisations'. See Hedley Bull, 'International relations as an academic pursuit', *Australian Outlook* 26, 3 (1972), p. 256. For a useful discussion, see also William Bain, 'Are there any lessons of history? The English school and the activity of being an historian', *International Politics* 44, 5 (2007), pp. 513–30.

[35] Rengger, 'Serpents and doves in classical international theory', pp. 218–19.

or national) nor to one form of government nor to one structure of political expression. Many states differ from one another fundamentally. To speak of a society of a variety of structures or movements or theories would seem to be meaningless, except in some semi-private essentialist sense.[36]

Rengger had read more IR than Jones had by the time he came to address this topic, so did not follow him down some of those paths. But he had similar concerns about the notion that we should treat states as unitary agents and about how the ES imagined them forming a society. Doing both privileged the state as a social institution and limited the kind of IPT (and practice) that could follow. It stood in the way of cosmopolitan theories, in particular. The ES, Rengger complained, treats the state as 'uniquely the carrier of the possibilities of international society' – as something '"qualitatively" different from other kinds of actors and agents in world politics'.[37] And that creates 'a pretty much unbridgeable gulf … between the English school … and the cosmopolitan emphasis on universalizeable norms' in which states are conceived as playing a 'purely facilitative and secondary role'.[38] As a result, the school is forced to fall back on its confused and relativistic 'ethics of statecraft', which he did not think passed muster.[39]

Unlike most of the scholars keen to revive the ES in the late 1980s and 1990s, who focused on what they saw as the possibilities inherent in the concept of international society, as opposed to the idea of an international system, Rengger thought it too flawed and fraught. There was something worth rescuing from the early school, but 'international society' was not it, given the way that it privileged the state above all other forms of political association. He argued that the idea should be set aside, as Jones had earlier argued, as muddled and unhelpful, especially to the projects of IPT and international ethics. Moreover, the inside/outside distinction implied by Wight also had to be discarded, not least because, as Rengger noted in an essay in *International Affairs* in 2000, Wight did not himself abide by it.[40] Wight 'gave his famous "three traditions" names associated with past *political* thinkers', Rengger observed, and much of his analysis of the history of international thought dwelt on the work of political theorists and political

---

[36] Jones, 'The English school', pp. 1, 5.
[37] Rengger, 'On cosmopolitanism, constructivism and international society', p. 194.
[38] Ibid, p. 195.
[39] Ibid., p. 196.
[40] On inside/outside, I am alluding of course to R.B.J. Walker, *Inside/Outside: International Relations as Political Theory* (Cambridge: Cambridge University Press, 1992).

philosophers.[41] Instead, Rengger was convinced, what should be recovered from the early school were its commitments to historicism and interpretivism.

The Rengger project

Understanding why Rengger made that argument requires a grasp of what he was up to, intellectually, during the first phase of his career. It also demands stepping away from IR, to a degree and back to where he began, in political theory. Rengger's PhD thesis had explored the political thought of the Enlightenment, especially the work of Immanuel Kant and David Hume, but the main purpose was addressing contemporary political theory and responding to the question of what that field ought to do and how. With that in mind, he welcomed its resuscitation by Alastair MacIntyre, John Rawls, Bernard Williams, and others two decades after its near-death at the hands of analytical philosophy and behaviouralist social science. But at the same time he argued that political theory had not yet recovered its purpose or strength, partly because of how the revivalists had framed their task.[42] If the field was to flourish, and properly and effectively to shape practice, Rengger insisted, it 'must take history, and what has been called [by John Dunn] the "view from here and now", much more seriously if it is adequately to perform the task'. It needed the 'self awareness [*sic*]', he argued, that could only come from a grasp of the contingent context in which reasoning and political practice takes place.[43]

This conviction carried over into Rengger's first book, *Political Theory, Modernity and Postmodernity*, and indeed into the rest of his work – it clearly underpinned, for example, the late writings about the anti-Pelagian imagination. It first emerges during his extended conversation in his PhD thesis with MacIntyre's argument that the Enlightenment project had failed, leaving us with the options of going back to Aristotle or somewhere else with Nietzsche.[44] Rengger dissented, insisting that there was in any case more than one Enlightenment project, and that some of what those projects produced could be useful today. But he did not think any of it was straightforwardly applicable to our world. The Cambridge school of the history of ideas – especially Quentin Skinner and J.G.A. Pocock – had

---

[41] Nicholas J. Rengger, 'Political theory and international relations: promised land or exit from Eden?' *International Affairs* 76, 4 (2000), p. 757, emphasis added. See also Wight, *International Theory* and Martin Wight, *Four Seminal Thinkers in International Theory: Machiavelli, Grotius, Kant, and Mazzini*, edited by Gabriele Wight and Brian Porter (Oxford: Oxford University Press, 2005).

[42] On this point, see also Rengger, *Political Theory, Modernity and Postmodernity*.

[43] Rengger, *Reason, Scepticism and Politics*, p. v.

[44] Alastair MacIntyre, *After Virtue: A Study in Moral Theory* (London: Duckworth, 1981).

convinced him otherwise, along with R.G. Collingwood, Michel Foucault, Michael Oakeshott, and Richard Rorty.

Rengger was persuaded by these thinkers' historicism, which placed everyone and every theory within what he called a 'grid' of time and place, concept and convention, though he was discomforted by what it might imply.[45] In his thesis, he wrote: 'It is surely true that part of our most basic assumptions are [sic] historically located in a very strong sense. It is this fact which gives the arguments of Rorty, Collingwood, Foucault and others their plausability [sic]. I have said that on the basis of these arguments we cannot escape that historical and cultural location'.[46] In other words, he was convinced we are in some fundamental sense trapped where we are, not just physically but also epistemologically, and this in turn both shapes the ways in which we behave politically and we must assess the actions of others, conscious of the incommensurability – a term he borrowed from Rorty – between our ethical frameworks and those of other places.[47] 'Our actions in the moral and political world', Rengger argued, 'will very largely be determined by what we consider to be of "decisive importance" and this … will be a product of historical and cultural location and our own reflection and articulations (perhaps inchoate) of this historical and cultural sense'.[48]

What this means for political theory is worked out – at least in part – in his somewhat convoluted book on modernity and postmodernity. Opening with the assertion that political theory should be, as Judith Skhlar wanted it, the meeting point between philosophy and history, Rengger there argued that the theory we need to inform practice must account for context. It was not sufficient to argue, as John Dunn did, that we need to revive and embed John Locke's concepts of trust and prudence in contemporary politics.[49] We have also to explain how those concepts will fit our world: 'we need an account', Rengger argued, 'of our contemporary condition that displays the character … of its politics much more concretely than simply suggesting that it is highly complex and multi-faceted (which is true but trivial)'.[50] We need

---

[45] Rengger, *Reason, Scepticism and Politics*, p. 157.

[46] Ibid., p. 178.

[47] For a longer discussion of incommensurability, see N.J. Rengger, 'Incommensurability, international theory and the fragmentation of Western political culture', in J.R. Gibbins (ed), *Contemporary Political Culture: Politics in a Postmodern Age* (London: Sage, 1989), pp. 237–50. I am grateful to Vassilios Paipais for highlighting that publication.

[48] Rengger, *Reason, Scepticism and Politics*, p. 181.

[49] Rengger, *Political Theory, Modernity and Postmodernity*, pp. 20–6. See also John Dunn, *Interpreting Political Responsibility* (Cambridge: Cambridge University Press, 1990) and Nicholas J. Rengger, 'Trust, prudence and history: John Dunn and the tasks of political theory', *History of Political Thought* 16, 3 (1995b), pp. 416–37.

[50] Rengger, *Political Theory, Modernity and Postmodernity*, pp. 25–6.

a political theory, in other words, 'sensitive to our embeddedness in the web on which we are all nodes, to the dual character of our impulses, the deeply contextual character of our circumstances'.[51] This demands some analysis of the various possible political languages available to us – and indeed discarded by us and our ancestors – and of the habits and rules and wider 'mood' of our age, as well as its social and economic organization.

Political Theory, Modernity and Postmodernity attempted to supply some of this necessary contextualization, but – it has to be said – the book never quite got to spelling out exactly what sort of political theory Rengger would prefer. It did hint at where he wanted to go next, however. Political theory could not 'remain corralled within the boundaries of the state', he concluded, even it 'should not ignore those boundaries and what they imply, or – worse – pretend they somehow do not exist'.[52] It needed to deal with IR, for all its messiness.

Order and history

International Relations, Political Theory, and the Problem of Order was Rengger's initial attempt to sketch out a political theory with that necessary international component.[53] It extended the earlier book in so far as it tried to locate the various theories it discussed in the broad historical context of modernity, which he argued was characterized by particular ways of thinking about political order that differed from earlier conceptions.[54] The rise of the sovereign state had 'instantiated, for better or worse, *a particular way of being political* [emphasis in original]', and a new manner of conceiving order: ' "inside" [the state], "order" increasingly became a province of legal regulation within such states while "outside" the whole problem became what could achieve "order" in the absence of the legitimacy conferred by sovereignty'.[55] And in essence, two kinds of order had come to dominate the modern imagination.[56] The first, inherited from the medieval world, and put best by Augustine, was an order that involved simply 'the minimizing of disorder, conflict and instability'. The realists, the ES, and some

---

[51] Ibid., p. 213.

[52] N.J. Rengger *Political Theory, Modernity and Postmodernity: Beyond Enlightenment and Critique* (Oxford: Blackwell, 1995a), p. 226.

[53] The book also followed closely the Master's level course on international theory that Rengger began to teach at St Andrews soon after he arrived in 1996. This course, which I took a year later, was my introduction to the subject.

[54] Rengger, *International Relations, Political Theory, and the Problem of Order*, p. 4.

[55] Ibid., p. 6.

[56] For an instructive analysis of how and why this occurred, see William Bain, *Political Theology of International Order* (Oxford: Oxford University Press, 2020).

institutionalists favoured that approach. The second, developed from more authentically modern sources, was an order that involved the imposition of some new 'pattern of authority' that will do away with those ills.[57] An array of progressivists advocated that alternative, from Kant and Marx onwards.

Now what is interesting here is not so much Rengger's categorization of the various theories, but the manner in which he approached the study as a whole. He stated, quite baldly, 'I would not wish to locate myself [in the ES] at all'.[58] But both the historicism of the *Order* book and the interpretivist preferences he reveals by the end of it align him more with the thinking of the early school than perhaps any other group of thinkers in IR. The theories he discussed are contextualized both in terms of the broad political, social, and economic developments, then in terms of 20th-century intellectual debates, and finally in terms of disciplinary history. There is a strong sense throughout that theories are products of their times – classical realism of the early Cold War; neorealism of the late – and may therefore lack universal applicability.[59] Equally, there is a strong sense that theories are not simply academic instruments for explaining what happens in IR, but that they are intertwined with practice, seeping into the minds of policymakers and other actors, and shaping their behaviour. This is especially clear in the chapter on 'Institutions', which dissects the liberalisms both scholarly and practical of the post-Cold War order.[60] There is a lot in common between the *Order* book, in other words, and the work of the early ES, especially Martin Wight's essays in *Diplomatic Investigations*. Of course, Rengger once again ruthlessly dispatches the concept of international society and the school's ethics (old and new), as he did in the earlier essays, but more pointedly and at greater length.[61] But his underlying assumptions are similar: the focus is on international thought more than just scholarly theory within a discipline; the 'point of view', as Butterfield and Wight put it, is 'historical'; and there is the same 'pervading moral concern'.[62]

Rengger ended his book by arguing that the central question students of politics and IR should ask is not the classic one suggested by Harold Lasswell – who gets what, when, how? – but rather Socrates' distinctly

---

[57] Rengger, *International Relations, Political Theory, and the Problem of Order*, p. 9.

[58] Ibid., p. 16.

[59] At the end of the chapter on realism, for example, it is suggested that the balance of power will likely have less of a role to play in managing 21st-century international relations than it might in the past (Rengger, *International Relations, Political Theory, and the Problem of Order*, p. 63).

[60] Ibid., pp. 102–42.

[61] Ibid, pp. 73–80, 87–92.

[62] Butterfield and Wight, Preface, pp. vi–vii.

normative 'how should we live?'[63] The answer he gave to that question, however, was somewhat opaque. He declared a preference for some kind of cosmopolitanism, but emphatically not a universalist one.[64] That cosmopolitanism had to be reasonable, he argued, and it had to recognize two things: that the problem of order is 'a permanent feature of politics' and that the problem can and does take different forms at different times and places, demanding a 'context driven' and 'casuistical' approach.[65] Such an approach 'will offer reasons, specific to context a or b, as to what actions are preferable, what institutions appropriate, where legitimacy lies in any given context'. 'It would not seek to create a Utopia, it would indeed be rooted in our world as we live it', he went on, 'but at the same time it would speak to the most powerful ethical and political impulses we have developed as a species'. And it would involve acquiring 'a highly developed, historically sensitive, conceptually sophisticated set of scholarly tools, many of which we have, some of which we have doubtless yet to develop adequately'.[66]

Progress and Pelagius

Much of what was sketched out at the end of the *Order* book is quite different to the early ES's preferred ethics, of course. The strongest influences upon it were a separate – and for Rengger, characteristically heterodox – set of thinkers, including Stephen R.L. Clark, Jean Bethke Elshtain, and Stephen Toulmin, and to a lesser extent Charles Beitz and Michael Walzer. But it has to be said too that Rengger did not develop the vision glimpsed in that book any further: he never published, or to my knowledge ever really considered, a *Cosmopolitan Theory of International Politics* to match Waltz or Wendt.[67] His later work – running from 2001 to his death in 2018 – turned to other issues, especially the 'uncivil condition' of war, in response to 9/11 and the 'War on Terror'. It also began to display other 'dispositions' – or at least to display more clearly dispositions latent but not obvious in his early work.[68] Michael

---

[63] Rengger, *International Relations, Political Theory, and the Problem of Order*, p. 201. See also Harold Lasswell, *Politics: Who Gets What, When, How* (New York: Whittlesey House, 1936).

[64] Rengger, *International Relations, Political Theory, and the Problem of Order*, p. 204.

[65] Ibid., p. 206.

[66] Ibid., p. 208.

[67] I am alluding here to Kenneth N. Waltz, *Theory of International Politics* (Reading, Mass: Addison Wesley, 1979) and Alexander Wendt, *Social Theory of International Politics* (Cambridge: Cambridge University Press, 1999).

[68] On war as an 'uncivil condition', see especially Nicholas J. Rengger, *Just War and International Order: The Uncivil Condition in World Politics* (Cambridge: Cambridge University Press, 2013a).

Oakeshott's thinking – clearly present in the wings in his PhD thesis and the essays that followed – became more central to Rengger's own. And so too did religious and theological concerns, reconnecting him to a different dimension of the ES and to Herbert Butterfield, as well as Martin Wight.

Butterfield and Wight were both believers and practising Christians, albeit of different kinds. The former was brought up a Methodist and became a kind of college chapel Anglican; the latter grew up and remained in the Church of England but held some quite radical and unorthodox beliefs at certain points. Both were historians by training – Butterfield eventually rose to be Regius Professor at Cambridge and Wight ended his career in a chair in that field at Sussex – and for both, their faith and scholarship were intertwined.[69] Their work on IR was also shaped by both: they insisted that the subject should be studied historically, with the evolution of international thought, both theoretical and pragmatic, at its core; and they resisted the progressivism that they perceived animated so much 20th-century scholarship on the subject. Secular history, for them, did not display moral progress, still less its inevitability; instead, it was a record of human folly and happenstance, full of ironic twists and turns.[70] And treating as a story of progress was un-Christian, in any case: to think of past people as 'mere stepping stones to the present day', as Butterfield put it, devalued them and their lives.[71] We must remember, Wight asserted, that '[e]very generation' is 'equidistant from eternity'.[72]

Rengger did not publicly endorse these views, but he was well aware of them, and in his work on the anti-Pelagian imagination ended up in a similar position for not dissimilar reasons.[73] The horrors of the first half of the 20th century convinced Butterfield and Wight that moral progress in history was illusory; I strongly suspect the events of 9/11 convinced Rengger of the same. To be sure, he denied that the attacks constituted some kind of rupture, transforming IR.[74] He even attacked – no softer word captures

---

[69] See Ian Hall, 'History, Christianity and diplomacy: Sir Herbert Butterfield and international relations', *Review of International Studies* 28, 4 (2002), pp. 719–36 and Hall, *International Thought of Martin Wight*.

[70] See especially Michele Chiaruzzi, *Martin Wight on Fortune and Irony in Politics* (New York: Palgrave, 2016).

[71] Herbert Butterfield, *Christianity and History* (London: G. Bell and Sons, 1949).

[72] Cited in Hall, *International Thought of Martin Wight*, p. 53.

[73] See, for example, Nicholas J. Rengger, 'Tragedy or scepticism? Defending the anti-Pelagian mind in world politics', *International Relations* 19, 3 (2005a), pp. 321–8 and Nicholas J. Rengger, 'Between transcendence and necessity: Eric Voegelin, Martin Wight and the crisis of modern international relations', *Journal of International Relations and Development* 22, 2 (2019a), pp. 327–45.

[74] Caroline Kennedy-Pipe and Nicholas J. Rengger, 'Apocalypse now? Continuities or disjunctions in world politics after 9/11', *International Affairs* 82, 3 (2006b), pp. 539–52.

what he did – Elshtain for suggesting otherwise and for over-reacting, in his view, in response.[75] But 2001 clearly marks a watershed in his work: the end of the search for a contextual and casuistical cosmopolitanism, and the start of his 'dealing in darkness', underpinned by the belief that IR is far less susceptible to being tamed by political theory and theorists. His tone shifts and his mood changes – it becomes less playful and more sombre. 'For much of the twentieth century', Rengger observed in the introduction to the *Anti-Pelagian Imagination*, in a passage without parallel in his earlier work, 'the realities of international relations have been an extended and grotesque lesson in the appalling ingenuity human beings can practise in their relations with one another: a seemingly endless catalogue of mendacity, special pleading, exploitation, naked self-interest, viciousness and barbarism, usually cloaked in the language of high ideals'.[76]

There are strong echoes here of Wight's famous description of IR as the 'realm of recurrence and repetition' but also, throughout the *Anti-Pelagian* book, of his insistence that the 'character of international politics is "incompatible with progressivist theory"'.[77] There are echoes too in Rengger's suggestion that political philosophers have retreated from 'darkness' to build 'ever more sophisticated castles [of ideal theory] in the air'.[78] This sounds a lot like Wight's observation that '[w]hen diplomacy is violent and unscrupulous, international law soars into the regions of natural law'.[79] Indeed, even the structure of the book follows a prompting from Wight, opening as it does with Kant, whom the former argued 'first channelled the doctrine of progress in international theory through his *Eternal Peace*' [that is, his *Perpetual Peace*].[80] For Rengger as for Wight, Kant is cast as the villain, even the archetypal Pelagian – a quite different role to the far more constructive part Kant played in Rengger's PhD thesis, 30 years before.

All of this, however, raises a question. In the end, Butterfield and Wight's denial of moral progress in history was grounded, in an entirely orthodox way, in Christian theology. They agreed with Augustine that the fallen nature of humankind meant that any order that could be established – either within the state or between states – would always be temporary and an imperfect reflection of God's just peace. For that reason, progressivism or Pelagianism was doomed to fail. By contrast, the grounding of Rengger's denial of moral

[75] Nicholas J. Rengger, 'Just a war against terror? Jean Bethke Elshtain's burden and American power', *International Affairs* 80, 1 (2004), pp. 107–16.
[76] Rengger, *Anti-Pelagian Imagination*, p. 3.
[77] Wight, 'Why is there no international theory?', pp. 46–7.
[78] Rengger, *Anti-Pelagian Imagination*, p. 3.
[79] Wight, 'Why is there no international theory?', pp. 49–50.
[80] Ibid., p. 48.

progress is less clear. It was not Christian or theological – he discussed those arguments and he appropriated the language some Christian theologians have used, but never openly endorsed a Christian worldview, still less publicly professed faith. The grounding appears instead to be empirical: we are invited to contemplate the 'calamitous century' just passed, littered with failed political projects and incessant conflict, and conclude that the anti-Pelagian imagination is simply more 'realistic' than its alternatives.[81]

Conclusion

In *Perpetual Peace*, as Wight pointed out, Kant argued that we must 'admit' that 'pure principles of right and justice have objective reality and … can be realized in fact' or else we will 'be driven to a position of despair'. This was 'surely not a good argument', Wight responded: it is really an appeal to faith, not reason.[82] A version of this critique applies, I think, to Rengger's anti-Pelagianism – and especially to the denial of moral progress on which it is based. It is not clear why we should accept it, except that if we do not, we will strive for unattainable things and then be disappointed by what results. The appeal to Oakeshott – and specifically to his concept of a 'disposition' – does not, it seems to me, help as much as Rengger might have thought. Oakeshott's invitation to entertain and to embrace his sceptical disposition were to some degree dependent on evidence and argument – his essays in *Rationalism in Politics* and *On Human Conduct* are reflections on instances of political action.[83] Rengger's work does something different: it catalogues various versions of anti-Pelagianism, but crucially, does not justify it, either historically or philosophically – or indeed theologically.

Rengger's early analyses of the ES are, I have suggested here, more penetrating and more constructive. He was surely right to argue that what was distinctive about it were its commitments to historicism and interpretivism. These – and not the concept of international society – are what mark it off from other IR theories, which draw to one degree or another on modernist political science. These too are the reasons why the ES has value to contemporary theorists, because it offers an alternative pathway for thinking about IR distinct from those shaped by behaviouralism and its modernist competitors. Ethically, it might be a 'dangerous place to be', but Rengger still recognized that, for all its flaws, it provided a starting point for people wanting to do the work he wanted to do.

---

81 Rengger, *Anti-Pelagian Imagination*, pp. 3, 163–8.
82 Wight, 'Why is there no International Theory?', pp. 48–9.
83 Michael Oakeshott, *Rationalism in Politics and Other Essays* (Indianapolis: Liberty Fund, 1991 [1962]) and Michael Oakeshott, *On Human Conduct* (Oxford: Clarendon, 1975).

From that point, of course, Rengger travelled a long way, far beyond the bounds of the ES to which he repeatedly said he did not want to belong. His *Order* book supplied a very different account of the history of modern IR to the one Bull or Wight, or indeed Adam Watson, laid out. It pushes the sovereign state, which was central to their narratives of the evolution of international society, into the background, to focus on deeper developments in European and then global political thought. Similarly, his contributions to the nascent fields of IPT and international ethics showed up the weaknesses of the early ES's ethics of statecraft, as well as the difficulties of grafting onto them progressivist cosmopolitan approaches. But Rengger ended up in a position not far, I think, from Wight's: affirming that arguments and practices must be interpreted in their historical contexts and warning of the limits of our capacity to improve our present circumstances.

6

Rengger's War on Teleocracy

Chris Brown

Introduction

N.J. (Nick) Rengger was one of the most influential figures in British International Relations (IR), and in the global discourse of international political theory (IPT) of the last 40 years, partly through his writings, but equally through his outsize personality and riveting conversation.[1] This last point is important because, now that he is no longer with us, future scholars will only have recourse to reading him, and, as a result, will get a very limited and imperfect impression of the impact he had on those of us who actually knew him and were fully exposed to the Rengger experience in all its Falstaffian dimensions.[2] In this chapter I will, of course, refer to his publications, but I also want to get across some of the impact of talking to him, arguing with him, sometimes being infuriated by him, but always realizing that you were privileged to be interacting with a quite extraordinary man and scholar.

In the first section, I will examine the way Nick Rengger exploded on the scene in the 1980s at a time when the discourse of IPT was forming, a

This chapter draws on Chris Brown, 'From serpents and doves to the war on teleocracy', a short essay written for a Forum on Rengger in *International Relations* 34, 4 (2020) pp. 616–20. I am grateful to Will Bain, Toni Erskine, Ian Hall, and Cian O'Driscoll for comments, and especially to Liana Hartnett for her comments on Augustine. The usual disclaimers apply – I alone am responsible for the final text.

Similar in this respect are the posthumous reputations of Isiah Berlin and H.L.A. Hart, neither of whom left behind a corpus of written work that truly reflected the great impact they had on their Oxford contemporaries.

discourse which he helped to form. His position then was supportive of, to use Richard Rorty's terminology, an 'edifying' rather than a 'systematising' account of the role of theory.[3] The second section fast-forwards by three decades to a period when Rengger's theme was anti-Pelagianism and opposition to teleocracy. Here I set out some of the, in my view, undesirable implications of these themes, and challenge his employment of Augustinian theology to support his espousal of a very conservative account of the possibilities of political theory. In the third and final section I look at some of the practical problems posed by the positions he adopted, in particular his opposition to progressivism and to what he saw as the perversions of modern just war thinking.

As will already be apparent, this will be a critical chapter; I shall have some harsh words to say about his writings in his final years and about the rhetorical language he employed. All I can say in my defence, if I need a defence, is that there is nothing here that I have not said to his face, and I can assure those readers who did not know Nick, that he would not have had it any other way.

In the beginning...

Nick Rengger's arrival on the academic scene in the 1980s was, in one respect, well timed. This was a time when the new discourse of IPT was slowly emerging out of a strange, and, it was to prove ultimately unstable, mix of newly christened ES thinkers, post-Rawls justice theorists, feminists, critical theorists, post-structuralists and even the occasional post-modernist.[4] A feature of the time was that many of the contributors to this new discourse were self-taught, their professional training having been in other areas of the social sciences – to name just three of the key figures of the period, both Terry Nardin, a leading normative theorist, and Michael J. Shapiro, a leading post-structuralist, had begun their careers in the academy as number-crunchers working with Harold Guetzkow and the InterNation Simulation Project at Northwestern University, while Cynthia Enloe, the most important feminist writer on IR, had written extensively on ethnic politics and political development before turning to gender issues. Other figures in the discourse, including the present writer, had backgrounds in conventional international studies and were reading themselves into writers

---

[3] See Richard Rorty, *Philosophy and the Mirror of Nature* (Princeton, NJ: Princeton University Press, 1980) esp. Chapter VIII.

[4] Rengger's own account of this discourse is 'Political theory and international relations: promised land or exit from Eden?', *International Affairs*, 76, 4 (2000): pp. 755–70.

such as Michel Foucault and Jacques Derrida, or, perhaps closer to home, John Rawls and Juergen Habermas.

In this context, Rengger's arrival on the scene was well timed because, as a product of the University of Durham's very strong team of political theorists, he came already equipped with much of the background knowledge which many of the rest of us were painfully acquiring. What was missing in the case of his training was a focus on the international, but that was soon remedied. Why did he turn to the international? Partly because it made sense given his interests in the nature of order which, he realized, had to include international order, but it is also worth remembering that the 1980s were a period of restructuring in British universities; government money dried up and the only way in which universities could expand was by attracting foreign fee-paying students – and while 'straight' Political Theory found it difficult to go down that route, IR was much easier to sell to rich foreigners. In short, there was a demand for new teachers of IR which he was happy to respond to.

I first met Nick sometime in the mid-1980s when he came to give a talk at the seminar series we ran at the University of Kent every Friday afternoon, largely for the benefit of exactly these fee-paying Master's students. I can't remember the title of the talk he gave, but I do remember how impressive this new kid on the block was. He brought to this discourse what was already an encyclopaedic knowledge of the literature of most of its components, and, most important of all, the training and background of a genuine political philosopher – while most of us aspired to a level of fluency that we didn't really possess, he genuinely was fluent. He could, as the saying goes, talk the talk and walk the walk whether the subject was Derrida's deconstruction, Foucault's archaeology, Frankfurtian critical theory, or Bull's international society. If he sometimes improvised and claimed a tad more fluency in a particular topic than he could justify, he improvised from a position of strength, at least by comparison with the rest of us.

But what was the content of his thinking back in the 1980s? For him then there were a number of key figures and particular positions around which he oriented his thinking, and the easiest way to get into his mindset is via one of his earliest papers, entitled 'Serpents and doves in classical international theory'.[5] This appeared in a Special Edition of *Millennium* on 'Philosophical traditions in international relations', a collection which brought together a good cross-section of writers who were constituting the emerging field of IPT including, inter alia, James Der Derian, Friedrich Kratochwil, Richard Ashley, R.J. Vincent, and the present author. In this paper he displayed the full range of his knowledge, engaging with the ES, asserting the importance

5   *Millennium: Journal of International Studies* 17, 2 (1988), pp. 215–25.

of classical political theory, and raising the issue of anti-foundationalism. He endorses Kant's position that 'there can be no dispute between political and ethical concepts', citing Kant (channelling St Matthew) that 'if politics were to say "be ye therefore wise as serpents" morality might add ... "and harmless as doves"' but adding that Kant did not have to come to terms, as we do, with modernity's discontents, especially our disillusion with objectivity.[6] The most important argument of his paper pulls together Richard Rorty's anti-foundationalism and Michael Oakeshott's notion of a mode of enquiry understood as a conversation (modified somewhat by the contextualism of Quentin Skinner and the Cambridge School). Rorty sees the notion that philosophy is about securing firm foundations for knowledge – what he calls foundationalism – as only one possible account of the task for the discourse, the other, which Rengger more or less endorses, is to attack this project.[7] 'Systematic' philosophers seek foundations, 'edifying' philosophers challenge the notion that knowledge needs foundations. For Rengger the model for edifying philosophy is Oakeshott's idea of a conversation. It is worth repeating here the extended quotation that Rengger cites because it is central to how he then thought of what he was doing when he did political theory: 'In a conversation, the participants are not engaged in an enquiry or debate; there is no truth to be discovered, no proposition to be affirmed, no conclusion sought ... the cogency of their utterances does not depend on their speaking the same idiom; they may differ without disagreeing.'[8]

Rengger argues that Rorty's anti-foundationalism can lead to extremes (he doesn't say, but, if memory serves, he had Derrida in mind) and sees Skinnerian contextualism as a way of pulling back from the brink of unreason – but rather than follow up on this, I want to keep the focus on conversation as a mode of enquiry, for two reasons. First, because conversation in the broadest sense was so central to Nick Rengger's intellectual life that it was more or less inevitable that he would be drawn to this way of describing the role of philosophy – and it is worth noting that in this essay and most of his later work the rhythm of his prose very much suggests a conversation, or, put differently, he wrote the way he spoke. Even though the conversation is, inevitably, one-sided, still his prose, with its engaging swagger and a sense of fun only just below the surface, invites us in – he is enjoying himself and wants us to join the party and engage with him. But the second reason I invite the reader to focus on the Oakeshott quote is rather darker; it is because,

---

6   Ibid., p. 222.
7   The best short summary of Rorty's complex and wide-ranging ideas is: Bjørn Ramberg, 'Richard Rorty', in Edward N. Zalta (ed), *The Stanford Encyclopedia of Philosophy* (Spring 2009 edition), available at: https://plato.stanford.edu/archives/spr2009/entries/rorty/
8   Michael Oakeshott, 'The voice of poetry in the conversation of mankind', in *Rationalism in Politics and Other Essays*. (London: Methuen, 1962) p. 197, cited here p. 218.

although Rengger never rejected the idea of enquiry as a conversation, his more recent work in the decade before his premature death no longer fitted quite so comfortably within this mode.

The war on teleocracy

Rereading this paper from 1988 today, it is striking how many of the themes it addresses are still present 25 years later in *Just War and International Order* and *The Anti-Pelagian Imagination in Political Theory and International Relations* and in his other late-period essays.[9] Present but, I want to argue, in a somewhat different form and one that is less consistent with the earlier conception of a conversation. The notion of social and political theory as a 'conversation' as presented by Oakeshott and endorsed by Rengger was clearly designed to undermine the view that political theory could have more practical implications for the world and, sure enough, in his 1988 paper Rengger is gently dismissive of international reformers and the prospects for international reform. In his later work this dismissal is firmed up and generalized; the possibility that the conversation might be transformative for its participants and actually lead to a change of views simply disappears.[10] Reformers who were gently chided in 1988 are now to be understood as 'Pelagians' (on which see later) and quite simply wrong – this is no longer a conversation where there is no truth to be discovered, no proposition affirmed, no conclusion sought. Instead, truth has been discovered and those who refuse to come to the conclusions that Rengger outlines are in error.

Anti-Pelagianism is one way of describing Rengger's position in the 2010s; another version of the same story is his critique of 'teleocracy'. Like the notion of conversation as a mode of enquiry, teleocracy derives from Michael Oakeshott's political philosophy. A key distinction for Oakeshott is between enterprise and civil association;[11] an enterprise association is an association that has come together with the intent of pursuing some common goal, while a civil association is an association of citizens whose goal is solely to arrange the common affairs of society. Enterprise associations are voluntary associations based on shared goals; civil associations are not voluntary but are based only on the shared goal of determining the rules under which citizens associate. For Oakeshott, politics, properly understood, is civil association. His thinking is nicely, if slightly confusingly, employed by Terry Nardin at

---

[9] Nicholas Rengger, *Just War and International Order* (Cambridge: Cambridge UP, 2013); Nicholas Rengger, *The Anti-Pelagian Imagination in Political Theory and International Relations* (London and New York: Routledge, 2017).

[10] Thanks to Liane Hartnett for pointing me to the potentially transformative nature of conversation.

[11] Michael Oakeshott, *On Human Conduct* (Oxford: Clarendon Press, 1975).

the international level to describe associations between states;[12] he renames civil association 'practical association' (because states are not citizens) and, more problematically, enterprise associations as 'purposive associations', which is problematic because practical association also has a purpose, albeit only that of living together peacefully and under the rule of law. To illustrate the practical implications of this distinction, Nardin sees the League of Nations as a practical association of states, its Covenant devoted simply to co-existence under law – the United Nations, on the other hand, is a purposive association, because the Preamble and the Purposes and Principles of the Charter of the UN commits its members to solving a range of social and economic problems.

Returning to Rengger's use of these distinctions, 'teleocrats' (a term occasionally used by Oakeshott) are people who see the *telos* (that is the end, the objective) of politics as lying beyond simply the association of citizens who come together to determine the terms of their co-existence in society. To employ the familiar 'ship of state' metaphor, teleocrats want to sail the ship in a particular direction rather than simply to keep it afloat. For most of us (I think it's most of us, but that may be presumptuous) the crucial issue here is the direction in which the ship is sailed; some hypothetical directions are clearly undesirable, but some are not. In liberal democratic, welfare-oriented states the direction could include the promotion of economic growth, the reduction of poverty and/or of inequality, the elimination of racial or other forms of discrimination and so on, and most of the citizens of these states are, I think, broadly content with these objectives, although they differ on priorities and the rigour with which they should be pursued. But Oakeshottians, including, it seems, Rengger, regard this as an illegitimate misuse of the idea of politics, exemplary of what Oakeshott called 'Rationalism in Politics',[13] the belief that political power can be properly directed towards such social goals. Interestingly, the argument here is not dissimilar to the position developed by Hannah Arendt based on her studies of republicanism in the classical world and totalitarianism today. Like Oakeshott, although for somewhat different reasons, she also believed that using political means to improve one's position in the world was somehow illegitimate (on this see the Little Rock controversy in which initially she appeared to side with segregationists against the civil rights movement).[14] But, given the way in which she rowed back from her original position on Little Rock, it is clear that Arendt was not happy with the practical implications

---

12 Terry Nardin, *Law, Morality and the Relations of States* (Princeton, NJ: Princeton UP, 1983).

13 Michael Oakeshott, *Rationalism in Politics and Other Essays* (London: Methuen, 1962).

14 The controversy was occasioned by Hannah Arendt, 'Reflections on Little Rock', *Dissent* 6, 1 (1959a) pp. 45–56. See also her 'Reply to critics', *Dissent* 6, 2 (1959b).

of her theoretical framework and tried to find ways of modifying it, while there is no evidence that either Oakeshott or Rengger had similar worries.

What, exactly, is wrong with the idea of wanting to improve society – or the world in the case of international reformers? Rengger argues that teleocracy leads to the alleged excesses of Pelagianism, defined by Rengger in terms of a belief in human perfectibility. I think there is sleight of hand occurring here. There have been some people – not many, but some – who believe in the 'perfectibility of man' (Passmore's title,[15] in those days sexist language went largely unchallenged) and they can perhaps, as Rengger and before him Voegelin[16] and others suggest, be seen as inheriting one or other Christian heresy about the possibility of human beings achieving salvation without God's grace – but does this critique actually apply to most reformers? I suggest it does not. Rengger choses to term such views Pelagian after Pelagius, the 4th-century British Christian theologian or heretic who was the target of St Augustine's wrath, but this is, I think, a deliberate attempt to use an unnecessary display of erudition to muddy the waters.

Why Pelagius? Pelagius was condemned as a heretic in 418 AD for arguing that human nature inclined towards goodness and that human beings possessed free will.[17] Why was this considered by Augustine to be heretical, and, more importantly, why should we, in today's largely secular society, follow in Augustine's footsteps? As to the first of these points, Augustine's views, there is space here for only a short and necessarily inadequate summary. In essence Pelagius' views contradicted Augustine on the doctrines of original sin, God's grace, and predestination.[18] On Augustine's account, drawn, he believed, especially from St Paul, human beings are born in a state of sin; we are naturally sinful, a position he believed to be supported by his observation of children. Metaphorically we are all sons and daughters of Adam and Eve, and we mirror their disobedience to the word of God. We cannot escape from this state of sinfulness by our own efforts, but only by the grace of God who may extend to us forgiveness that we do not deserve and cannot earn. But for Augustine, God's grace is not offered to all humanity, but only to those whom God knows in advance will accept it – they are the saved, everyone else will be damned. This is predestination understood as

---

[15] John Passmore, *The Perfectibility of Man* (Carmel, IN: Liberty Fund, Inc, 2000).

[16] For example, in Eric Voegelin, *Science, Politics and Gnosticism* (Wilmington, DE: ISI Books, 2005).

[17] Ali Bonner, *The Myth of Pelagianism* (Oxford: Oxford University Press, 2018) argues that these views were not, in fact, heretical.

[18] This account draws heavily on Augustine, *The Confessions* (London: Everyman's Library, 2001); Robin Lane Fox, *Augustine: Conversions to Confessions* (New York: Basic Books, 2015); and Peter Brown, *Augustine of Hippo*, 45th anniversary edition, (Berkeley: University of California Press, 2013).

preordination; God, who exists outside of time, knows who will accept His forgiveness for their sins and thus who will be saved, saved not through any effort on their part but through His grace. Thus, contra Pelagius, human nature inclines to sin rather than goodness, and we do not possess free will because our apparently free choices are, in fact, preordained by God.

Augustine's position appeared to triumph at the time, as witnessed by the condemnation of Pelagius, and has been enormously influential ever since, for example being central to the Reformation theology of Luther and Calvin in the 16th century. Luther's critique of the sale of indulgences is based precisely on the fact, as he saw it, that we do not possess the ability to save ourselves – we can only have faith that we are saved; *sola fide* was the battle cry of the Reformers. But the case against Augustine's position is also straightforward and has never really gone away. It is that his position denies the universal relevance of Christ's sacrifice on the cross. The appeal of Christianity in the late Roman Empire and through to our time has always rested on the claim that if we accept God's sacrifice of his Son in atonement for our sins we will be saved. Augustine is clear that this is not the case, only a small part of humanity, an Elect few, will be saved, and, to repeat the point, saved not because of any special merit on their part, or by virtue of their decision to accept Christ, but as the decision of God made before time began. This has never been an easy sell to ordinary people, and the Church (Catholic and Reformed) has usually played down Augustine's theology in its practical teaching, for example, in the Catholic tradition, inventing the notion of Purgatory, unknown to Augustine and the Early Church, to give hope to the sinner. In short, Pelagius' optimism and his belief in our ability to shape our own futures has never lost its appeal.

It is obviously beyond the scope of this chapter – and my competence as a non-theologian – to go further than sketching the issues involved in this controversy, but it is legitimate to ask searching questions about how this theology is being employed by Rengger in his account of contemporary ethical and political studies. We are entitled to ask what this controversy has to tell us about our attitude towards attempts to improve the conditions of life in domestic societies and internationally. To put the matter bluntly, even if we accept a broadly pessimistic view of human nature – as many IR realists do – it is not clear why we would adopt the whole package of Augustine's case against Pelagius. Augustinian realists generally rely on Augustine's nuanced account of the exercise of power in a fallen world, focusing on his account of the relationship between the two cities set out in *The City of God*, not on his condemnation of Pelagius[19] – Augustine is such an interesting thinker that there are many directions in which his

---

[19] Augustine, *The City of God* (London: Penguin Books, 1984).

thought can take us, and there is no reason to go down this latter path.[20] But Rengger does, and it is, I think, difficult to avoid the conclusion that his anti-Pelagianism is simply a rhetorical device designed to add force to a position that badly needs to be reinforced from somewhere. More, it is difficult to dispel the impression that he references Pelagius not because he expects us to be familiar with the theological issues that name conjures up, but rather precisely because he doesn't expect us to be clued in on 5th-century theological disputations, and therefore he can oppose Pelagius safe in the knowledge that most people won't realize what the implications of his position are. Perhaps this is a little harsh, but it is certainly fair to say that, outside of Theology Faculties and Seminaries, knowledge of Pelagius' work is not exactly widespread, as Rengger would have been aware.

The point is that it is quite obviously not the case that most modern reformers rely on assumptions about perfectibility in order to buttress their positions. Most reformers just want to make things a bit better; to take over Karl Popper's phrase, they are piecemeal social engineers.[21] Certainly they usually don't buy into Augustine's pessimism about human nature, much less his doctrine of original sin, and they often adhere to ideas about progress that the sophisticated would set to one side, but most reformers do not believe in a grand narrative of Progress with a capital 'P'. Nor do they believe that progress is necessarily inevitable and irreversible, although they may hope that this is the case, that, to cite a favourite quote of Martin Luther King and Barrack Obama, 'the arc of the moral universe is long, but it bends towards justice'. Instead of relying on grand narratives, they try to make the world a better place one step at a time, sometimes failing, sometimes succeeding, trying to learn from their mistakes and, if they fail again, to fail better – something the Augustine of *The City of God* would have no difficulty understanding and empathizing with. The welfare states of post-war Western Europe were built in that way and, for all their failings, have made for their citizens a better life than their forebears could have dreamed of. It is wholly reasonable to deny that progress is inevitable, and very few people nowadays adhere to that Victorian dream, but it is another thing altogether to deny that sometimes things can get better, that human suffering can be lessened and life-choices widened. Of course, there is no guarantee that such advances cannot be reversed, but whether such reverses

---

[20] It is an interesting illustration of the fecundity of Augustine's thought that two such radically different thinkers as William E. Connolly and Jean Bethke Elshtain should both have devoted books to him; see William E. Connolly, *The Augustinian Imperative: Reflections on the Politics of Morality* (London: Sage, 1993); Jean Bethke Elshtain, *Augustine and the Limits of Politics* (Notre Dame, IN: Notre Dame Press, 1997).

[21] Karl R. Popper, *The Poverty of Historicism* (London: Routledge and Kegan Paul, 3rd edition, 1961).

happen or not is down to us as political actors – there is no need to posit some wider narrative that guarantees either success or failure. Oakeshott's critique of the rationalist success-guaranteeing narrative is apposite, but neither his thought nor Rengger's application of it justifies adoption of an alternative grand narrative of inevitable failure.

Progress in the world and justice in war

To recap: Rengger's principled hostility to teleocracy and his campaign against Pelagianism appear to rest on shaky foundations, a question-begging account of the implications of Augustinian pessimism and an unrealistic vision of the motivations of progressivist reformers. Still, so far, the argument remains at an abstract level and now it is necessary to bring things down to earth by examining the more concrete issues he raised in his late works, especially on the subject of intervention and justice in war. But before moving to the latter topic I want to cash out something I promised in the introduction to this chapter, and reference a conversation with Nick, or rather a clutch of conversations.

As might be imagined from what is set out earlier, we quite frequently clashed on these issues, usually in a good-humoured way, but one of the few times Nick lost his temper with me was when I defended Steven Pinker's position that violence and intolerance have become less salient over time.[22] The story Pinker tells is of a long-term decline of violence in all its forms, war, civil war, domestic oppression, racism, and prejudice. Because Pinker is not by training a student of things international many scholars in international relations were sceptical of his data, yet well-established IR scholars such as Joshua Goldstein and John Mueller have come to much the same conclusion.[23] Interstate war has been in decline for decades; civil wars now are much more in evidence than the interstate variety, but even counting the two together, the number of lives lost to war has been in decline for some time. That this is so is actually rarely challenged in the IR literature – the debate nowadays is about whether this fall reflects a genuine change in the nature of international order or is the product of contingent factors, that is, factors that may change in the future. International anarchy, the absence of an effective global government, remains in place and one cannot be sure that the decline in war will continue. Moreover, if a great power war did return – perhaps between China and America, see books by Graham Allison

---

22 Steven Pinker, *The Better Angels of our Nature* (NY: Viking Books, 2011), also *Enlightenment Now* (London: Penguin, 2019).

23 Joshua Goldstein, *Winning the War on War* (New York: Dutton, 2011); John Mueller, *The Remnants of War* (Ithaca, NY: Cornell University Press, 2007).

and Christopher Coker[24] – the potential level of destruction would be such as to defeat any optimistic account of the future of war.

It is important to note that the decline in the kind of mass violence associated with war and civil conflict is also accompanied by declines in the less dramatic forms of violence represented by racism, homophobia, and other forms of prejudice. In the United States and the UK groups such as 'Black Lives Matter' draw attention to White racism, and similar pressure groups highlight other forms of prejudice in those countries and elsewhere in the Western world. No one would deny that these forms of prejudice still exist – but the contrast with the situation 50 or even 25 years ago is obvious in the case of racism and, in particular, homophobia. The number of countries that have enacted laws providing for same-sex marriage is striking, and the kind of routine disparagement of gay people that used to be so prevalent that it was simply taken for granted has all but disappeared. Nowadays in the UK a major issue in the media is whether Black and Minority Ethnic people are adequately represented in British public life, or on television or as news readers – but as recently as the 1970s and 1980s popular culture was steeped in racially offensive stereotyping. Moreover, extreme poverty has substantially lessened globally over the last 20 years; most of the UN's Millennium Development Goals have been met and hundreds of millions of people have been pulled out of poverty.

To return to my conversations with Nick, from my point of view the last two paragraphs are full of empirical propositions which are either true or false, and, with all due respect being paid to the proposition that all data is socially constructed, I think they are true. There is indeed less violence in the world today than there was in the past, racism and homophobia certainly haven't disappeared, but they are less salient than they were, grinding poverty and malnutrition affects fewer people than previously, average life expectancy globally is rising and so on. None of this is any comfort if you are one of the 'bottom billion' still in extreme poverty, or suffering the effects of the Syrian civil war, or under persecution for being gay in Uganda or Christian in Pakistan or living in Russia where life expectancy is falling – but still, taken in the round, progress has been made. To Nick this was a clear and distressing example of my Pelagian tendencies, and he was visibly upset that I could believe such, as he saw it, nonsense. But as far as I was concerned, these propositions could only be nonsense if they were used to construct a narrative of Progress which couldn't be reversed and would inevitably lead to the end of all suffering. Even in his most optimistic

---

[24] Graham Allison, *Destined for War: Can America and China Escape Thucydides' Trap* (London: Scribe UK, 2017); Christopher Coker, *The Improbable War: China, the United States and the Logic of Great Power Conflict* (London: Hurst & Co., 2015).

moments, Pinker doesn't go there, because there's no notion of perfectibility here. Rengger's dismissal of Pinker wasn't based on contesting the evidence but rather on the patently false position that to believe that the condition of humanity has improved and could be improved further entails a belief that such improvement is irreversible or is leading to perfected end-state. It was perfectly understandable that he should refuse to assimilate Pinker's data into a grand narrative of progress, but in order to avoid this step he found it necessary to ignore the obvious fact that change for the better does sometimes take place.

We can see something of the same kind of movement when we turn from conversation to Rengger's writings on intervention and the just war, most of which are to be found in his book *Just War and International Order*, but also relevant are his essays on Jean Bethke Elshtain in *The Anti-Pelagian Imagination in Political Theory and International Relations*.[25] His basic position here is summarized by him thus:

> [for] most of the modern period ... the scope of justifications for the use of force has in fact – and contrary to a widely believed narrative – been expanding not contracting, and the most influential tradition that is supposed to be about the restraint of war (the just war tradition) has in fact been complicit in this.[26]

One justification for the use of force that has been employed occasionally – though not as often as is widely believed or as one would imagine from reading Rengger – is summarized by the term 'humanitarian intervention'. He is, predictably, highly critical of such interventions, seeing them as attempts to put the world to rights by one state interfering in the affairs of another, pointing out that such interventions are usually unsuccessful, making matters worse. Such is, he argues, the inevitable result of perfectionist approaches to world politics, and the unwarranted teleocratic belief by liberal powers in their capacity to identify good and evil and act to promote the former, if necessary, by violence. Much of this is good sense. He is, of course, right (and hardly unusual), in pointing out that interventions often fail and indeed can make things worse. It would be difficult to find anyone reflecting on the events of the last 30 years who would disagree. What is less clear is what conclusion ought to be drawn from this sorry history? His seems to be 'don't ever intervene' but this doesn't automatically follow; another approach might be to try to learn from past errors and look at those few cases where intervention has been relatively successful (Sierra Leone, East Timor,

---

25 See Footnote 3.
26 Rengger, *Just War and International Order*, p. xii.

on some counts, Kosovo) to work out why these cases were different from the obvious failures. In other words, the story here is much like the story of domestic reform – piecemeal international social engineering, learning from one's mistakes and trying to do better. Of course, one response to this is that the interveners don't have the legitimacy required to act as global reformers, which may well be true but isn't an argument that would cut much ice with, for example, the victims of the Rwanda Genocide, where the world did stand aside, or of the current genocide of Uighurs in China where the world is again standing aside, this time with more justification considering the costs of action. The key point here is that a pragmatic case-by-case approach to intervention would seem on the face of it not to warrant the condemnation Rengger offers.

His case against certain just war thinkers who have contributed to the debate on intervention is much more interesting because his targets here are figures who would be difficult to characterize as teleocrats. Jean Bethke Elshtain and James Turner Johnson, the targets in question, are both Augustinians with unimpeachable anti-teleocratic credentials; Elshtain's book *Augustine and the Limits of Politics*[27] is precisely a critique of over-reaching political action, and Johnson's work on religious ethics and the just war is, again, resolutely Augustinian. The choice of these targets is interesting in particular because there is a branch of contemporary just war that comes much closer to being, in Rengger's terms, teleocratic – the revisionist work of figures such as Jeff McMahan.[28] But, crucially, these thinkers are generally opposed to Western interventions so do not fit the bill.[29] Elshtain and Johnson, on the other hand, were supportive of the War on Terror and the invasion of Iraq in 2003; Elshtain's *A Just War Against Terror*[30] tells the story through the title while Johnson's *The War to Oust Saddam Hussein: Just War and the New Face of Conflict*[31] is a defence of this intervention. Both writers were also signatories of the open letter 'What We're Fighting For: A Letter from America' in which 60 academics (also including such important just war thinkers as John Kelsay and Michael Walzer) set out an ethical defence of the war on terror.[32]

---

[27] See Footnote 18.

[28] See, for example, McMahan, *Killing in War* (Oxford: Oxford University Press, 2009).

[29] Generally opposed, but not always, see Jeff McMahan, 'Syria is a modern-day holocaust: we must act', *The Washington Post* (30 November 2015), available at: www.washingtonpost.com/news/in-theory/wp/2015/11/30/syria-is-a-modern-day-holocaust-we-must-act/.

[30] Jean Bethke Elshtain, *A Just War Against Terror* (New York: Basic Books, 2003).

[31] James Turner Johnson, *The War to Oust Saddam Hussein: Just War and the New Face of Conflict* (Lanham, MD: Rowman & Littlefield, 2005).

[32] See *The Washington Post* (12 February 2002) for the text of the letter, available at: www.washingtonpost.com/wp-srv/nation/specials/attacked/transcripts/justwar_letter020102.html.

His case against Elshtain and Johnson is simply put, and, on the face of it, compelling. The notion of the just war, he argues, is at root a doctrine that is meant to restrain the drive to war, but becomes, for these two writers, a doctrine that justifies war. The war on terror and the invasion of Iraq are seen as fulfilling the requirements of justice – and perhaps, he argues, this is telling us something more generally applicable to the idea of a just war, namely that by describing a war as 'just' the tradition turns a political act into a moral crusade. This is not a wholly original argument – Carl Schmitt makes a not-dissimilar point[33] – but it has considerable force when applied to the events of the last two decades. In effect, the charge is that just war thinking has been weaponized by international teleocracy to justify attempts to remake the world in its image.

Is this a valid bill of indictment delivered against Elshtain and Johnson or, indeed, against the modern reading of the Just War tradition taken as a whole? A key point here is whether the tradition is, as Rengger repeatedly asserts, unambiguously in favour of restraint, and here we need to draw a distinction between the just conduct of war and the justice of engaging in war, or, to use the Latin tags that have become customary, *ius in bello* and *ius ad bellum*. Restraint is certainly basic to the just conduct of war, and there is nothing in the writings of Elshtain and Johnson to suggest that they disagree with the restrictions nowadays built into the Law of Armed Conflict, nor does Rengger suggest that any such critique of restraint is to be found there. The key question is whether restraint is also basic to the idea of justice in the resort to force. Here things are a lot less clear-cut. Certainly, in classical just war thinking there is a presupposition against the use of force, a requirement that all plausible peaceful routes to correcting an injustice are pursued before force is resorted to, and a requirement that there is a reasonable prospect of success before force is engaged in. So, indeed, an element of restraint is required. But the most basic definition of the *ad bellum* principle is that there is a just cause, that a serious wrong has occurred and must be responded to, assuming these other criteria, *in bello* as well as *ad bellum* are met. In short, the tradition in itself is neither permissive nor restrictive – it says act if, and only if, it can be judged that there is a just cause and that the other conventional criteria can be met, which may restrict action in some cases but may require it in others.

Elshtain and Johnson believed that overthrowing Saddam Hussein met these conditions, that his regime was tyrannical and by its existence constituted a threat to its neighbours. Rengger disputes this judgement, and,

---

[33] See Chris Brown, 'From humanised war to humanitarian intervention: Carl Schmitt's critique of the Just War tradition', in Louiza Odysseos and Fabio Petito (eds), *The International Political Thought of Carl Schmitt* (London: Routledge, 2007b), pp. 56–79.

with some reason, argues that they and other just war thinkers dismissed far too readily the fears of those who argued that the consequences of action would be worse than inaction. This is not an open-and-shut case, and Rengger is right to suggest that just war is an 'ambiguous tradition',[34] but that very ambiguity tells against the notion that there is a simply teleocratic story to be told here. His judgement that the Just War tradition is complicit in expanding the justifications for the use of force is rather too one-sided in its failure to recognize this ambiguity. In the final chapter of *Just War and International Order* he joins many just war thinkers in attacking the notion of 'supreme emergency' associated with the doyen of just war thinkers, Michael Walzer, precisely because it is thought to open the door to an expansion of justifications for the use of force – even though his argument is explicitly directed towards *in bello* issues.[35] But as ought also to be recognized, although Walzer did sign the Letter from America, he did not support the war in Iraq, and has not supported subsequent interventions such as the overthrow of the Gaddafi regime in Libya in 2011. Effectively he used the same criteria as Elshtain and Johnson, but came to different conclusions, nicely illustrating the point that while the Just War tradition can be used to support interventions it can also be used to oppose them.

In summary, it seems to me that when he turned to these issues in his later writings, Rengger's tendency was to close down rather than to open up the conversation. There is a good case for arguing that the Just War tradition consists of a set of pertinent questions about the use of force, rather than a set of answers, and that the recent turn towards an attempt by analytical philosophers to produce such answers is misguided.[36] This seems, on the face of it, to be a debate to which the conversational, edifying Rengger might have contributed to in a positive way. He clearly had the wherewithal for such a contribution but his commitment to opposing international reformism led him in another direction, in opposition to figures who one might think would be his allies. He believed that by their adoption of a particular position on the war on terror they were closing down the conversation, but by focusing on their errors he, arguably, acted to the same effect.

---

[34] Rengger, *Just War and International Order*, Chapter 3.

[35] Ibid., Chapter 5. On Walzer as a just war thinker, see Chris Brown, 'Michael Walzer', in Daniel Brunstetter and Cian O'Driscoll (eds), *Just War Thinkers: From Cicero to the 21st Century* (London: Routledge, 2018).

[36] See Chris Brown, 'Just war and political judgement', in Anthony F. Lang, Jr, Cian O'Driscoll and John Williams (eds), *Just War: Authority, Tradition and Practice* (Georgetown, DC Georgetown University Press, 2013) and 'Justified: just war and the ethics of violence and world order', in Lothar Brock and Hendrik Simon (eds), *The Justification of War and International Order* (Oxford: Oxford University Press, 2021), pp. 435–48.

Conclusion

I am not sure whether there is any empirical support for the widely held belief that mathematicians and theoretical physicists do their best work early in their careers, but I think it plain that political philosophers such as Nick Rengger come into their own in middle and late-middle age – Rawls' *Political Liberalism* and Oakeshott's *On Human Conduct* are just two of the many seminal books that were written by scholars older than Rengger was when he died.[37] This being so, what might we have expected from him over the next decade, the decade that should have seen him establish his reputation for the ages? My first inclination is to think that perhaps we might have hoped for a substantial book setting out the positive side of his anti-Pelagianism, an account of what politics could be, rather than the orientation towards the wrong beliefs of others which was the default setting for his writings in the 2010s. In my critique of these works earlier, I have suggested that a politics based on opposition to teleocracy would be a politics that was insensitive to the demands of ordinary people that their condition be improved – would he have accepted this proposition or, perhaps, explained why it was wrong-headed?

Probably not. One of Nick's favourite anecdotes related how Oakeshott had refused an invitation to join the Mont Pelerin Society which was formed in 1947 by inter alia Friedrich Hayek, Karl Popper, and Ludwig Von Mises to combat what was then seen as the near-inevitable march of socialism in the world. His rejection was based on the principle he had clearly expressed in a review of Hayek's *The Road to Serfdom*: '[A] plan to resist planning may be better than its opposite, but it belongs to the same style of politics'.[38] To ask for a broad account of politics from a standpoint that is suspicious of all broad accounts of politics is unlikely to be productive. Those of us who are unwilling to participate as combatants in the war on teleocracy or to identify as anti-Pelagians would not have been presented with a full-scale account of what an anti-teleocratic politics would look like. Had he lived Rengger would not have produced a systematic political philosophy.

Fair enough, but would his future work have been edifying? Such was his commitment in the 1980s, where his endorsement of Rorty and Oakeshott was tied up with a refusal to systematize – but does his work of the 2010s suggest that this commitment remained in place? This is, I think, an open

---

[37] John Rawls, *Political Liberalism* (New York: Columbia University Press, 1993); Oakeshott, see Footnote 7.

[38] The quotation may be found in Oakeshott, *Rationalism in Politics and Other Essays*, p. 21. For context see Andrew Gamble, 'Oakeshott and totalitarianism', in Terry Nardin (ed), *Michael Oakeshott's Cold War Liberalism*, (New York: Palgrave Macmillan, 2015), pp. 83–98.

question. While the style he employed in these late writings remained relatively light-hearted and welcoming – in other words, edifying – the content, as I hope I have shown, became much darker and less tolerant. While still refusing to systematize, he became, it seems to me, less concerned to keep the conversation going, less committed to the idea that there was no truth to be discovered, less open to diverse viewpoints. We all of us change over time, and he was no different from the rest of us in that respect; the Rengger of the 1980s reading the Rengger of the 2010s would have recognized and appreciated the style, but, I suspect, would have been surprised and not altogether pleased by the content. One can only regret that we can no longer debate this issue with him.

7

Conservatism, Civility, and the Challenges of International Political Theory

Michael C. Williams

Dark times require that we peer deeply into the darkness, and we seem to live in times where the will and ability to peer into the darkness is increasingly vital. Much that has been taken as progress in politics both domestic and international seems at risk of unravelling. Most strikingly, across the globe radical conservative and avowedly 'neo-reactionary' movements are challenging the principles, practices, and institutions of the liberal world order that (for better or worse) for at least a quarter of a century seemed firmly 'embedded' as the dominant international order – with often worrying success.[1] Autocracy, illiberal democracy, racial exclusion, and extreme nationalism – to name but a few – are today powerful forces in world politics. Democracy, human rights, toleration, and even civility are on the back foot in many places, and in rapid retreat in others.

Despite these pressing challenges, the main traditions of thought in IR and international political theory (IPT) seem largely ill-equipped to respond to them. Most liberal-rationalist theories have lost their ability to understand the ideas, interests, and emotions associated with today's right wing and other 'populist' movements, never mind to address them.[2] Conventional constructivists and postmodernists might well be able to

---

[1] See Rita Abrahamsen, et al., 'Confronting the international political sociology of the New Right', *International Political Sociology* 14, 1 (2020), pp. 94–107.

[2] For a more sympathetic reading of 'populism', see David Goodhart, *The Road to Somewhere* (London: Hurst, 2018).

trace and record the contours of reactionary 'populisms', but it is far from clear that they have the tools for assessing their claims, not to mention confronting them. In the face of radically reactionary strategies that take as their foundation the claim that 'nothing is true and everything is possible',[3] the unspoken optimism that has often accompanied these views looks suspiciously thin. Realism, with its focus on the gloomier prospects of politics, its stress on nations and their clashes of interest and power, seems on the surface better attuned to the shifting geopolitical landscape – but, at least in its 'structural' forms, it has (and can have) little to say about the deeper political questions involved and the challenges they raise, including their extreme nationalism and alternative visions of international order.[4] And while 'classical' realism may be more well equipped to provide a basis for such an engagement, few of its recent proponents have shown much inclination to do so. As a result, IR theory, despite its ever-increasing mathematical rigour, methodological virtuosity, and seemingly endless proliferation of novel theoretical 'turns' has little to say in response to some of the most striking challenges to the international order seen in half a century.

Yet the ideas and impact of the radical Right cannot be easily dismissed or ignored, uncomfortable as that fact may be. While it is reassuring to see them as little more than incohate 'know nothing' reactions to social and political change and dislocation, the reality is more complex. Today's radical conservative movements are far from anti-intellectual. On the contrary, key parts of the movement have spent decades seeking to generate, in the words of Alain de Benoist, a new 'metapolitics' that can provide philosophic foundations for a renewed politics of the radical Right. In an interesting survey of contemporary ideas on the far Right, Andrew Sullivan has bravely noted both their sense of attraction and importance:

> I know why many want to dismiss all of this as mere hate, as some of it certainly is. I also recognize that engaging with the ideas of this movement is a tricky exercise in our current political climate.

---

3   Peter Pomerantsev, *Nothing is True and Everything is Possible: The Surreal Heart of the New Russia* (New York: Public Affairs, 2015); the 'postmodern' dimensions of the thinking of one of the New Right's most important thinkers, see Alain de Benoist, *View From the Right*, (London: Arktos, 2017 [1977]). For the relationship between these movements and the 'critical' movements in international political theory that Rengger had a role in debating, see Jean-Francois Drolet and Michael C. Williams, 'From critique to reaction: The New Right, critical theory, and international relations', *Journal of International Political Theory* (2021b), pp. 1–17.

4   For a recent attempt, see John Mearsheimer, 'Bound to fail: the rise and fall of the liberal international order', *International Security* 43, 4 (2019), pp. 7–50.

Among many liberals, there is an understandable impulse to raise the drawbridge, to deny certain ideas access to respectable conversation, to prevent certain concepts from being 'normalized'. But the normalization has already occurred – thanks, largely, to voters across the West – and wilfully blinding ourselves to the most potent political movement of the moment will not make it go away. Indeed, the more I read today's more serious reactionary writers, the more I'm convinced they are much more in tune with the current global mood than today's conservatives, liberals, and progressives. I find myself repelled by any of their themes – and yet, at the same time, drawn in by their unmistakable relevance. I'm even tempted, at times, to share George Orwell's view of the neo-reactionaries of his age: that, although they can sometimes spew dangerous nonsense, they're smarter and more influential than we tend to think, and that 'up to a point, they are right'.[5]

In his last book, tellingly subtitled *Dealing in Darkness*, Nicholas Rengger opens with a famous passage from Milton's *Paradise Lost*: 'No light, but rather darkness visible / Served only to discover sights of woe'.[6] I want to suggest that few thinkers in IR in recent decades had a firmer sense of the power of these kinds of ideas that tap into currents of 'darkness', and of the challenges they present, than Nicholas Rengger. Although his commitment to IPT rarely manifested itself in explicit political pronouncements, and though in both philosophy and temperament he was sceptical of the ability (and claims) of theory to direct practice, it is precisely the depth of his thinking and the sensibilities it sought to advance that are most strikingly pertinent today. Through his engagement with political 'darkness' (not only epistemic uncertainty, but also like many theologically inclined thinkers, with darker 'Augustinian' themes concerning human conduct and motivation), Rengger engaged indirectly key issues on the contemporary global 'New Right' in ways that few thinkers in IR are able to achieve. It is this aspect of his legacy that I want preliminarily to explore here.

The argument comes in two parts. In the first section, I propose to look at two areas where the 'dark' themes Rengger interrogates and contemporary reactionary ideas intersect in revealing ways. In the second section, I examine two of Rengger's searching appraisals of responses to the politics of reaction, appraisals that raise crucial questions for contemporary IR, both theoretically and practically.

---

[5] Andrew Sullivan, 'The reactionary temptation', *New York Magazine* (1 May 2017).

[6] Nicholas Rengger, *The Anti-Pelagian Imagination: Dealing in Darkness* (London: Routledge, 2017), p. 1.

Part one: liberalism, realism, and the New Right

Part of the reason that IPT has so little engagement with radical conservatism lies in the fact that it is not much concerned with conservatism per se. In the early phases of the discipline's development, its theoretical 'menu for choice' mirrored political theory's defining triumvirate of liberalism, conservatism, and Marxism, – but IR replaced conservatism with realism – often leaving the mistaken impression that realism and conservatism were two sides of the same coin, however much the historical record suggests a much more complex story.[7] Rengger's international theory does not suffer from these limitations. Grounded in the history of political thought rather than IR theory, it is more attentive to both conservative thinking and to the limitations of straightforwardly equating realism and conservatism. In this section, I would like to explore two areas where this openness allowed him to engage themes that intersect with those on the contemporary NR. But before doing so, it is necessary to examine in slightly more detail key elements of the NR's view of global politics that distinguish it from views commonly associated with conservatism today.

Rationalism and globalization

Conservatism is not often identified with a critique of capitalism and globalization. In recent decades, conservatism has tended to be lumped together with neoliberalism and neoconservatism as a champion of the market all that goes with it. Yet, as Ian Hall and Rengger argued, this significantly constrains our view of conservatism's intellectual sensibilities, which often hold nuanced suspicions about market individualism and capitalism.[8] To summarize briefly a very wide set of ideas, traditional conservatism saw the values and social forces of market society eroding traditional bonds of community and obligation (and, one should never forget, hierarchy), leaving a world of individual anomie, unconstrained

---

[7]   See the revealing treatment in William Scheuerman, *Morgenthau* (Cambridge: Polity Press, 2009) and, more broadly, Nicolas Guilhot, *After the Enlightenment: Political Realism and International Relations in the Mid-Twentieth Century* (Cambridge: Cambridge University Press, 2018); an attempt to trace some of the historical dynamics involved is Jean-Francois Drolet and Michael C. Williams, 'Realism, radical conservatism, and the evolution of post-war international theory', *Review of International Studies* (2021a), pp. 1–22.

[8]   Ian Hall and Nicholas Rengger, ' "The Right that failed"?: The ambiguities of conservative thought and the dilemmas of conservative practice in international affairs', *International Affairs* 81 (1) 2005.

collective passions, and instrumental domination.[9] Over recent decades this scepticism (and sometimes outright hostility) towards market society has largely disappeared as conservatism has been co-opted and supplanted by what are in reality neoliberal ideas that it once steadfastly opposed.[10]

Yet this fusion between conservatism and neoliberalism has not gone uncontested. In fact, many parts of the intellectual vanguard of today's NR explicitly reject this synthesis and provide implacable critiques of global liberal capitalism based not simply in economic populism or hostility toward migration, but in a much wider critique of liberal modernity and political rationalism. In this view, the real driving force behind economic and cultural globalization lies not in capitalism or realpolitik as traditionally conceived by Marxists or Realists, but in the dynamics of a rationalist episteme with intrinsically universalizing aspirations linked to powerful new social and political structures of liberal managerialism. In a view that found its most powerful early formulation in James Burnham's 1941 study *The Managerial Revolution*, liberal modernity is synonymous with the emergence of a New Class of technically skilled administrators who had succeeded in gaining power in government, business, and the media by exploiting redistributionist slogans was not exclusive to Soviet Russia, but also a key feature of fascist and welfare state democracies across Europe and North America.[11] According to Burnham, these different managerial experiments were built on neither a market economy nor true socialist equality. Rather, they elevated a managerial class that already had positioned itself in a corporate economy and would now provide state-authorized social services, thereby displacing older elites lacking the functional skills required to operate in a world being reconfigured rapidly by new technological developments. Devaluing tradition, presenting individuals as capable of continual re-fashioning, and espousing an experimental approach to social issues that almost seamlessly matched the emerging claims to expertise and institutional capacities of the

---

[9] An insightful account of how reactionary thinkers influentially framed the Enlightenment in these terms is Darren M. McMahon, *Enemies of the Enlightenment: The French Counter-Enlightenment and the Making of Modernity* (Oxford: Oxford University Press, 2001).

[10] Different accounts of this shift can be found in George H. Nash, *The Conservative Intellectual Movement in America, 1945–1980* (Wilmington DE: Intercollegiate Studies Institute, 1996); Quinn Slobodian, *Globalists: The End of Empire and the Birth of Neoliberalism* (Cambridge MA: Harvard University Press, 2018); Paul Gottfried, *Conservatism in America* (London: Palgrave, 2007).

[11] James Burnham, *The Managerial Revolution: What is Happening in the World* (New York: John Day Co., 1941). See also Samuel T. Francis, *Power and History, The Political Thought of James Burnham* (Lanham MD.: University Press of America, 1984); *James Burnham: Thinkers of Our Time* (London: Claridge Press, 1999); Samuel T. Francis, *Leviathan and its Enemies* Washington DC: Washington Summit Publishers); Paul Gottfried, *After Liberalism: Mass Democracy in the Managerial State* (Princeton, NJ: Princeton University Press, 2001).

New Class, pragmatism became an important component of the new forms of liberal power and the *dis*empowerment of previous forms of conservatism.

In this view, global liberal ideology relentlessly targets 'traditional' social orders, states, ideas, and identities that oppose its expansion, a strategy radical conservatives believe is exemplified in liberal international human rights campaigns and support for mass immigration. Reducing individuals to economic maximizers and values to subjective hedonism, they argue that liberalism does not enhance 'diversity'; on the contrary, it flattens the world, stripping cultural diversity of any real substantive content and social grounding, commodifying individuals and cultures, eroding non-liberal societies and refashioning them in its image. Liberal cosmopolitanism is thus nothing of the kind. Rather than promoting diversity, it reduces all values to subjective 'lifestyles' and then subjects those lifestyles to their manipulation by the market and the regulation by bureaucratic, therapeutic, and cultural elites who prescribe acceptable forms of diversity and proscribe those they find offensive or politically incorrect.[12] The primary methods for dealing with this resistance are the 'soft' powers of liberal 'global governance' – therapeutic social and education policies, cultural stigmatization, and legal activism – though recourse to violent coercion is also frequent, as the wars advocated and conducted by managerial liberal elites and states in the name of liberal democracy and human rights (not to mention free markets) demonstrate. Contemporary globalization, from this perspective, is simply the latest and perhaps highest expression of rationalist attempts to govern, thought, action, and politics – to establish the universal rule of liberal reason.

Today's NR applies these insights to contemporary global politics, and although this account overlaps with some more familiar critiques of globalization and American hegemony, it stands outside most of the conceptual frameworks that dominate IPT. Rengger, however, provides a rare engagement with a series of analogous themes in political thought, and through them to global politics. In an extended analysis of John Gray's increasing liberal 'pessimism' and engagement with realism and IR, for instance, Rengger stressed how Gray's critique of globalization connects to the wider assaults on rationalism and utopianism surveyed earlier. As Gray puts it in his 2007 book *Black Mass*:

---

12 From an American 'paleo'conservative perspective, see Samuel T. Francis, *Leviathan and its Enemies* (Washington DC: Washington Summit Publishers, 2005); and Paul Gottfried, *After Liberalism: Mass Democracy in the Managerial State* (Princeton, NJ: Princeton University Press, 2001); for a wider treatment, Jean-Francois Drolet and Michael C. Williams, 'The view from MARS: American paleoconservatism and ideological challenges to the liberal international order', *International Journal* 74, 1 (2019), pp. 15–31; and from an icon of the European *Nouvelle Droit*, Alain de Benoist, 'Confronting globalization', *Telos* 108 (1996), pp. 117–37.

Since the French Revolution, a succession of utopian movements has transformed political life. Entire societies have been destroyed and the world changed forever. The alteration envisioned by utopian thinkers has not come about, and for the most part their projects have produced results opposite to those they intended. That has not prevented similar projects being launched again and again right up to the start of the twenty-first century, when the world's most powerful state launched a campaign to export democracy to the Middle East.[13]

Globalization, in Gray's view, too, is not simply an economic process. On the contrary, it is the outcome of the continuing 'rationalist attachment' dating from the Enlightenment.[14] In Gray's telling, Rengger notes, the endgame of this project is both near and dismal, concluding 'with the stark warning that with the end of *laissez-faire* – an end he had spent the book foretelling – "a deepening international anarchy is the human prospect"'.[15]

For Gray, avoiding this dire situation demands a different liberal alternative, one that rejects rationalist globalism, recognizes the inescapable plurality of the world, and seeks to construct a modus vivendi in which the irreducible plurality of forms of life are recognized, to some degree embraced, and managed with as little conflict as possible. The cracks in rationalist dreams of the Enlightenment and the challenges posed by the at least partial unravelling of laissez-faire and globalization (which have become even more apparent in the last decade) require a renewed if rather chastened liberalism. Interestingly, as Rengger points out, Gray identifies political 'realism' as a key part of this project: realism in the sense of recognizing the inevitability of pluralism, the potential for conflict it entails, and the need for practices that can manage both.

Understandably, much of the discussion of Gray's ideas has taken place in 'mainstream' political theory. But it is significant that these themes also echo, or even mirror, critiques on the radical Right in ways that challenge both liberalism and realism far more than Gray is willing to countenance. In fact, analogues to Gray's critique of liberal rationalism and its 'utopian' universalism are easy to find on today's radical Right. From Alain de Benoist in France to Alexander Dugin in Russia, as for a myriad of their associates in

---

[13] John Gray, *Black Mass: Apocalyptic Religion and the Death of Utopia* (New York: Farrar, Strauss and Giroux, 2007), p. 3.

[14] Starting from figures like Gray rather than in IR also allows Rengger to engage widely with analogous critiques, including with other influential conservative figures and themes, such as Voegelin's attack on political Gnosticism. Rengger, *The Anti-Pelagian Imagination*, p. 105.

[15] Rengger, *The Anti-Pelagian Imagination*, p. 100; Gray, *Black Mass*, p. 3; John Gray, *False Dawn: The Delusions of Global Capitalism* (New York: New Press, 2008).

between, the idea of an international 'pluriverse', a multi-polar international order based on fundamentally different cultural groupings, has become a common geopolitical imaginary across the Right.

Strikingly, and yet logically, in fact, a central move of the radical Right has been towards geopolitics. Parts of this appear at first glance to fit quite well with realism. The focus on nations, irreducible plurality, and so on, have long also been staples of realist geopolitics, and the two even claim some of the same antecedents, such as Halford Mackinder. In the hands of radical conservatives, however, geopolitics are transformed from being a post-liberal play of differences in some kind of reconfigured 'neo-medieval' system into an international order centred around a return to the 'ethnos', to what Roger Griffin has evocatively captured as a 'basic unit of homogenous cultural energy' distinct from the modern nation (and state).[16] Unlike Gray's rather forlorn call for a new liberalism whose social foundations he seems to find hard to see, the NR believes that the historical dynamics of liberalism are opening avenues for its success, as the economic and cultural dislocations caused by globalization, and resentment against the proliferation of 'liberal wars' provide propitious conditions for a conservative counter-movement. In this context, it seeks to develop an alternative: a new political theory, a vision and narrative beyond the outmoded categories of Left and Right, and a sustained campaign of cultural and political mobilization based upon it.[17]

In geopolitical terms, this narrative takes a number of novel turns. American paleoconservatives have argued for a decentralized nationalism based on the social power and cultural hegemony of Middle America. This would be achieved through an aggressive process of de-bureaucratization and power devolution, as well as a sharp reversal of the immigration policies associated with the liberalism of East Coast elites and the interests of global capital.[18] European New Rightists seek a similar return to literally 'grounded' political communities of substantive culture and history (and in some cases – De Benoist – subsidiarist local democracy) as an alternative to

---

[16] Quoted in Mark Bassin, 'Lev Gumilev and the European New Right', *Nationalities Papers: The Journal of Nationalism and Ethnicity* 43, 6 (2015), p. 842. For a further analysis, see Jean-Francois Drolet and Michael C. Williams, 'Radical conservatism and global order: international theory and the New Right', *International Theory* 10, 2 (2018), pp. 285–313.

[17] See De Benoist, and particularly his support of Dugin's call for a new 'fourth political theory' for the 21st century that can supplant the liberal, socialist, and nationalist theories that successively dominated the previous three. Alexander Dugin, *The Fourth Political Theory* (London: Arktos, 2012).

[18] See, for instance, Samuel T. Francis, 'Nationalism: old and new', *Chronicles* June (1992), pp. 18–22; and Paul Gottfried, 'Reconfiguring the political landscape', *Telos* 103 (1995), pp. 111–26.

liberal modernity, globalism, or the technocratic structures of the European Union. Here, the legacy of the German 'conservative revolution'[19] can be seen clearly, with old ideas of technological elitism and communal solidarity fused in a revolutionary embrace requiring both restraining capitalism and intensively exploiting (and yet controlling) technology without rejecting either.[20] This might in their geopolitical imaginings yield a form of subsidiary and neo-medieval order – but it would be one based on an exclusive commonality in 'European' culture that explicitly excludes 'non-European' forms of life.

Both the myth of an ethnos-based polity, and a technologically liberated elite are at work in these visions. The goal is not to replace the state with some more comprehensive form of the same universal logic but to move beyond it. To remain within a statist logic is to be trapped by outdated ideas and institutions that need to be transcended. That these ideas may sound suspiciously like some advocated on the anti-globalization Left is to NR thinkers like De Benoist another illustration of the need to transcend outdated political dichotomies, accepting environmental and economic positions antithetical to free-market conservatives, while rejecting the Left's cultural cosmopolitanism.

This reconfigured order would restrict membership in the political community by excluding or even expelling those who do not or will not adopt its way of life. The NR is quick to argue, in some eyes disingenuously, that this does not mean that these Others should be hated or despised; they, too, should have their own polities, that should be equally valued in their own ways. The NR thus claims to be pluralist, yet anti-liberal; identitarian, but not necessarily racist (the NR's position on race in fact varies a great deal depending on authors and factions). Nor, they assert, is it a return to the fascist glorification of the state. Identity, Benoist claims to follow Martin Buber, is 'dialogical'. The NR should therefore oppose cultural and economic globalization internationally as well as locally, and support counter-globalization (anti-imperial) efforts by such peoples globally (while

---

[19] Armin Mohler, *The Conservative Revolution in Germany, 1918–1932* (Washington, DC: Washington Summit 2018).

[20] As De Benoist puts it, 'European civilization is not in danger because of technical progress, but because of the egalitarian utopia which seems to be gaining ground nowadays and is proving to be in contradiction with the needs of society – born of, amongst other things, precisely this technological progress', quoted in Alberto Spektorowski, 'The New Right: ethno-regionalism, ethnopluralism and the emergence of a neo-fascist "Third Way"', *Journal of Political Ideologies* 8, 1, p. 120. This position is echoed in the techno-elitism of popular online figures such as Curtis Yarvin (aka Mencius Moldbug), a computer scientist and 'neo-reactionary' political theorist; see Rosie Gray, 'Behind the internet's anti-democracy movement', *The Atlantic* (10 February (2017).

dismissing/rejecting Leftists who attempt to do so in the name of some abstract 'humanity').[21]

These themes are frequently connected to yet another idea that the NR seeks to redeem historically – that of empire. In this view, smaller 'ethno'-political units could form a wider regional order that is not simply an extension or enlargement of the modern state or an interest-maximizing structure, which the NR equates with the quintessentially managerial-liberal EU. Instead, they suggest it would be possible to construct neo-regional orders among 'grounded' ethno-polities sharing broadly similar cultural foundations. Empire in this narrative is not oppression and domination: it is a form of autonomy and subsidiarity – a possibility for intra-order pluralism impossible within the universalizing logic of the modern state but capable of sustaining itself on different principles. De Benoist's version of these arguments draws specifically on Julius Evola's influential 1934 work *Revolt Against the Modern World*: 'What distinguishes the empire from the nation? First of all, the fact that the empire is not primarily a territory but essentially an idea or a principle. The political order is determined by it – not by material factors or by possession of a geographical area. It is determined by a spiritual or juridical idea.'[22]

Despite some affinities, this is not necessarily 'the West' portrayed by Samuel Huntington or, for that matter, senior officials in NATO. As we have seen, for many NR thinkers 'the West' as a civilizational entity now scarcely exists. Moreover, some European NR thinkers even insist that contemporary America should not be seen as part of the natural order of 'Eurasia', and that Russia quite possibly should be. This is a key element in the 'Eurasianist' view of the future advocated by Russian conservatives like Alexander Dugin, and provides another bridge between NR thinkers IR scholarship via geopolitics.[23] De Benoist, for instance, argues that: 'It seems to me that we have to take very seriously the notion of "Eurasia" which, far from being only Dugin's property, links up directly to the theories of the main geopoliticians since the time of Rudolph Kjellen, Alfred Mahan, Nicholas Spykman, and Halford Mackinder.' Commenting on Dugin, he continues:

---

[21] Thus 'the concept of differentialist ethno-pluralism … sets the basis for a right-wing theory of multiculturalism pitted against liberal multiculturalism.' Spektorowski, 'The New Right', p. 113.

[22] Alain de Benoist, 'The idea of empire', *Telos* 98–9 (1993/1994), p. 84.

[23] Dugin's ideas derive in part from the influence of the Soviet historian Lev Gumilev, though Gumilev would have been unlikely to share his protégé's enthusiasm for Europe; for Gumilev's connections to and divergence from today's NR, see Bassin, 'Lev Gumilev and the European New Right', and for claims about his influence on Putin see Charles Clover, *Black Wind, White Snow: The Rise of Russia's New Nationalism* (New Haven, CT: Yale University Press, 2016).

What is interesting is that he adds to this general perception the idea of the Empire as opposed to the Western idea of the nation-states. This has prompted him to stress that Empire is always a multicultural space, and thus he takes a firm stand against all forms of racism and xenophobia.[24]

For Dugin, this conservative Traditionalism (as opposed to traditional conservatism)[25] can provide a binding force, a shared commitment linking Europe, Russia, and stretching variably even to the Middle East, particularly Iran. Indeed, in Dugin's view, the diversity of the New Right is the source of its potential strength, providing the basis for multiple conservative forces to make common cause against their defining liberal adversary. As he puts it in a statement worth extended attention:

> Another question is the structure of a possible anti-globalist and anti-imperialist front and its participants. I think we should include in it all forces that struggle against the West, the United States, against liberal democracy, and against modernity and post-modernity. The common enemy is the necessary instance for all kinds of political alliances. This means Muslims and Christians, Russians and Chinese, both Leftists and Rightists, the Hindus and Jews who challenge the present state of affairs, globalization and American imperialism. They are thus all virtually friends and allies ... That is the basis for a new alliance. All who share a negative analysis of globalization, Westernization and postmodernization should coordinate their effort in the creation of a new strategy of resistance to the omnipresent evil. And we can find common allies even within the United States as well, among those who choose the path of Tradition over the present decadence.[26]

Across national and intellectual boundaries, NR thinkers concur on the need to challenge rationalism and modernity. But this vision of plurality is far from liberal. It is a plurality of Identitarian political groupings, a vision that prizes ethno-pluralism between such groupings, but that is strongly (sometimes virulently) anti-pluralist within them. Their appeal to pluralism

---

[24] Quoted in Arthur Versluis, 'A conversation with Alain de Benoist', *Journal for the Study of Radicalism* 8, 2 (2014), pp. 84–5.

[25] For an analysis of Traditionalism see Mark Sedgwick, *Against the Modern World: Traditionalism and the Secret Intellectual History of the Twentieth Century* (Oxford: Oxford University Press, 2009).

[26] Quoted in George Hawley, *Right Wing Critics of American Conservatism* (Lawrence: University Press of Kansas, 2016), p. 237.

is far from liberal – in fact, it is the very opposite. Seen from this vantage point, as Rengger was well aware, the adequacy of the liberal move such as Gray's thus becomes an issue of considerable contemporary salience. But before turning to this question, it is useful to turn to another of Rengger's areas of concern that mirrors the agenda of the New Right: the 'dark side' of human rights.

Liberal universalism and human rights

Although the antipathy of the NR towards universal human rights is widely acknowledged, the theoretical foundations of this hostility are less well understood.[27] As we saw earlier, among its most important sources of inspiration is a critique of contemporary power structures that, following Burnham, the NR terms 'liberal managerialism'. In this view, contemporary life is dominated by the 'organizational revolution' that transformed the political life of industrialized societies from the late 19th century, and led to the emergence and continuous expansion of a transnational 'New Class' elite that supplanted the old bourgeois elites that had become incapable of running the mass world they created.

By the mid-20th century, corporations were run by managers, governments by administrators, and both were linked to mass communications and educational institutions that shared their organizational structures and much of their underlying ideology. Whereas classical liberalism emphasized the merits of distributed powers, the virtues of self-government and the importance of protecting civil society from state interference, contemporary liberalism aims primarily at fighting prejudices, providing social services and welfare benefits, and punishing infringements on expressive and lifestyle liberties.[28] Exploiting redistributionist slogans and manipulating the centralizing mechanisms of mass organization,[29] the New Class possesses a vested interest in the 'war on poverty', progressive reforms, and bureaucratic expansion that rewards itself and the client groups associated with it. It expresses and consolidates this power through a professed commitment to the interests of others, to universal justice, equality, and human rights.

In this view, managerialism and its rationalist logic tend towards liberal universalism and cosmopolitanism. For the NR, therefore, the very idea of international human rights developing towards and around purportedly

---

[27] The following paragraphs draw on Drolet and Williams, 'Radical conservatism and global order', which develops a more extended account.

[28] Samuel T. Francis, 'Paleoconservatism and race', *Chronicles* 1 December (2000), p. 10.

[29] Burnham, *The Managerial Revolution*.

universal principles is not only a questionable or misguided philosophic position. It is also a political strategy and a form of power characteristic of liberal managerialism. Under the guise of pluralism and tolerance, universal liberalism effectively forecloses the legitimacy of any appeal to 'native' values or particularist definitions of rights, and opposes the right of national publics to effectively and democratically support particularist values. Under the guise of pluralism and tolerance, it effectively forecloses the legitimacy of 'native' definitions of values or rights and opposes the right of national publics to effectively and democratically support particularist values.

From this perspective, liberal international institutions are the global expression of the managerial state and the interests and values (universalism, egalitarianism) of the New Class, carried out through largely undemocratic institutions such as courts (both domestic and international), regulatory agencies and expert tribunals, and bureaucratic networks. The processes of international 'institutionalization' and 'juridicalization' applauded by liberals worldwide[30] are for the NR illustrations of the power (and, in their view, pathologies) of the liberal state and its elites. Such an order seeks subtly yet incessantly to transform the world in exactly the same way as it succeeded within liberal states – through elite educational and managerial networks, and by severing the normative basis of international legitimacy from the political principle of national democratic consent, as liberal's continual assaults on the dangers of 'populism' attest.[31] Liberal structures of intellectual and institutional power place such decisions in the hands of elites including international courts and tribunals, international organizations, and NGOs who claim the right and increasingly possess the ideological and institutional power to adjudicate such rights and enforce their decisions. However, and crucially, for the NR this power also generates increasingly substantial reactions against it as those who subscribe to 'traditional' values across the globe find themselves pressured and disempowered by liberal values, institutions, and elites. This provides the potential for counter-movements to mobilize the resentment this generates, something the NR sees (and seeks to foment) in reactions against global human rights and institutions such

---

[30] See, quintessentially, Anne-Marie Slaughter, *A New World Order* (Princeton, NJ: Princeton University Press, 2001).

[31] Consider Habermas' characteristic formulation on behalf of global liberal governance for example: '[at the global level] the democratic procedure no longer draws its legitimizing force only, indeed not even predominantly, from political participation and the expression of political will, but rather from the general accessibility of deliberative processes whose structure grounds an expectation of *rationally accepted results*'. Jürgen Habermas, *The Postnational Constellation*. Cambridge: Polity Press, 2000), p. 110; see also Drolet and Williams, 'Radical conservatism and global order'.

as the International Criminal Court.[32] As the influential American 'paleo' conservative, Samuel Francis, evocatively declared:

The first thing we have to learn about fighting and winning a cultural war is that we are not fighting to 'conserve' something; we are fighting to overthrow something. Obviously, we do want to conserve something – our culture, our way of life, the set of institutions and beliefs that distinguish us as Americans. But we must understand clearly and firmly that the dominant authorities in the United States – in the federal government and often in state and local government as well, in the two major political parties, the major foundations, the media, the schools, the universities, big business, and most of the system of organized culture, including the arts and entertainment – not only do nothing to conserve what most of us regard as our traditional way of life but actually seek its destruction or are indifferent to its survival. If our culture is going to be conserved, then, we need to dethrone the dominant authorities that threaten it.[33]

Once again, these criticisms have received relatively little attention in IPT. But Rengger was acutely sensitive to the principles at stake, even if he did not address the developments surveyed earlier. Consider his incisive interrogation of Onora O'Neill's modulated scepticism towards universal human rights – an analysis that touches directly on analogous themes in NR analyses of resentment and global managerialism. Strikingly, Rengger highlights O'Neill's concern that the universalism of human rights will generate resentment against increasingly abstract and distant but empowered agencies – particularly global legal regimes. As he puts it, this reflects a worrying 'and for some, no doubt, depressing … thought' concerning the:

reification of an attitude that marks much contemporary moral theory, and very problematically so I think – to wit, the encouragement of a way of seeing the moral life largely (or perhaps wholly) as a matter of 'praise or blame'. O'Neill calls Nietzsche in aid here, who brilliantly, as she says, captures the sense in which rights holders become grudge holders, and grudge holders victims: 'I am suffering. Someone or other must be to blame for that.' While she does not suggest that what she calls the 'human rights culture' inevitably produces this rancorous

---

[32] For a further analysis, see Drolet and Williams, 'The view from MARS'; and Jean-François Drolet and Michael C. Williams, 'America first: paleoconservatism and the ideological struggle for the American right', *Journal of Political Ideologies* 25, 1 (2020), pp. 28–50.

[33] Samuel T. Francis, 'Winning the culture war', *Chronicles*, December (1993), p. 12.

approach to life, she does think it has, to use the title of her essay, a dark side, one that is not often commented upon.[34]

Yet, as I suggested earlier, while it is certainly true that these concerns are not often commented on in mainstream political (and IR) theory, they have long been central to the radical Right. Indeed, O'Neill's concerns echo criticisms of the managerial state that are staples among radical conservatives. Equally importantly, and with reference to John Vincent's pioneering work on human rights and world politics, Rengger echoes O'Neill's worry that:

> By sustaining the belief that ethical claims in politics (whether international or domestic) are best seen in terms of rights and obligations not only does it continue to spread that 'rancorous' conception of politics (as O'Neill called it) but it also places more and more power in the hands of states, or state-sanctioned and -supported agencies – together with some non-governmental agencies whose authority is, to say the least, questionable and whose commitment to liberty at best instrumental. We may well find, in due course, that 'working human rights into the cracks in international society', rather than becoming, as Vincent hoped, the 'handle for further progress', merely tightened the noose around the neck of civil conceptions of politics.[35]

What Rengger feared at the end of this essay – the 'irony' that the increasing prominence of universal human rights might turn against 'civil conceptions'[36] of politics, is no longer speculative. It is in fact a pressing political reality: these are two of the most powerful themes *strategically mobilized* by radical conservatives – as envisaged by thinkers such as Francis, and executed or advocated by strategists like Steve Bannon.[37]

Part two: an anti-Pelagian response?

As I have tried to show, a number of the themes raised by those who 'deal in darkness' to probe what they see as the limits of contemporary liberal theory and practice resonate closely with those animating important parts of the radical Right. As Rengger was well aware, part of the power of the ideas of the Right lies in its ability to tap into currents and lineages of thought well

---

[34] Rengger, *The Anti-Pelagian Imagination*, p. 57.

[35] Rengger, *The Anti-Pelagian Imagination*, p. 58.

[36] Ibid., p. 58.

[37] An interesting treatment of the practical strategies of Traditionalists, centred on Steve Bannon, see Benjamin Teitelman, *War for Eternity: Inside Steve Bannon's Far Right Circle of Global Power Brokers* (New York: Harper Collins, 2020).

beyond the shallow 'populism' to which it is often reduced today. The radical conservative critique of modernity, liberalism, progressivism, and utopia cannot be easily dismissed. It evokes and reworks a series of long-standing themes in conservative thought, as well as echoing the doubts (though *not* the politics) of a number of sceptical or 'dystopic' liberals as well. Although these ideas are generally overlooked in IPT, they are too important to be ignored today. Taking them and their intellectual lineages seriously is an essential challenge to be met.

A further challenge, however, lies not only in understanding these radical conservative ideas, but also in responding to them theoretically and politically. Here, the lessons of those willing to deal in darkness also provide important insights and inspiration, and Rengger's ideas are particularly powerful and suggestive, though unfortunately more fully developed in critique than in providing a fully articulated alternative. Let me turn briefly to each dimension.

A critique of the limits of liberalism

If the power of many of the positions on the Right develop directly from its radicalization of dilemmas within liberal, rationalist, and progressive ideas that have dominated Western political thought over the past century or more, where are we to turn for responses to reaction? One response, often heard, is akin to those who when confronting someone in a foreign language they do not understand simply resort to saying the same thing over and over again, only louder. This is the tactic of many progressive social movements and political parties. It can have some success, if shouting down one's interlocutor is the definition of success. But as the substantial rise in popularity of the radical Right might indicate, it is unlikely to achieve much when confronted with opponents who systematically reject its premises and principles, and who have powerful discursive strategies (and shouting voices) of their own. One can even argue that it actually contributes to further energizing and empowering the radical Right rather than reducing its appeal.[38]

A different tack is to take seriously the criticisms of liberal progressivism developed by conservative thinkers, recognizing many of their misgivings without taking them to such radical conclusions and adjusting, revising, and amending liberal ideas so as to enter the battle of ideas with more solid armour and improved weapons. Doing this takes IPT far beyond conventional conceptual divides between 'sunny' liberalism and 'dark' realism, seeing instead the complex interactions between the two. Indeed, some of the most powerful of such responses can be found in positions that meld

---

[38] Again, see Goodhart, *The Road to Somewhere.*

realist and liberal themes, including those expressed in what Rengger calls 'dystopic liberalism', a position he admires, in many ways supports, and yet subjects to searching criticisms that are also crucially important to attempts to challenge the Right today.

Illustrations of this are found in Rengger's searching assessments of Judith Shklar's 'liberalism of fear' and Bernard Williams' political realism, as well as their important links to IR thinkers such as Raymond Aron and Stanley Hoffmann.[39] Rengger holds that, like Gray, these dystopic liberals show a clear sensitivity to many realist themes and to the anti-Pelagian politics that he sought to trace and, to some extent, to endorse. Both Shklar and Williams try to disconnect liberalism from rationalist and abstract formalism, lately very much tied to Rawlsian frameworks. For Shklar, liberals need to give up transcendental foundations and focus instead on restraining the worst that humans are capable of (cruelty, for instance) as well as the 'ordinary vices' we all commit in one way or another. For Williams, contemporary liberal thought has become increasingly divorced from the messy, power-infused, and imperfect reality of politics. As ideal theory it may be philosophically powerful, but it is politically obtuse. For both thinkers, saving the best of a tolerant, reasoned liberal politics demand giving up on what liberalism has become, not only because it is philosophically questionable, but because its political practices damage rather than further the values it claims to uphold. For both, bringing liberalism into conversation with realist themes is essential to propagating, and even saving, liberalism itself. A non-ideal 'liberalism of fear', to use Shklar's famous formulation, provides a sounder and more engaged position than scholarly abstractions about the 'veil of ignorance' or 'ideal speech situations' will ever muster. Sharing a basic scepticism, and stressing the limits of reason, the power of emotion, the attractions of irrationalism, and a host of other themes, these dystopic liberals appealed to a certain kind of political realism, attempting as Rengger put it 'to tie a certain sort of realism and a certain sort of liberalism together'.[40]

The key question that follows from this attempt (as in Gray's) is 'whether it is possible to tame realism without betraying liberalism'.[41] Are these liberal realists sceptics first and liberals second – or the other way around? Can their scepticism support their liberalism, or must their liberalism overwhelm their scepticism? Shklar, Rengger notes, presents the two as parallel. But they logically do not have to be: a sceptic need not be a liberal – as Rengger points out, Gray has become so sceptical and dystopic that he often seems barely liberal at all.[42] More pressingly, to return to my concerns here, in the

---

[39] Rengger, *The Anti-Pelagian Imagination*, p. 70.
[40] Ibid., p. 73.
[41] Ibid., p. 74.
[42] Ibid., p. 75.

hands of radical conservative thinkers like de Benoist or Dugin, scepticism towards Enlightenment universalism is transformed into 'ethnopluralism' where 'difference' is construed in relational but radically exclusionary and illiberal terms. Toleration (they rather optimistically claim) is only between polities; within them, it is strictly confined by 'traditional' values. If this is the case, Rengger's concern about the weaknesses of liberal scepticism is no abstract question: it is a core practical issue in an age where 'illiberal democracy' is presented as a viable alternative.

These considerations lead us to reconsider the question of conservatism and political realism. If liberal realism is worryingly weak at key points, might conservatism provide a better way forward? In an astute analysis, occasioned in no small part by the invasion of Iraq and the ascent of 'democratic globalism' in Western foreign policies, Rengger and Ian Hall argued that the insights of traditional conservatism have been obscured by the ascendance in conservative politics of individualistic neoliberalism masquerading as conservatism, or by the neo-conservativism of figures like Irving Kristol, who fuse a belief in free markets with a deep commitment to universal ideology and military intervention.[43] Traditional conservatism has few contemporary theorists and even fewer political proponents in a political landscape that, for all the heated conflicts between liberalism and conservatism, liberalism reigns supreme.

A central question thus becomes, is it possible to save conservative insights, and maybe even conservative politics, from its capture by these forces, or from those on the radical Right? Rengger explored many aspects of this question through the prism of Michael Oakeshott's engagement with Hans Morgenthau. At the centre of this engagement is Morgenthau's claim, developed most fully in *Scientific Man versus Power Politics*, that political life is inescapably tragic, involving moral compromises and the inevitable exercise of power and domination, even with the best of intentions. For Oakeshott, the anti–utopian and anti–perfectionist insights embraced in Morgenthau's realism, and the tragic vision of politics in general, is valuable – and a salutary counter to contemporary liberal rationalism and optimism. However, he warns that it risks reproducing and reinforcing the very dilemmas it seeks to overcome, precisely because it actually accepts their categories of thought, terms of debate, and possible alternatives. As Rengger nicely captured the argument, Oakeshott felt that Morgenthau's tragic vision of politics involved an aestheticizaton or 'romanticization'[44] of politics that remained trapped in a struggle with a utopian alternative, and thus risked unnecessarily radicalizing the choices and the alternatives of political life:

[43] Hall and Rengger, '"The Right that failed"'.
[44] Rengger, *The Anti-Pelagian Imagination*, p. 165.

Morgenthau's 'tragic' view runs the risk of becoming a mirror image of the views about progress that it opposes, for the rosy future of the scientistic progressives is mirrored in Morgenthau by the nostalgia for a better-ordered past. While Morgenthau is right to challenge the assumptions they make, the assumptions that he makes are equally open to challenge, at least from someone who thinks, as Oakeshott did, that the danger of Morgenthau's tragic vision (and, we might add, those more recent attempts to revive it) is that it still makes 'the world' the standard. 'Realism' in international relations is still for those who share the anti-Pelagian imagination, a child of the world; to be sure, a chastened child, one aware of the problems and pitfalls that lie in store for the world's children, but a child of the world for all that.[45]

What Oakeshott accuses realists like Morgenthau of might well apply equally to the radical Right. Far from being a radical alternative to liberal rationalism or the desire for universal certainty, the radical Right simply mirrors it at a different level, finding an alternative to Enlightenment universalism in metaphysics of ethnicity, race, history, or Tradition that betray the same longing. An important lesson here is that attempts to salvage liberal politics from the proponents of darkness must avoid adopting a critique of liberalism and modernity that ends up sharing the categories, if not the conclusions, of the radical Right. To fail to do so is already to concede much of the ground of political debate. This is a temptation that many left-wing critics of liberalism have been all too eager to give in to, as their fascination with Carl Schmitt in recent decade attests. While the critiques drawing on this lineage are often bracing, avoiding their illiberal consequence often demands that 'left Schmittians' continue to rely on the continuation of the very liberal political order they decry to insulate them from their less savoury possibilities of their positions. The rise of the radical Right as a salient political force renders this comfortable stance questionable in ways that can no longer be ignored. To return to Rengger's core insight, playing the 'realist' card is replete with danger as well as insight.

So far, so good, we might say. An anti-Pelagian sensibility helps us diagnose important aspects of contemporary political life, and may even help avoid some of the most grievous errors that modern political understandings are susceptible to. This is no small achievement, and it is no small part of Rengger's legacy in IPT. But if this is not simply to be a negative position – a useful strategy of deconstruction but one that, like the dystopic liberalism it criticizes, cannot generate a positive position – then where are we to turn?

---

45 Ibid., p. 166.

Here, Rengger's views are suggestive, but at best partial and promissory. Oakeshott's thinking, he argues:

> does enable us to see more clearly the character of that world and thus resist false attempts to portray the world in a different light. What it cannot do, however – and what I am suggesting he is right to suggest it cannot do – is to become 'practice'; to become, of itself, an engagement in the world or give rise to such an engagement ... Thus, what I am here calling the anti-Pelagian sensibility runs counter to one of the most general assumptions made about scholarship in international relations (and indeed elsewhere in the social and political sciences) – that it can have a direct and positive impact on the world of practice, that it can help build a better world.[46]

Yet if this is the case, where is one to turn in such a quest? Is the goal, however chastened, of a better (or even somewhat less miserable) world simply to be abandoned? Rengger suggests that intimations of an answer can be found in Oakeshott's appeal to different modes of experience, and to conservatism as a valuable mode of 'civil association' and civility between inescapably (and valuably) plural groups and forms of life. The attractions of this position are easy to see, and they involve mining a vein of conservative thought so long marginalized as to be almost lost to sight in political theory, and especially in International Relations (IR). Recovering it, he suggests, is essential if one is to circumvent the dangers and limitations of liberalism and contemporary mainstream (and, I would add, radical) conservatism.

However, here realism again raises its head. For as the evolution of conservative thought and practice over past decades has shown, it is far from clear (to put it charitably) that the rather genteel, even aesthetic, sensibility that Oakeshott proposes is capable of commanding the kind of support, much less raising the passions, of potential adherents today. In fact, as I suggested previously, rejecting this view of civility and conversation and replacing it with rhetorics of division, outrage, and enmity is an important discursive and aesthetic strategy of the NR, a strategy enabled and amplified by digital communications and social media.[47] As a consequence, it is difficult to escape the same conclusion that Hall and Rengger once reached concerning older forms of conservatism – that this is a 'right that failed' as conservative

---

46 Ibid., p. 167. See also the insightful treatment in Vassilios Paipais, 'Between faith and scepticism: Nicholas Rengger's reflections on the "hybridity" of modernity', *International Relations* 34, 4 (2020), pp. 627–33.
47 See, for instance, Alan Finlayson, 'YouTube and political ideologies: technology, populism and rhetorical form', *Political Studies* (July 2020), pp. 1–17.

thinking and politics have gone in almost exactly the opposite direction. It is thus a serious question to ask whether these commitments could in any realistic sense be recovered, what politically powerful intellectual resources it could draw on, and what social forces it might be attached to. Without considering such issues, an Oakeshottian politics becomes elegiac at best, irrelevant at worst. Conversation risks looking like a weak and thin form of political aesthetics at a time when politics are being radically aestheticized through digital and visual technologies that are arguably hostile to the very principle of conversation itself. And it provides a weak rejoinder to the more radical formulations of conservative ideas that increasingly mark politics today. Older ideas of 'civility' may yet have important roles to play in response to this situation, but to have such a role they must confront realistically their substantial marginalization in political life – and from political power – in recent decades.

PART III

The Uncivil Condition in World Politics

8

Rengger the Reluctant Rule Follower

Anthony F. Lang, Jr

Introduction

What rules govern the conduct of warfare? Do state and non-state actors conduct themselves in accordance with rules? These are long-standing questions in the study and practice of war. There are, however, some underlying questions that may also be worthy of investigation. How stable are those rules? What foundations do they have? Even more provocatively, are rules the best way to govern the conduct of warfare? Many areas of public life are conducted in terms of rules, yet rules and rule following can become fetishized. Judith Skhlar's famous critique of law and international criminal law introduced the idea of 'legalism', or the use of rules and laws to cover over ideological or political conflicts.[1] Rules guide us through complex situations; at the same time, rules can constrain and limit our ability to respond when those situations change or when a rule simply does not work.[2] In fact, rules can even generate their own forms of violence, especially when yoked to ideas like the national interest.[3]

Nicholas Rengger did not address rules directly in his scholarship. Instead, the idea of rules and law formed a backdrop to many of his critical

---

[1] Judith Shklar, *Legalism: Law, Morals and Political Trials* (Cambridge, MA: Harvard University Press, 1964).

[2] Anthony F. Lang, Jr, Nicholas Rengger, and William Walker, ' "The role(s) of rules: some conceptual clarifications', *International Relations* 20, 3 (2006), pp. 274–94.

[3] Anthony F. Lang, Jr, 'The violence of rules: rethinking the 2003 war against Iraq', *Contemporary Politics* 13, 3 (2007a), pp. 257–76.

interventions in world politics. From his studies of order to just war, Rengger engaged with and contested the idea that law and rules alone could structure our political lives.[4] At the same time, as I will argue in this chapter, Rengger did not set aside rules in their entirety, for he understood the necessity of rules in both domestic and international political order more broadly. Instead, Rengger argued for a more casuistic approach to political life. Drawn from ancient and medieval moral and political theory, this idea highlights the importance of the contexts within which rules operate. Rules and laws still play a role, but they cannot be seen as the only way to approach political conflict. As such, the focus of this chapter will be on Rengger as a reluctant rule follower.

The chapter will use Rengger's writing on just war and violence to orient the argument. The first section sets out his understanding of rules and their relation to political order. Following this, and building upon it, the next section explores his reading of the Just War tradition as found in his book *Just War and International Order*. In that work, Rengger develops a critical perspective on the Just War tradition which draws out its reliance on the contemporary state system and the problems which result from that linkage. As part of that critique, he brings forward a theme that has been central to much of his earlier writing – a focus on the contexts, traditions, and frameworks within which politics takes place. The following section of the chapter looks to how he develops this idea of a context and his worries that contemporary politics locates such contexts primarily in the nation or state. As an alternative, he proposes a turn to prudence and judgement when deciding to use force. But even here, he worries that a turn to judgement will avoid the complexities of the contexts within which judgements take place. In the last section, I suggest some ways Rengger's ideas about rules and judgement might speak to debates about cyber warfare, a contemporary form of war that does not sit easily within the sovereign state system precisely because it undermines the spatial contexts of the community. Rengger's insights reveal how we might think about judgement and rules in this new form of war.

The problem of rules

In 2006, Rengger, William Walker, and I published a paper entitled 'The role(s) of rules: some conceptual clarifications'. The article introduced a

---

[4]   Nicholas J. Rengger, *International Relations, Political Theory and the Problem of Order: Beyond International Relations Theory?* (London; New York: Routledge, 2000a); Nicholas J. Rengger, *Just War and International Order: The Uncivil Condition in World Politics* (Cambridge: Cambridge University Press, 2013a).

special issue published in the journal *International Relations* that looked at rules and rule-making from a broad range of perspectives. One of the key points of the article is the following:

> We conclude by locating ourselves between a realpolitik dismissal of rules and an overly legalistic insistence that rules are the answer to all social and political conflict. We end by suggesting that rules are an essential element of any political order but that the ways in which they are understood and deployed must display great finesse and take into account the specificity of context.[5]

As one way to make our point, we introduced the distinction between formal and informal rules, seeking to develop the importance of both and highlighting the benefits and limits of rules. We noted that there is a movement back and forth between formal and informal rules in the governance and practices of the international system, a movement that participants in those activities do not always recognize or acknowledge. This inability to keep these two kinds of rules distinct has led, we argued, to assumptions about what rules can and cannot do. Rather than assume that they will always function effectively, it is important to recognize when the different kinds of rules are being employed.

A second point we make about rules in that article is to emphasize the importance of the contexts within which rules function. We argued that

> Rules in human life take many forms, forms that are often dictated by the contexts in which they emerge. A problem at the global level is the numerous contexts in which rules can and do emerge … rules only make sense, only become meaningful, in certain contexts … Moreover, contexts generate certain informal rules that underlie the creation of formal rules, but the link between them is often confused or ignored.[6]

In the article, we go on to link this idea of contexts to the philosopher Ludwig Wittgenstein's idea about language games, though we suggest that Wittgenstein's ideas here perhaps do not capture the nuance of how rules are linked to politics. Turning to debates around the 2003 Iraq war, and drawing on the work of H.L.A. Hart, we suggest that international rules (that is, international law) should be seen within the political contexts that generate them. To locate rules in relationship to such political contexts is not to diminish the rules as standards, but only to recognize their origins.

---

[5] Lang et al., 'The role(s) of rules', pp. 275–76.
[6] Ibid., p. 280.

And, importantly, the idea that rules can change and adapt requires attention to their original political context. After reviewing other aspects of rules concerning legitimacy, enforcement, and technology, we focus again on the idea of contexts:

> [The] contexts are constantly changing at the international level in ways that cannot be predicted accurately if at all in advance. This means that rule-making must be flexible enough to accommodate unexpected situations and power configurations. In some cases, rules made in one context do persist into a new context. But in other cases, old rules not only fail to reflect changes but actually prevent needed change and development.[7]

While this was a jointly written article, the emphasis on contexts came largely from Rengger. His focus on this idea helped to shape the overall argument of the paper, and the project of which it was a part.[8] In other words, understanding rules requires an understanding of contexts, especially the political contexts in which the rules arise and where they play themselves out. Rather than see this as a reflection of power politics overriding rules, it is important to see rules as part of an ongoing and adaptive political dynamic.

Just war according to Rengger

Which contexts matter? And how do they matter? Rengger provides one way to see these contexts and their import in his 2013 book on just war. The book is, in fact, a critique of contemporary just war thinking rather than a defence of it. Rengger begins the book by noting that contemporary just war theorizing is enabling war rather than limiting it. This is not because those writing about just war are realist warriors but rather because the underlying justifications for the limits placed on war (both *ad bellum* and *in bello*) rely on the contemporary state system as their background condition. Drawing on the work of Michael Oakeshott, Rengger argues that just war thinking since World War II has become 'teleocratic'. This concept draws from Oakeshott's idea that politics more generally has become an activity directed to a specific endpoint rather than the more conservative idea of politics as a continued attention to the arrangements of communal life.

Oakeshott introduces this idea in his book *On Human Conduct* where he uses several overlapping terms to describe two different types of politics.[9]

---

7   Ibid., p. 290.
8   For a further iteration of that project, see Anthony F. Lang, Jr and Amanda Beattie, *Torture and Terrorism: Rethinking the Rules of International Security* (London: Routledge 2008).
9   Michael Oakeshott, *On Human Conduct* (Oxford: Clarendon Press, 1975).

He summarized the argument of the book in a talk he gave in the year of its publication, in which he explains that there are two kinds of human associations: an enterprise association and a civil association. The former is an association of persons directed towards some specific goal or endpoint, while a civil association is one that has rules enabling individuals to interact and live together without proscribing what the goal of their communal life should be. Oakeshott argues that one of the problems with contemporary politics is that it assumes the state should be a kind of purposive association, one that seeks to advance liberalism, democracy, or even something so vague as the national interest. He links this to war: 'And this vision intrudes, of course, when a state is at war, and all the more decisively when the war is thought of as a crusade.'[10]

Oakeshott introduces the term teleocratic as a shorthand for describing this enterprise association, one which is drawn from the Aristotelian idea of a *telos*, or end state. Following Oakeshott, Rengger sees the danger of this purpose-oriented statism coming out most clearly in war, which contemporary just war theory further reinforces when it advances the use of force for humanitarian or even self-defence reasons. That is, warfare in the service of the contemporary nation-state allows political leaders to use the underlying moral claims of the Just War tradition to reinforce their uses of force, making war more acceptable. Rengger notes that:

Taken together, I want to suggest (and I think Oakeshott wanted to suggest) that all of these things have created in modern states an orientation that is heavily disposed to see itself in terms of an enterprise association, and a central component of this understanding is the ordering of a society for 'war'. Of course, the common enterprise for which force may be used will shift over time; it may be obviously material in one generation – access to the goods and services of the empire, the 'expansion of England'; and so forth – and more ideational in another – 'intervention for humanitarian purposes' perhaps, as we shall see. Nonetheless, central to the understanding of a modern state as an enterprise association is a willingness to see a 'common purpose' for which, under at least some circumstances, force is an entirely appropriate response; as Oakeshott says, the habits learned through endless preparation for war are retained in times of relative peace.[11]

---

[10] Michael Oakeshott, 'Talking politics', in *Rationalism and Politics and other Essays, New and Expanded Edition* (Indianapolis: Liberty Fund, 1991 [1975]), p. 453.
[11] Rengger, *Just War and International Order*, p. 33.

As he states further on: 'Where injustice is everywhere, the reasons to use force to oppose it are not hard to find.'[12] Finding injustice everywhere, the modern liberal state has become an agent of justice, one that seeks to right all wrongs through the continued use of force. Perhaps the clearest example of this is the 'war on terror', a never-ending war on terrorism because it is a wrong that will continue to define the modern political condition for some time to come. Especially when terrorism is defined as the use of force by non-state actors, the importance and virtuousness of the state and its leaders is further reinforced. While Rengger does not explore this example at any length, his worries about the justice-seeking teleocratic state system find their clearest evidence in this dynamic, one that once led to a ground war in Afghanistan and Iraq and now manifests itself as an ongoing drone war.[13]

How does this relate to rules and rule following? In Chapter 3 of *Just War and International Order*, Rengger provides a thorough genealogical study of how the just war tradition arose out of the dual emergence of the modern state and international law. He highlights developments such as the split between *ad bellum* and *in bello* elements of the tradition, resulting in three different kinds of just war theorizing – the juridical, the Christian, and the cosmopolitan. All of these rely in important ways on the teleocratic nature of the state which has become linked to a liberal positivist international legal order. In so doing, they reinforce the tendencies that Rengger notes at the outset – that is, the enabling function of the just war as a tool for ridding the world of injustice while reinforcing the centrality of the nation state. As he concludes the chapter: 'Rather than allowing the *jus in bello* to balance competing demands and competing claims, it tended to force the *in bello* constraints into one particular shape: that of modern, positive international law and of the state forms that have given birth to that idea.'[14]

Rengger makes concrete the problem of the teleocratic state and its reliance on legal rules in a critique of Michael Walzer's defence of the supreme emergency. In *Just and Unjust Wars*, Walzer argues that the rules of war may be set aside in moments of emergency, but that the limits on such exceptions must be very carefully policed. Walzer explores two cases, both from World War II: the British bombing of German cities and the dropping of the atomic bombs on Japan.[15] In both cases, Walzer argues that

---

[12] Ibid., p. 66.

[13] Rengger did explore, briefly, the nature of drone war in a co-authored essay: Caroline Kennedy-Pipe and Nicholas J. Rengger, 'The new assassination bureau: on the "robotic" turn in contemporary war', Carnegie Ethics Online Monthly Column, (November 2012), available at: www.carnegiecouncil.org/publications/ethics_online/0075

[14] Rengger, *Just War and International Order*, p. 101.

[15] Michael Walzer, *Just and Unjust Wars: A Moral Argument with Historical Illustrations*, 5th edition. (New York: Basic Books, 2015).

we cannot rely on utilitarian calculations alone, but we must confront our competing moral commitments. He concludes that the British bombings were justified but the dropping of the atomic bombs was not. This is an interesting, and perhaps counterintuitive conclusion, one that opens many interesting questions on the limits imposed by just war and how to keep to those limits in situations of conflict.

Rengger highlights the fact that throughout Walzer's book, and especially in this section, he is defending the state and the state-based system. As should be obvious by now, Rengger finds this kind of defence problematic. It puts the existence of this particular political construct before the ultimate purpose of the just war tradition, which was to restrain rather than enable the use of force. As Rengger argues, Walzer fails to recognize that the just war tradition is:

> in a very important sense constituted by and through its rules, and they cannot be 'trumped' or overridden by any particular social or contextual circumstance. That, indeed, is what it means, I think, to see the just war tradition as Walzer at least claims to do as a casuistic tradition. Any given action, the bombing of German cities, for example would have to be examined in the context of the 'rules' which are not merely laws, and nor are they fixed, but they certainly have a centre of gravity around a common set of precepts. Political communities may have a putative right of defence under these precepts, for example, but such a right is always conditional on other precepts being met and is never absolute.[16]

This captures Rengger's overall concern with the tradition, but also hints at the importance of rules. While Walzer presents his argument as one that relies on a shared morality and a certain form of legalism (not the one that Shklar critiques, but one that overlaps with our shared morality), Rengger is highlighting how that common morality depends on the nation-state system. And its dependence on that system further enables the use of force that is so problematic in the contemporary order. But we should notice that Rengger states that the tradition is 'constituted by and through its rules', something that suggests rules remain important.

Judgements, contexts and rules

The international legal order and the just war tradition, while seemingly different at times, both rely on the nation-state. And the most powerful

---

[16] Rengger, *Just War and International Order*, p. 154.

nation-states have for some time promoted a positivist, legalist, and liberal idea of the nation-state. Combined, this legal positivism and statism have generated a global political context within which rules and rule following are the sole way to justify and understand the use of force. Rengger's insights here help us to see this more clearly.

Is there any alternative to this nation-state context? One alternative can be found in Rengger's reflections on political theology.[17] In a review essay from 2013, he looks to Charles Taylor's *A Secular Age* for insights into global political life, drawing on Taylor's reading of the parable of the Good Samaritan.[18] Taylor, who is himself drawing on the philosopher Ivan Illich, argues that one reading of the Good Samaritan parable can lead to a kind of cosmopolitan embrace of all persons no matter their identity of political community. But rather than creating a rule which establishes that we ought to help all persons at all times, Taylor (and Illich and Rengger) suggest that we should instead see this story as one about an individual responding in a particular moment to an embodied person in pain. The decision to help the Samaritan is not one about moral rules. Instead, it is a judgement, one that enables us to look beyond rule fetishism towards a different way of imagining how we might be in the world. And, while the story of the Good Samaritan does highlight the two communities (Jews and Samaritans) it does not tell us that such differences will disappear and that rules within or between those communities will no longer matter. Rather, it tells us that Jesus' message was that rules can constrain us in moments when we encounter others whom rules may define in one way but who are embodied persons we need to accept and embrace. Communities and rules will continue to exist; the point is that we must sometimes make judgements about how to respond when those communities and rules blind us to the reality of suffering and pain.

This idea of judgement that is not directly tied to rules is something that Rengger develops throughout his work. As Rengger notes, the tradition drew heavily in the medieval period on the idea of casuistry, or the ability to make judgements about political life which relied heavily on the contexts within which such judgements were made. Rather than apply rules blindly or assume that decisions can be made without reference to the particularities of a situation, a casuistic moral framework demands attention to the complexities of the world in which we live. Drawing on the work of Stephen Toulmin, Rengger suggests that this casuistic tradition might provide something worth pursuing. Indeed, in his 1995 book on

---

[17] Thanks to Vassilios Paipais for pointing me to this article.

[18] Nicholas J. Rengger, 'On theology and international relations: world politics beyond an empty sky', *International Relations* 27, 2 (2013b), pp. 141–57; Charles Taylor, *A Secular Age* (Cambridge, MA: Harvard University Press, 2007).

modernity, he concludes that such a theory of judgement is sorely needed as a way to balance counter claims in moral and political life, suggesting that uncovering and reinvigorating such an approach to judgement must be one of the tasks of political theory.[19]

What is judgement? How does it differ from rule following? The easiest way to see the difference is to contrast two moral theories, virtue ethics and deontology. As any introductory textbook in ethics will explain, there are three primary types of ethical theory in the contemporary world: consequentialism, deontology, and virtue ethics. The first evaluates actions and behaviours on the basis of consequences; the second evaluates actions and behaviours on the basis of rules; and the third does not evaluate actions and behaviours but rather focuses on the character of the one undertaking those actions. The virtues that define a virtue ethics approach can include courage, temperance, empathy, charity, and civility. Some of these are specific to military affairs (courage) while others are more general (charity). Two virtues play a more central role than others – justice and prudence. Justice, one of the four classical virtues, has two meanings in the tradition. First, it is the virtue of finding balance or fairness in one's actions. It requires an individual to know how to distribute goods when interacting with others. Second, it links up the internally driven character traits with a political community. Without justice, virtue ethics can become a self-obsessed moral theory, one that is only about pursuing personal happiness rather than being happy within a community.

The second master virtue and, indeed, the most important, is prudence. Prudence is one translation of the word *phronesis*, the Greek term that can also be translated as (practical) wisdom. It is the ability to make right judgements in relation to the multiple competing demands on the human person. In Aristotle's philosophy, it is also a way to combine the intellectual and practical virtues, or how to combine knowledge of the world with right action. Prudence is not easy to define, for it requires attention to the contexts and situations within which individuals must make choices about how to act. But without it, all the other virtues lose their force. And, importantly, prudence provides us with an understanding of political life that does not rely on rules alone; as Harry Gould notes, we can 'resist the urge to make prudence a matter of following rigidly delineated, general procedures and instead be more willing to focus attention on the particular. It is a call to bear in mind the inability of general rules to determine outcomes'.[20]

---

[19] Nicholas J. Rengger, *Political Theory, Modernity and Postmodernity* (Oxford: Basil Blackwell, 1995), p. 224.

[20] Harry Gould, 'Prudence, relevance and the scholastic disposition', *International Studies Review* 19, 4 (2017), p. 710.

One other way to understand the idea of prudence is to link it to judgement. To make judgements using prudence is to connect the particular with the universal. As Rengger points out, this was the form of reasoning that informed political philosophy throughout the classical and medieval periods. It came to be discredited during the early modern period when universalizable rules came to be seen as the way to conduct inquiry across all fields, from the sciences to the humanities, as described by Stephen Toulmin. Chris Brown has also drawn upon Toulmin's understanding of casuistry to propose an alternative to the rule-based approach to the use of force. In essays on humanitarian intervention and pre-emptive uses of force, Brown has suggested a turn back to what he calls a neo-Aristotelian understanding of judgement. He suggests a form of virtue ethics training when he writes that: 'We need our leaders to cultivate the habits of political judgment and we should not seek refuge in the illusion that there can be moral rules that can substitute for such judgment.'[21] Brown combines this claim with a focus on realism, arguing that classical realists such as Hans Morgenthau also found in a form of casuistry a means by which to make judgements in international affairs.[22]

But making judgements requires not just attention to the particulars of the situation facing an individual agent, but a shared understanding of what kinds of virtues might enable those judgements. Aristotle argued for a set of virtues that defined what it meant to be an Athenian citizen in the 4th century BCE. Those virtues may not be the exact ones of relevance to contemporary contexts. Indeed, though he found in the virtue tradition and the casuistic method of judgement great benefit, Rengger also recognized this problem of what contexts are most relevant when making such judgements. In a festschrift dedicated to Chris Brown, Rengger highlights this problem. While he is appreciative of Brown's idea of judgement, Rengger argues that it lacks what the medieval theorists of casuistry and judgement had; a shared cultural, political, and ethical framework within which making judgements made sense. The ability to make judgements in the contemporary global order would require a much greater consensus about what counts as legitimate evaluative standards than we currently have; in fact, to suggest that such standards can be found and cultivated in the world today is, perhaps, 'wishful

---

[21] Chris Brown, *Practical Judgement in International Political Theory: Selected Essays* (London: Routledge, 2010), p. 245.

[22] Morgenthau drew from Aristotle a number of insights, including his view that the prudence of diplomats is the one hope for using power to bring about peace; see Anthony F. Lang, Jr, 'Morgenthau, agency and Aristotle', in Michael C. Williams (ed), *Reconsidering Realism: The Legacy of Hans J. Morgenthau in International Relations* (Oxford: Oxford University Press, 2007b), pp. 18–41.

thinking'.[23] Rengger's critique of Brown parallels his critique of Walzer; that is, both of them propose forms of judgement that do not reflect carefully enough on the state-based system in which they are making those judgements. They do not recognize the way that the context of their reflections is shaping the judgements they are able to make.

Where does this leave us? Rengger has highlighted the importance of a more virtue-oriented, prudential form of reasoning about when we should use force. Rather than abiding by rules, we need to act after seeking to combine the existing rule-based frameworks with the particulars of the situation. He is worried that the rules defining the contemporary order are too much shaped by the particular context of the state-based system combined with a positive legal order. And, he is concerned that those who propose using prudence may not recognize that this context shapes them in ways that enable more violence.

But Rengger is also perhaps setting a standard for judgement that cannot really be achieved. Here, I would push back against his account and note that the very nature of judgement does not allow for too much specificity, a point that Brown also makes in response to Rengger's critique.[24] Moreover, Rengger has never given much specificity to what kind of contexts or forms of judgement are possible outside of the state system; indeed, his later work seems to move away from the possibility of judgement towards a more pessimistic response to the contemporary global order. He concludes his last book with a turn to a more sceptical, and perhaps pessimistic position, one that leaves a small glimmer of hope but is very resistant to making claims about how any form of ethical or political practice can truly change the world in which we live.[25]

Rengger's critical reflections on rules, however, do not necessarily lead me to the same scepticism. Rather, they lead me to an appreciation for the contexts in which rules get made and enacted. The final section will explore one area of global politics where force is being used in different ways. Its context is parasitic upon, but perhaps not wholly reliant on, the state system. It does not 'solve' the problems highlighted by Rengger in his work; rather, Rengger's work helps us to see that paying attention to the

---

[23] Nicholas J. Rengger, 'Practical judgement: inconsistent – or incoherent?', in Mathias Albert and Anthony F. Lang, Jr (eds), *The Politics of International Political Theory: Reflections on the Work of Chris Brown* (London: Palgrave Macmillan, 2019b), p. 63.

[24] Chris Brown, 'In response', in Mathias Albert and Anthony F. Lang, Jr (eds). *The Politics of International Political Theory: Reflections on the Work of Chris Brown* (London: Palgrave Macmillan, 2019), p. 247.

[25] Nicholas J. Rengger, *The Anti-Pelegian Imagination in Political Theory and International Relations: Dealing in Darkness* (London: Routledge, 2017), p. 168.

'context' of this new realm is just as important as it is in understanding more traditional uses of force.

The context(s) of the cyber realm

In November 2020, the British Prime Minister announced an increase in defence spending for the next few years. An important part of this increase will be devoted to developing a new National Cyber Force, whose role will be to consider and perhaps undertake offensive cyber operations in response to cyber attacks and informational warfare already being waged by different powers in the international system.[26] The decision to create this unit and to support cyber war capabilities more generally arises from threats faced by countries like Russia, China, and Iran, all of whom have used (or are accused of using) various forms of cyber warfare against European and North American states. Rather than simply identify ways to better protect the British cyber facilities, the decision to create an 'offensive' capability is a step into a new domain for the UK. While all militaries have both offensive and defensive capabilities, this new realm of conflict has very few states acknowledging that this is a form of military action they will deploy.

The literature on the cyber and informational war is extensive and continues to grow.[27] Alongside the general literature on this topic, a number of scholars are exploring cyber and informational warfare from the perspectives of ethics[28] and

---

[26] Dan Sabbagh, 'Hackers HQ and space command: how UK defense budget could be spent', *The Guardian Online* (18 November 2020), available at: www.theguardian.com/uk-news/2020/nov/18/hackers-hq-and-space-command-how-uk-defence-budget-could-be-spent; Dan Sabbagh and Patrick Butler, 'Boris Johnson agrees 16bn rise in defense spending', *The Guardian Online* (18 November 2020), available at: www.theguardian.com/politics/2020/nov/18/boris-johnson-agrees-16bn-rise-in-defence-spending

[27] Brandon Valeriano and Ryan Maness, eds, *Cyber War versus Cyber Realities: Cyber Conflict in the International System* (Oxford: Oxford University Press, 2015); Brandon Valeriano and Ryan Maness, 'International relations theory and cyber security: threats, conflicts and ethics in an emergent domain', in Chris Brown and Robyn Eckersley (eds), *The Oxford Handbook of International Political Theory* (Oxford: Oxford University Press, 2018), pp. 259–72; Anthimos Alexandros Tsirigotis, *Cybernetics, Warfare and Discourse: The Cybernetisation of Warfare in Britain* (New York: Springer, 2017); Jacob Oakley, *Waging Cyberwar: Technical Challenges and Operational Restraints* (New York: Springer, 2020).

[28] Fritz Allhoff, Adam Henscke, and Bradley Jay Strawser (eds), *Binary Bullets: The Ethics of Cyberwarfare* (Oxford: Oxford University Press, 2015); Michael L. Gross and Tamar Meisels (eds), *Soft War: The Ethics of Unarmed Conflict* (Cambridge: Cambridge University Press, 2017); George Lucas, Jr, *Ethics and Cyberwarfare: The Quest for Responsible Security in an Age of Digital Warfare* (Oxford: Oxford University Press, 2016); Martha Finnemore, 'Ethical dilemmas in cyberspace', *Ethics & International Affairs* 32, 4 (2018) pp. 457–62.

law.[29] Almost all of this ethical and legal literature seeks to provide rules for how to respond to cyber-attacks. Perhaps the clearest example of this comes from the Tallinn Manual, now in its second edition. Convened by NATO in 2009, a group of international legal scholars came together to develop new rules for the governance of this realm drawn from existing international legal principles and norms. The first iteration of the manual, named after the Baltic city where the meetings took place, was mainly the work of scholars and appeared in 2013. After the success of the manual, a decision was made to revise and update it, and to have the manual discussed by State representatives. The Netherlands convened over 50 representatives from states around the world in 2016, referred to as the Hague Process. In a Chatham House context, this allowed states to provide input into the process, though the editors of the final volume clarify that the final version does not represent any particular state nor can specific changes to the manual be linked to any specific state.[30] While it is unclear to what extent states will use this legal guidance, the editors and experts involved designed it to be so used; as they stated, the 'primary audience [for the manual] consists of State legal advisors charged with providing international law advice to governmental decision makers, both civilian and military'.[31]

So clearly Rengger's insight that the state-based system is shaping the rules governing the use of force in cyberspace has much truth to it. However, it is also complicated by the very nature of this use of force. First, it is unclear whether cyber war should even be called a use of force. Michael Gross, a scholar who has written extensively on just war, proposed the term 'soft war' to describe this form of conflict (along with other forms, such as economic sanctions). This concept of soft war 'includes all non-kinetic measures whether persuasive or coercive'.[32] In the cyber realm, this means that everything, from a denial of service attack (DoS) intended to bring down a country's health care infrastructure to an informational war designed to disrupt a country's elections, counts as a soft war. While this concept is helpful in highlighting the idea that war should be understood outside of the battlefield, determining whether or not these different actions merit a

---

[29] Heather Harrison Dinniss, *Cyber War and the Laws of War* (Cambridge: Cambridge University Press, 2012); Jens David Ohlin et al., *Cyber War: Law and Ethics for Virtual Conflicts* (Oxford: Oxford University Press, 2015); Michael N. Schmitt (ed), *Tallinn Manual 2.0 on the International Law Applicable to Cyber Operations* (Cambridge: Cambridge University Press, p. 207).
[30] Schmitt, *Tallinn Manual 2.0*, p. 6.
[31] Ibid., p. 2.
[32] Michael L. Gross and Tamar Meisels (eds), *Soft War: The Ethics of Unarmed Conflict* (Cambridge: Cambridge University Press), p. 1.

military response requires something closer to Aristotelian judgement than it does to following a rule.

Even more concerning is that the international legal approach undertaken in the Tallinn Manual might enable retaliatory uses of force. Eric Heinze and Rhiannon Neilsen highlight this potential in a recent article.[33] Their article highlights the growing tendency to discard the international legal rules against reprisals. Reprisals were an accepted form of military force until the UN Charter explicitly banned them. However, various developments in the international system have encouraged their use. The authors note that the Tallinn Manual, while highlighting the problems of reprisals, does leave space for their use because some participants in the drafting process understood such actions to be justified.[34] Here we find one of the problems with seeking to put into a set of rules all possible scenarios. Rules cannot cover all contexts, and the cyber realm creates contexts that we have not yet seen. Because of this, any effort to provide rules for all scenarios will undoubtedly leave open possible uses that skirt around the general view. Moreover, following Rengger's point about contexts, when such rules and rule-making take place within a state-based context, the defence of the state will remain the most important standard by which to make judgements. Rather than judgements based on limiting uses of force or reprisals, rules will be seen through the lens of the national interest. And, because in the cyber realm, with uses of non-kinetic force being possible, the use of reprisals seems more justified.

And it is here that Rengger's focus on contexts can help us in making such judgements. For instance, determining the relevant context of a DoS relies on several considerations: was the event the result of an intentional action by an adversary or was it the result of a simple overload of a computer system? Was the attack the result of human intentionality or did it arise from an algorithm designed to disrupt a website based on a set of rule-like commands? Was the attack undertaken by a profit-seeking entity (a multinational company seeking to secure a contract) or by a political group ('hacktivists' seeking to advance a political cause) or by an adversarial state? Is the attack targeted at civilians, at the military, or at an entity that sits somewhere between the two? To even consider such questions requires an understanding of the context of the cyber world. That is, the cyber world is not controlled by states alone but by agents without links to states and some with links to states. It has commercial uses which have become more prominent for states which have undertaken a neoliberalization of their public services. The cyber world

---

[33] Eric Henize and Rhiannon Neilsen, 'Limited war and the return of reprisals in the law of armed conflict', *Ethics & International Affairs* 34, 2 (2020), pp. 175–88.

[34] Ibid., p. 182.

gives freedom to many to find information and engage in political activism without having to leave their homes. Its military uses often overlap with its political and civilian uses. The flow of information in the cyber world is one of its most important contexts, but it is a context within which the distinction between truth and lies becomes more complex.

As can be seen from this short list of questions, the context of the cyber world is not one that is defined by the state system in the same way that military intervention or pre-emptive action is, the two issues explored in Rengger's just war critique. This suggests that the state-based teleocratic context that Rengger focused on throughout his writing on just war and force does not necessarily fit as easily here. This context may well have some of the teleocratic elements that Rengger identifies; using Oakeshott's language, the cyber world often has a strong element of an enterprise association about it. However, at the same time, the cyber world with the multiplicity of agents and interests might well be closer to a civil association, one that enables multiple purposes to intersect and which is guided by the simple desire to create a space in which agents can communicate and pursue the shared and divergent interests.

To return to the use of force, and to the creation of a new cyber offensive military capacity by the UK military means considering how this new and different context fits into the teleocratic purpose of the nation state. Rather than self-defence, the new British military project appears more designed to advance a particular agenda, one that seeks to defeat adversaries (unnamed at this point, but undoubtedly led by Russia and China). To enable this form of military capability to develop without recognizing the cyber context, and to seek to create rules to govern this context, rules that will have more to do with advancing particular ideological agendas than with solely engaging in self-defence, is to fall into the trap that Rengger identifies.

So, is there an alternative? We have the suggestion from Rengger, never fully developed in his work, that we need a form of practical wisdom that would allow us to make practical judgements when faced with cyber conflict. Practical wisdom is not simply knowledge but the ability to deliberate on the basis of various forms of knowledge. For the cyber realm, this would include, but is not limited to: the technical side of the cyber world; the political knowledge of which agents are pursuing which interests; the strategic understanding of how different actions will or will not bring together different online resources. Coupled with these forms of knowledge, one also needs a set of practical or moral virtues. These could include virtues such as temperance, or the ability to control one's emotional response to an online disruption (which might or might not be from an adversary); courage, or the ability to act when necessary even if there is a chance that it might lead to harm to one's self or country; justice, or the ability to determine the fairness of an action in terms of its impact on other agents in the cyber realm; magnanimity, or the ability to be generous with one's resources in the cyber world; and empathy, or the ability to understand and appreciate the position of others in the cyber world who may hold radically different positions than oneself but who need the cyber world to continue to function.

These are just suggestions. A full description of the virtues necessary for the cyber world context can be found in a recent work by Shannon Vallor. In her book, *Technology and the Virtues*, Vallor combines the insights of Aristotle with those of Buddha and Confucius to create a global virtue ethic, but one specifically designed for the cyber realm.[35] While she does treat the military as one element of that cyber world, her approach is broader than this, seeking to create a set of virtues that might help to govern the way we interact online. As with the virtue ethics traditions, these are not rules or specific guidelines, but character traits that we should cultivate that will enable us to be better citizens in the specifically global cyber context. Whether Vallor's list or others are best requires further investigation; the benefit of her account, and what I have tried to introduce here, is that a context-sensitive approach to the cyber realm cannot be one of simply introducing rules, but must combine knowledge of this realm with sets of character traits that will enable a less violent cyber world.

Conclusion

Nick Rengger was wary of rules. He argued that rules alone cannot help us to understand the world of military force. Instead, he wanted us to pay attention to the contexts in which military force takes place. I have taken this insight and linked Rengger more closely to a virtue-oriented framework, one in which a combination of knowledge about the world and a particular form of judgement will enable us to act in ways that may decrease incidences of violence rather than enable them.

Aristotle ends his ethical and political reflections by highlighting the importance of education. For it is only through education that a virtuous person can be constructed. But virtue is not disconnected from rules and laws. Indeed, his reflections at the end of the *Nicomachean Ethics* point us to the importance of legislating as a way to achieving a virtuous citizenry:

The best thing, then, is for there to be correct public concern with such things. But if they are neglected in the public sphere, it would seem appropriate for each person to help his own children and friends on the way to virtue, and for him to be able to do this, or at least

---

[35] Shannon Vallor, *Technology and the Virtues: A Philosophical Guide to a Future Worth Wanting* (Oxford: Oxford University Press, 2016).

rationally chose to do so. From what we have said, however, it would seem that he will be better able to do this if he has the chance of legislating, because care at the public level is evidently demonstrated through laws, and good care through good laws.[36]

Rengger was not an Aristotelian theorist, so my effort to link him to Aristotle reflects my own interpretation of his work.[37] However, I think he shares with Aristotle the idea that education into the virtues enables a better way of being in the world. And, I would argue that one solution to the dilemmas he lays out in his reflections on war and our inability to see the contexts that enable war can be found in a virtue ethics approach, one which privileges an education that reveals contexts that are not so obvious. Indeed, Rengger spent his life in the academy, where his prowess as a teacher was undeniable. Importantly, his approach to education was not one of giving students clear answers or carefully worked-out formulae. Instead, his approach is perhaps best seen through the framework of Socrates, the one who questioned those who thought they knew the answers. In so doing, Rengger helped students to see that the assumptions they have about democracies, liberalism, and war were not as clear as they might have imagined. By forcing his students, and all of us, to map out the contexts within which politics and war take place, Rengger advanced his own form of virtue. His approach to education enabled students and fellow scholars to see that the world as it is cannot be our only world. He proposed a wary or perhaps reluctant form of rule following, one that could only work if virtuous individuals were the ones making and following those rules. I have suggested how this might work in the realm of cyber conflict. Whether or not we can uncover the depth of that context, or those that we will face in the future, is not clear. But to realize we need to look for them is perhaps what Rengger gives us, and for which we should be thankful.

---

[36] Aristotle, *Nicomachean Ethics, Revised Version*, edited by Roger Crisp (Cambridge: Cambridge University Press, 2000), p. 199.

[37] There are certainly a number of points in his early work where Rengger highlighted his affinity for Aristotle; for instance, see his agreement that habit is a crucial dimension of ethical behaviour in Rengger, *Political Theory*, pp. 148–51. Thanks to Vassilios Paipais for reminding me of this affinity.

9

Rengger and the 'Business of War'

Caroline Kennedy-Pipe[1,2]

Introduction

It is becoming increasingly interesting to write about Nick Rengger and what I term the business of war. Reading his manuscripts inevitably reveals his (much commented upon) preoccupation with just war theory and his anti-Pelagianism.[3] A careful scrutiny of the written words and a recall (perhaps mistaken) from memories of many conversations, however, yield very little insight into his view of the business of war. This absence is quite remarkable given that Rengger would have agreed that war was both the curse of the international system but also the very stuff from which International Relations (IR) had been created. In this chapter, I want to explore why Rengger had little if nothing to say about the actual conduct of war[4] and how this silence weakens his position as a scholar of war if

---

[1] By business of war, I mean the reality and brutality of the experience of war but also the responsibilities of command, the agony of the battlefield and the shifting scales of death as calculations are made about who or what to sacrifice – this on all sides.

[2] I am very grateful to the following for their recollections of the late Nicholas Rengger: Chris Brown, Sophia Dingli, Richard English, Noël and Margo O'Sullivan, Vassilios Paipais, James Rogers, Thomas Waldman.

[3] Nicholas Rengger, *The Anti-Pelagian Imagination in Political Theory and International Relations* (London and New York: Routledge, 2017).

[4] One exception was a piece that Nick and I co-authored in 2012 for the Carnegie Council Ethics online monthly column. In it we explored the use of drones in extra-judicial killings under the Obama Administration, but our primary purpose was to highlight the 'bending' or 'breaking' of international law to justify drone assassinations.

not, of course, his status as a political theorist of some note. The omission I highlight though is especially puzzling given that towards the end of his life he had grown somewhat impatient with the subject area (he never considered it a discipline)[5] as both too 'critical' in methodology and too wedded to a highly partisan view of democracy as a 'cure all'. Many scholars were for him far removed from appreciating the essential 'darkness' of the human condition in all its guises and how the aftermath of 9/11 with its multiple consequences had in his view further darkened politics. In this sense he was infuriated with the ideas, for example, of Stephen Pinker and any claims that the world had become and was becoming more peaceable. But in typical Renggerian fashion, he had no real evidence to oppose that thesis, no facts, no data but merely the conviction, perhaps the hope,[6] that Pinker was quite simply wrong.[7]

Gathering empirical evidence or doing fieldwork was not in the Rengger canon. It did not need to be perhaps,[8] but I think there is in general a problem with discussing war simply in abstraction. So I end this chapter with the thought, perhaps a harsh one, that Rengger often evaded the hard realities of looking at the business of war in favour of a position which seemed to accept that politics ended when the fighting began; that there was little that could be done apart from a reliance on the power of conversation to raise if not resolve the points of contention. Here, Rengger owed much of his reliance on the idea of conversation to Michael Oakeshott, one of his formative influences.[9] I reiterate a point

---

See Nicholas Rengger and Caroline Kennedy, 'The new assassination bureau: on the "robotic" turn in contemporary war', Carnegie Ethics Online Monthly Column (6 November 2012).

[5] See Caroline Kennedy-Pipe, Nicholas Rengger, 'BISA at thirty: reflections on three decades of British International Relations Scholarship, *Review of International Studies* 32, 4, pp. 665–76. See also my article which I discussed at length with Nick: Caroline Kennedy-Pipe, 'At a crossroads – and other reasons to be cheerful', *International Relations* 21, 3 (2006a), pp. 351–4.

[6] Hope is not usually an emotion that we associate with Rengger, and his position on it is the subject of disagreement between many of his friends and colleagues!

[7] It is to Chris Brown that we owe the memory of Nick and other colleagues sitting one evening in a restaurant in St Andrews arguing with some vehemence over the Pinker thesis. See Chris Brown, in this volume.

[8] As the editor of this volume has pointed out to me questions of empirical evidence would and were summarily dismissed by Rengger as not relevant to his position. Empirical evidence does not speak for itself; it was only one part of an interpretive framework. Rengger and I simply disagreed on this point as do many of our colleagues in the field.

[9] I am indebted to Thomas Waldman for this insight after his many conversations with Rengger on Clausewitz, including in his doctoral viva at Warwick University.

that Noël O'Sullivan has observed to me, in our many discussions about Rengger and this was that Oakeshott:

> used the term conversation to characterise the nature of philosophy once the old metaphysical quest for an absolute reality had been abandoned in favour of the view that all knowledge is conditional (this does not mean relative). In other words, he did not apply it to the political relationships if only because that involved rhetoric and persuasion.[10]

That last line is interesting because, as I will go on to argue, Rengger, like Oakeshott, did not do rhetoric or even much persuasion. I will though in this chapter highlight a short period in the late 1990s when Rengger directly addresses the issue of sub-state war and proclaims that something must be done! He even advocates hope![11] This was not typical of him and so this phase has not really been noticed by his contemporaries: increasingly I have come to believe that the idea of hope is threaded across his work; I will turn to my particular reading of Rengger later.

But to return to the business of war, Rengger had no direct experience of violent conflict nor indeed much inclination to stray far from the places that he felt most comfortable – first as a student at Durham University[12] and later as a Reader and Professor among the convivial surroundings and colleagues of the University of St Andrews. He was not latterly a traveller nor indeed someone particularly eager to witness global politics first-hand. Indeed, what was striking at his funeral were the comments made by his brother Patrick and his vivid evocation of a Nick enraptured as a child by his toy soldiers, his models, and the obsession, which would last until his death, with the fantastical if blood-soaked world of Tolkien.[13] The work produced over a 40-year career forms a tapestry rich with reference to those obsessions: war films, Westerns, and contemporary action movies,[14] images of classical and modern warriors and allusions to spy novels,[15] and the

---

[10] Noël O'Sullivan in correspondence, December 2020 and January 2021.
[11] Nicholas Rengger, 'The beginning of the end of modernity? Honour, ethics and the practises of civil war at the fin de siècle', *Civil Wars* 1, 2 (1998), pp. 38–51.
[12] He was taught at Durham by, among others, Henry Tudor and Noël O'Sullivan as well as David Manning.
[13] See his reference to J.R.R. Tolkien, *The Lord of the Rings* (London: Harper Collins, 1961) in Rengger, *The Anti-Pelagian Imagination*, p. 130.
[14] Nick noted that we had become friends because of our shared enthusiasm for Westerns. See Nicholas Rengger, *Just War and International Order* (Cambridge: Cambridge University Press, 2013a).
[15] Nick often talked about his own 'spy thriller' which he claimed would appear at some point in the future!

intelligence intrigues of the Cold War.[16] His version of war was derived from what I increasingly came to regard as an idealized, perhaps even fictional, and ultimately ambiguous set of assumptions.[17]

Avoiding the ugly face of war?

Although Rengger had been engrossed with a variety of issues throughout the late 1980s[18] and 1990s,[19] it was really only after the events of 9/11 that he began to be agitated by the state of war.[20] His monograph *International Relations: Political Theory and the Problem of Order* published in

---

[16] Rengger was a great admirer of Richard Aldrich and his work: Richard J. Aldrich, *The Hidden Hand Britain, America and Cold War Secret Intelligence* (London: John Murray, 2001).

[17] I am not the only friend and colleague of Nick to note the ambiguous nature of his thinking on war. In conversation with Chris Brown, he recalls an occasion just after the Balkan Wars had started in the early 1990s. He remembers Nick somewhat enthusiastically advocating that Western planes/bombers should fly low over Serbia just to show the Serbian dictatorship what damage could be rained down should the path of ethnic cleansing against the Muslims be taken. As Chris Brown points out this position was at considerable odds with Rengger's later position opposing military intervention. This ambiguity was also present on the occasion when Professor Lawrence Freedman (War Studies, Kings College London) and Professor Paul Rogers (Peace Studies, Bradford University) debated the prospects of war with Iraq at the BISA Conference. Both speakers gave rousing and opposing speeches for and against war. Nick applauded both colleagues with equal gusto explaining later that both had made compelling cases. Vassilios Paipais sees this apparent contradiction as part of Rengger' s Oakshottian sensibility. He enjoyed a good debate/conversation for purely aesthetic pleasure. He thought theory should have no impact whatsoever on, or serve as a justification to, the world of practice (politics). Note though in my chapter my memories of Nick as pro-intervention in the late 1990s.

[18] Again, I am indebted to Chris Brown for his account of the way in which during the 1980s political theorists such as Rengger were both pushed to engagement with IR because of burgeoning student demand for the subject but also how Nick had begun to see the international as part of the wider issue of order. Rengger's first monograph was N.J. Rengger, *Political Theory, Modernity and Postmodernity* (Oxford: Blackwell, 1995a).

[19] Nick published an extremely interesting essay on ideas of culture and International Relations in 1992. In it he sets out his stall as a pluralist, again seeing competing traditions as an obstacle to any idea of world order. See Nicholas J. Rengger, 'Culture, society and order in world politics', in John Baylis and N.J. Rengger (eds), *Dilemmas of World Politics: International Issues in a Changing World* (Oxford: Oxford University Press, 1992a), pp. 85–103. The book was dedicated to the late John Vincent.

[20] Rengger published an impressive array of articles and chapters throughout the 1980s and 1990s, many of which study the subject of IR and its relationship to the Social Sciences. See, for example, with his great friend Mark Hoffman, Nick Rengger: Mark Hoffman, 'Modernity, postmodernism and international relations in J. Doherty, E. Graham, and M. Malek (eds) *Postmodernism and the Social Sciences* (London: Palgrave Macmillan, 1992), pp. 127–47.

2000 summed up his intellectual trajectory until that point: it was a deft summary of, and challenge to, the idea of order in the writings of scholars drawn from Political Theory and from IR. The index contains only three references to any discussion of war within the text.[21] It is quite a curious experience to read the manuscript again, as in my case, hunting, expecting, and hoping for a discussion of war in a book, which was after all about international order, but it is quite simply absent or perhaps subsumed under wider considerations.

To be fair though even if the business of war is missing in this book, Rengger had during the end period of the Cold War and in the decade or so afterwards mused at some length about what any supposed new world order might entail. He had never really been drawn into the major debates about nuclear deterrence or nuclear strategy which was rather surprising as it was in the years of Mutually Assured Destruction (MAD), Flexible Response and the Revolution in Military Affairs that much of the debate about morality in world politics had taken place.[22] Rather Rengger spent much of the 1990s jousting with the advocates of the then fashionable (along with the end of history thesis[23]) and influential Democratic Peace thesis.[24]

In this period he was also beguiled by the ideas of the public intellectual Michael Ignatieff, as expressed through his many lectures, his talks, and his books; *Blood and Belonging*,[25] *Virtual War*[26] and with a fair degree of enthusiasm the treatise of the *Warrior's Honour*.[27] The second and third books appealed to Rengger's sense of a classical tradition betrayed by the influx of technology and the subsequent demise of chivalry, leaving even the professional warrior, in his view, in need of a code of honour, so as to in his words understand 'why they fight and how they fight'.[28] How such

---

[21] Nicholas Rengger, *International Relations: Political Theory and the Problem of Order* (London: Routledge, 2000).

[22] As Turner Johnson argues in his review of Rengger's work; he, unlike Rengger, locates moral visions of just war thinking in the 20th century and 'specifically in response to the challenges posed by nuclear weapons and deterrence and by the arguments over the Vietnam War. See James Turner Johnson, Review Essay: 'Three perspectives on just war', *International Relations* (2017b), pp. 511–22.

[23] Francis Fukuyama, *The End of History*, various editions. (London: Penguin, 1993).

[24] N. Rengger, 'On democratic war theory', in A. Geis, L. Brock, and H. Müller (eds), *Democratic Wars* (London: Palgrave Macmillan, 2006), pp. 123–41.

[25] Michael Ignatieff, *Blood and Belonging Journeys into the New Nationalism*, (London: Vintage, 1994).

[26] Michael Ignatieff, *Virtual War* (London: Vintage, 2001).

[27] Michael Ignatieff, *The Warrior's Honor Ethnic War and the Modern Conscience* (London: Vintage, 1999).

[28] See Nicholas Rengger in 2002, 'On the just war tradition in the twenty-first century, *International Affairs* 78, 2. For an interesting view of how Rengger regraded Ignatieff

a code was to be implemented in the post-Cold War era of stand-off and vicarious war[29] was a question Rengger never really answered apart from to insist that war must remain a human activity fought with a human face.[30] As he wryly remarked, drones did not have faces.[31]

But just before technology such as drones began to exert a powerful grip on the business of war, a turn that we can date to the beginning of the Afghan War,[32] Rengger, influenced by Ignatieff, spent time and some of his considerable intellectual energy reflecting on the literature which had emerged in the closing days of the century on the increasing prevalence of ethnic (or as Mary Kaldor characterized them 'New Wars'[33]) war. Hopes for a New World Order had rapidly receded after the US debacle in Mogadishu, the Rwandan genocide, and the Bosnian conflict; the incompetence of the United Nations had been starkly highlighted by the failure of its peacekeepers to halt the tragedy of Srebrenica. In fact, in the period of engagement with Ignatieff in the 1990s there is something that I had forgotten about Rengger. That is until now.[34] He had actually argued against the mainstream (not that that in itself was unusual given his love of debate) but in this instant, he disputed the overtly pessimistic

---

see the fascinating response by Rengger to Ignatieff in Nicholas Rengger, 'A global ethic and hybrid character of the moral world', *Ethics & International Affairs* 26, 1 (2012), pp. 27–31.

[29] Thomas Waldman, *Vicarious Warfare American Strategy and the Illusion of War on the Cheap* (Bristol: Bristol University Press, 2020). Nick had acted as external examiner for Tom Waldman's doctoral thesis on Clausewitz. Nick was also a tremendous admirer of the work of Christopher Coker and recommended his book *Warrior Geeks* to all.

[30] The New Assassination Bureau. In 2014 Rengger hosted a workshop on drone warfare in St Andrews which was funded by the Oxford Research group. It brought together scholars to discuss the use of drones under President Obama.

[31] The New Assassination Bureau. Rengger especially enjoyed his interactions with the American scholar, Mary Ellen O'Connell. He profoundly disagreed with her advocacy of drone use in the 9/11 wars. This was apparent in the debate of February 2012 at Westminster Abbey organised by the University of Exeter and Notre Dame Law School.

[32] James Rogers, 'Drone warfare: the death of precision', *Bulletin of the Atomic Scientists* BF1, 1 (2017).

[33] Mary Kaldor, *New & Old Wars: Organised Violence in a Global Era*, multiple editions (Cambridge: Polity, 2012).

[34] I had founded the journal *Civil Wars* in 1996 with the good offices and encouragement of the publisher the late Frank Cass to reflect the growing interest academically in the study of Civil Wars. As anyone who has founded a journal knows, in the early years you have to count on friends and colleagues for support! Nick kindly wrote the 1998 article at my request for our first volume. I regard this article as reflecting the best of Nick's style. It is based on a breadth of reading and is rather mischievous. See his comment about the hopeless nature of the new neo-medievalists!

accounts pervading the academy.[35] He contested the idea of a coming anarchy,[36] argued against the advent of a neo-medievalism,[37] and he challenged the general liberal handwringing (as he termed it) over the state of the world. (Note here that Rengger had a somewhat sunnier view of the Middle Ages than was generally held, again partly because he emphasized it as an age of chivalry and honour.) That aside, for once, or the once, I can find he adopted a line that 'we' with the caveat 'whoever we may be', must not just address in conversation the mayhem of civil wars – or as he termed them – 'uncivil' wars – but actually do something about them. Thus, in the 1998 essay he writes the following:

> Civil or uncivil war has slipped from its clear and established moorings. It seems to me that understanding it and its various trajectories is about as good a check on the pulse of the modern era as any. If we fail to check the virus like spread of the 'uncivil' wars of our own time, then, in the opening decades of the twenty-first century, perhaps it will be time to talk of an 'end' to the modern era ... we will need to work on trying to deal with such wars ... Recognising their inevitability, but also recognising their limits and seeking to check them where we must and prevent then where we can.[38]

Rengger is commonly accepted as opposed to the business of humanitarian intervention.[39] But here it was: a rallying cry. Adopting a position that rejected Kaplan's dire view of the coming anarchy, Rengger rather sides with Ignatieff: 'We are not in control, says Kaplan and of course that implies we – whoever "we" are (again that phrase) cannot be and should not try to be in control. Well I side with Ignatieff, sometimes "we" should try, must try, to be in control.'[40] It was not Rengger's style to offer practical solutions as to how to stem what he termed the virus of civil wars, but he did hint that looking at the just war tradition might help.[41] But it was just a hint. Then something changed for Rengger.

---

[35] See N.J. Rengger, 'The beginning of the end of modernity? Honour, ethics and the practices of civil war at the fin de siècle', *Civil Wars* 1, 2, pp. 38–51.

[36] Robert Kaplan, *The Ends of the Earth: A Journey at the Dawn of the Twentieth-First Century* (New York: Random House, 1996).

[37] Philp Cerny, 'Neomedieval, civil war and the new security dilemma: globalisation as durable disorder', *Civil Wars*, 1/1 (Spring, 1998). Phil also very kindly also appeared in the first volume of *Civil Wars*.

[38] N.J. Rengger, 'The beginning of the end of modernity?'

[39] Turner Johnson, 'Three faces of just war; Review Essay', pp. 511–22.

[40] Rengger, 'The beginning of the end of modernity?'

[41] Ibid.

9/11: Not apocalypse now?[42]

It was the myriad justifications for the global war on terror (later the long war) that galvanized his curiosity, taking him as far as he ever strayed into anything close to a policy debate. Writing in 2002 on contemporary war and again in 2005, after what he termed 'the return of force and war' to the international system, he clearly laid out the three positions that for him formed the relationship between war and politics.[43] The first was that war was quite simply never a legitimate endeavour: this stance he found in its purest and perhaps most honest form in a type of Christian Pacifism. (This, I think is the position he was moving towards at the end of his life. It is a theme to which I will return). The second proposition was one in which during the harsh reality of war 'anything and everything' becomes permissible – even the wanton destruction of civilians. Rengger recognized that it was this second position that had gained dominance through the development of the European state system and then throughout the 20th century. It was through the interrogation and questioning of the third position – that restraint was possible and indeed preferable in war – that increasingly formed the basis of his work. Specifically, he found the co-option of the just war theory into the pretensions and ambitions of modern politicians such as Tony Blair and George Bush a matter of expediency dressed up as principle.[44] But he also objected across a number of years to the academic scramble to lay claim to that Christian tradition to encourage military interventions under the guise of progress, benevolence, or democratization. Usually, much to his annoyance, all three of these claims were linked together.

The co-optation of the just war tradition arose most obviously in the debates about liberal values and how war should be conducted against a variety of enemies, whether it be a Slobodan Milosevic, a Saddam, Osama bin Laden and his Al-Qaeda, the Taliban, or any one of the gallery of dictators, pariahs, and rogues that formed the so-called Axis-of Evil. Rengger noted here that there was scant discussion about why war was or should be considered an appropriate mechanism for dealing with any of these unsavoury individuals or groups. But what provoked ire, inspiring some scintillating paragraphs, were the public justifications for the British (and as it turned out disastrous) intervention in the 2003 Iraq War. Surveying the accounts

---

[42] Caroline Kennedy-Pipe, Nicholas Rengger, 'Apocalypse now? Continuities or disjunctions in world politics after 9/11', *International Affairs* 82, 3 (2006b), pp. 539–52.

[43] Nicholas Rengger, 'The judgment of war: on the idea of legitimate force in world politics', *Review of International Studies* 31 (2005), pp. 143–61.

[44] Rengger, *The Judgment of War*.

given by the Blair Government and the legal justifications provided by the then Attorney General for war, Rengger posed the question:

> Why did it matter if the war was legal? At no point that I am aware did anyone seriously discuss the surely related question, that even if it was legal, was it morally justified? Or rather in as much as they did, the assumption seemed to be that morality and legality were effectively, in this instance, at least one and the same. Yet a moment's reflection should serve to underline that this could not possibly be the case.[45]

Taking many sideswipes at Blair and his fellow travellers, Rengger highlighted the route from the initial legal justifications for war, into the oft-stated public position that melded the legal with the moral case. Somehow in a moment of political trickery, a 'look no hands affair', a state-led morality was created which required, indeed demanded, the overthrowing of the (in Blair's words) 'evil' Iraqi regime.[46] This trickery laid dangerous turf for Rengger, who like others, saw this as perhaps, even inevitably, foreshadowing the abuse of state power and more pertinently making war a moral choice not a pragmatic necessity. In this unease over the extension and abuse of state power, Rengger has much in common with the thinking of the late Judith Shklar, a scholar he greatly admired.[47] Indeed, it is perhaps some of her words, not his, that capture the essence of the challenged posed by any rush to war. Shklar writes:

> The instinct for personal and collective self-preservation may be taken as a force of nature and as such necessary. When people defend themselves against aggressors bent upon pure extermination, they have been forced to return to the state of nature where there is no justice, only a struggle for bare survival. How many wars are really like that in the first place? And how many such wars could be avoided? If we answer these questions *honestly*, it is clear that the necessity of self-preservation is rare and that a return to peace is generally possible.[48]

She continues: 'This is scarcely a novel observation', but it is surely a pertinent one. She then goes on to ask:

---

[45] Rengger, *The Judgment of War*.

[46] For Tony Blair, the purpose of the war was to set the Iraqi people free from the evil of Saddam Hussein. Quoted in *The Guardian*, Wednesday 6 July 2016, during a press conference in which Mr Blair rejected the findings of the Chilcot Inquiry.

[47] Judith N. Shklar, *The Faces of Injustice* (New Haven, CT: Yale University Press, 1990). Nick foregrounds his debt to her in his book on International Order.

[48] Shklar, *The Faces of Injustice*, emphasis added.

What can be just about an enterprise in which the innocent perish more frequently than the guilty and that is nothing but a test of strength and endurance, even if these contests are sometimes rule-governed? To be drawn into a war for sheer survival may be a misfortune that the victims cannot avert but it cannot be just.[49]

Just – indeed. What is just or can be deemed as just? This was increasingly the most important issue in Rengger's later writing, creating a series of provocative confrontation with a range of scholars. He objected/located the modern tendency to utilize the just war tradition in the example of the strategic bombing campaigns of World War II. The work of Michael Walzer was in many ways his touchstone.[50]

But to return briefly to my opening point about Nick and his meditations on war. Although he wrote, talked about, and taught about Michael Walzer and his seminal book *Just and Unjust Wars*, Nick was curiously silent (even disinterested) as to the detail of the raw human material on which Walzer drew in his descriptions of the strategic bombing campaigns. There is nothing in Nick's analysis of the human costs of the bombing campaigns. Nothing in terms of that chilling phrase 'body counts' or anything really of the ugly business of what area bombing as opposed to (supposedly) precision bombing had entailed. This is curious in several ways. Rengger did not seem particularly or even especially interested in the dead or the dead cities (as Grayling would have it[51]) of that war. Indeed, in the 2005 essay he spends only a few lines on those who opposed the Allied bombing campaign against German cities and civilians. This is odd as he was keenly aware (in conversation) of the debates which had locked figures as formidable as George Orwell and Vera Brittain in opposition and in acrimonious exchanges the legacies of which lasted well beyond Orwell's death.[52] He merely notes that this type of public exchange over civilian deaths had embarrassed the wartime British Government. Actually, as we now know, the Government *had* permitted, if not obviously encouraged, some forms of criticisms over strategic bombing by those such as Orwell,[53] fearing that a complete prohibition on dissent might have drawn down on its head comparisons with Hitler's pernicious regime. But that is not really my point here. Rather

---

[49] Shklar, *The Faces of Injustice*.

[50] Michael Walzer, *Just and Unjust Wars: A Moral Argument with Historical Illustrations* (New York: Basic Books, 1977).

[51] A.C. Grayling, *Among the Dead Cities. Is the Targeting of Civilians in War ever Justified?* (London: Bloomsbury, 2006).

[52] See Richard Westwood, 'Vera Brittain versus George Orwell', The Orwell Society (12 February 2012), available at: https://orwellsociety.com>vera-brittain-versus-george-orwell

[53] Westwood, Vera Brittain.

I wonder how the scholar who could write the following paragraph did not display any real interest in the calamity (calamities) that occurred in war:

For much of the twentieth century – and indeed also now in the twenty-first – the realities of international relations have been an extended and grotesque lesson in the appalling ingenuity that human beings can practise in their relations with one another: a seemingly endless, viciousness and barbarism, usually cloaked in the language of high ideals ... an honest observer would have to conclude that, overall, it is the twentieth century that truly deserves the title famously bestowed by the historian Barbara Tuchman on the fourteenth, a 'calamitous century' – and that the twenty-first century hardly promises, so far at least, to be any better.[54]

In this sense his position is radically different to Shklar who wrote with passionate intensity about the victims of war and their rights.[55] To return to strategic bombing, Rengger did not address the politics of the decision-making making to bomb German (and Japanese) cities, which, whatever the evidence, mandated the destruction of buildings and civilians alike. Given that he always said that he wanted to understand politics and war there is no discussion of the strategy of Unconditional Surrender (later regarded by many as having prolonged the agonies of war), nothing on the first use of nuclear weapons or what the conduct of war may do to the process of peace afterwards. Rather, Rengger skates through Walzer's secular interpretation of the just war theory, his opposition to the Vietnam War and on to the more contemporary iteration of just war theory. Along the way Rengger acknowledges the manner in which the Cold War permitted and encouraged the Manichean trends in US politics to shape the Liberal confrontation against an 'evil' Soviet Union.[56] Again though there is a strangely disembodied discussion of evil, reliant both on C.S. Lewis and his Screwtape Letters[57] (a book Rengger liked to point out, dedicated to J.R.R. Tolkien) but also on Hannah Arendt and her thesis of the banality of evil.[58] Indeed, it has been left to the scholar and former St Andrews student, Renee Jeffrey, to

---

[54] Rengger, The Anti-Pelagian Imagination.

[55] Shklar, The Faces of Injustice, pp. 83–126.

[56] I was indebted to Nick Rengger for his conversations while I was writing my 2013 article on moralism in US foreign policy. See Caroline Kennedy-Pipe, 'The Manichean temptation: moralising rhetoric and the invocation of evil in US foreign policy', International Politics, 50, 5 (2013), pp. 623–38.

[57] C.S. Lewis, The Screwtape Letters (London: Geoffrey Blis, 1942).

[58] Hannah Arendt, Eichmann in Jerusalem: A Report on the Banality of Evil (New York: Viking Press, 1963).

develop to a fuller extent what Nick's discussion of and thinking about evil may mean for contemporary war.[59]

To those of us fortunate to know him it was obvious Rengger did not trust politicians. Perhaps this is why he refused for most of his career to engage in policy debates or get into the dirty business of practical politics. He was working on a review of Nick Wheeler's monograph and his long-standing interest on Trust just before he passed away.[60] We can only really speculate as to what his reaction might have been to Wheeler's overall thesis but part of his essay in 2005 is a scathing attack on the political skulduggery of both Mr Blair and President Bush.

However, it was in 2008 that Nick finally placed his cards on the table. In an essay published that year by Caroline Soper in International Affairs, he comes the closest to revealing his view of war and indeed politics. In an essay entitled 'The greatest treason? On the subtle temptations of preventive war', he describes how those scholars who sought to justify the Bush doctrine of 'preventive war' were probably well intentioned but simply wrong and their thesis subversive to order in multiple ways. He rejects the attempt to make just war theory the speedy vehicle for war and comes the closest I can recall of admitting that his version, his own reading of Realism, could be seen as a form (albeit a version lightly worn) of Pacifism. Finally, the authentic Rengger?[61]

The essay lambasts the way President Bush and those around him utilized the tragedy of 9/11 to bring the rhetoric and reality of 'preventive war' to the centre of American strategic doctrine. Starting with the Presidential address at Fort Bragg in 2005, Rengger traces exactly how Bush ended the distinction between preventive and pre-emptive war, making it perfectly clear that the United States would act preventively, if it was decided that it was in its best interests to do so: to quote the sentiments of the President: 'This nation will not wait to be attacked again. We will take the fight to the enemy. There is only one course of action against (those who subscribe to this murderous ideology) to defeat them abroad before they attack us at home.'[62]

---

[59] See Renee Jeffrey, *Evil as Thoughtlessness. Human Suffering in an Age of Terror* (New York: Palgrave Macmillan, 2008).

[60] Rengger had greatly enjoyed the lecture given by Nicholas Wheeler on Trust at Chatham House.

[61] N.J. Rengger, 'The greatest treason? On the subtle temptations of preventive war', *International Affairs*, 84, 5 (2008), pp. 949–61. Here again Vassilios Paipais has reminded me, or rebuked me perhaps, that annoying as it may be Rengger was reticent to take a fixed position on anything that may bring the conversation to an end; he never wanted to be held accountable or described. Yet I began to see/believe that in later years he had developed far more of an aversion to violence than in his younger days.

[62] See President Bush, speech at Fort Bragg, 29 June 2005, available at: https//aaa.nbcnews.com>wbna8404774

To disagree with George W. Bush was not necessarily a difficult task but Rengger's quarry was not just the President. It was rather those in IR studies who sought to legitimize and champion the adoption of preventive war through adapting/perverting the just war tradition. For nearly a decade and a half Rengger demolished the arguments made by a series of scholars who all sought to shift the burden for war away from the traditional basis of restraint to a more permissive (in his view reckless?) use of military force. Their pretext was to prevent any harm such as had occurred on 9/11, to halt hurt before it could again be inflicted on the United States. Rengger discusses at length the pro-preventive war arguments of academics such as Buchanan, Keohane, and in considerable detail those of Michael Doyle,[63] opposing any idea that norms on the use of force should in the wake of 9/11 be transformed. His first objection was that the practice of preventive war made conflict more likely, hence:

> The advantage of the existing prohibition is that it at least requires actual harm to have occurred before we act; thinking we know harms are on the way is all too easy, but we may be mistaken; but then if we take preventive action, we have let the genie of war out of the bottle and will have the devil's own job putting it back.[64]

And here's the rub: his second objection was that (and this is the connection to his appreciation for Shklar's work) politicians, and their handling of state power during a supreme emergency may prove (surely would) prove to be expansionist, opaque, and frankly 'all too human'. To quote directly from Rengger: 'The Just War tradition, as I read it, has always been very sceptical not only about human motivation but also about human reasoning capacities.'[65] He was also profoundly opposed to any idea that 9/11 had fundamentally altered, in the way that Doyle claimed, the realities of global politics.[66]

At some point along the way Rengger though seemed to lose some of his much-prized objectivity or as others have suggested his appetite for uncertainty. All of us who knew him had recognized his commitment to pluralism, his respect for the views of an opponent, and, as noted, the value of conversation. Sometimes, much of the time, he was slippery in his views and this could be infuriating.[67] It was tricky to pin down what he believed – but

---

[63] Michael Doyle, *Striking First: Pre-emption and Prevention in International Conflict* (Princeton, NJ: Princeton University Press, 2011).

[64] N.J. Rengger, 'The greatest treason?', p. 957.

[65] Rengger, *The Greatest Treason*.

[66] Kennedy-Pipe and Rengger, 'Apocalypse now?'

[67] See the comments by James Turner Johnson in 'Three perspectives on just war'. He comments: 'I suggest that Rengger owes his readers more.'

the conversation was for Nick the thing. In his final few years he became more opinionated and indeed more querulous with those who disagreed with him or with whom he disagreed. Indeed, in a somewhat uncharacteristic and waspish earlier barb he accused the military historian John Keegan of 'foolishness' after Keegan had written in his much-admired book *The Face of Battle* that 'the suspicion remains that battle is abolishing itself'.[68]

It was in Rengger's powerful criticisms (both public and private) of Jean Bethle Elshtain that I think he revealed the older perhaps more reflective man. His objections to the pronouncements of Elshtain,[69] someone he counted as a friend centred on her pivot to act not just in defence of American patriotism, but as stalwart of the Bush Administration. This along with her very public endorsement of the use of torture as an instrument in the wider war on terror was for Rengger just startling. For Rengger, her turn caused offence in two ways: one was the endorsement of the brutality of the state apparatus and the dressing up of it as patriotism – a sentiment which trumped that of anyone or anything else. But the second was that she had become mired in the politics – that is, how actually to do the ugly business of war. I have elsewhere written on his (our) deep disappointment with Elshtain.[70]

What Rengger resisted was her endorsement of the excesses and the breaking of crucial norms of state behaviour. These included some practices such as extraordinary rendition, the operation of the so-called black sites and an easy acceptance of physical abuse by the United States and its allies. He especially objected to the Elshtain line of questioning what might or should constitute torture; he disliked her musing on whether a slap constituted torture or something else. For him it was in fact something else: it was characteristic of the overreach of the state. In this respect he heartily endorsed Nancy Sharman and her view that 'torture did not happen by accident', that it took legions of doctors, administrators, and soldiers, all officially sanctioned to make abuse happen.[71] (Note here the link to C.S. Lewis and his own description of bad decisions taken by faceless bureaucrats in well-lit offices.)

---

[68] John Keegan, *The Face of Battle: A Study of Agincourt, Waterloo and the Somme* (London: Pimlico, 1976).

[69] Elshtain was Laura Spelman Rockefeller professor of Social and Politics Ethics at the University of Chicago. Jean Bethke Elshtain, *Just War Against Terror. The Burden of American Power in a Violent World* (New York: Basic Books, 2003). See also Jean Bethke Elshtain, *Woman and War* (Chicago: University of Chicago Press, 1987).

[70] Caroline Kennedy-Pipe, 'Nick Rengger and Two Wars', *International Relations*(2020). See also Caroline Kennedy-Pipe, 'Jean Bethke Elshtain (1941–2013): a woman's refuge, Baghdad, summer, 2015', in Richard Ned Lebow, Peter Schouten, and Hidemi Suganami (eds), *The Return of the Theorists: Dialogues with Great Thinkers in International Relations* (Houndmills, Basingstoke: Palgrave Macmillan, 2016), pp. 352–61.

[71] Nancy Sherman, *Stoic Warriors: The Ancient Philosophy of the Military Mind* (Oxford: Oxford University Press, 2005).

Rengger's disquiet also arose from a profound disagreement over Elshtain's role as public intellectual (a problem he did not seem to have with Ignatieff but then Ignatieff was not really of the Academy). Elshtain's visibility as a public figure clashed with his own view of a scholar as standing above or outside the stormy clouds of politics. But his objections to Elshtain lay also with his lifelong antagonism towards the imposition of ideals on others. In perhaps one of his finest reviews in 2012 he was asked to respond to Michael Ignatieff's view of a Moral World.[72] Based on Oakeshott's view that ethics are to be found in 'the exercise of habitual affection and good conduct' Nick noted that inevitably any form of global ethics involved subordination, power, and ultimately the exercise of violence because we live in a world of plurality. There it is again; his view that no one ideology, no one state should dominate. Elshtain had therefore in her later years committed the sin of 'ceding to one state – one sovereign – the power to act in the world in an unlimited way – whether much of the world wanted it or not'.[73]

Conclusion

I am keenly aware that any chapter about a close friend can easily turn into a chapter about oneself. Although, on reflection, one of Rengger's great gifts was his pliability; his very elasticity intellectually allowed one to find shape in him. My own work on war though, supportive as he always was, seemed to increasingly upset him, not in the way that Elshtain's had done, but in its weary and sometimes intimate trajectory of death across the battlefields of the Middle East and beyond. It perhaps (as did so many of the other scholars of war that he valued)[74] challenged his view of war (and certainly warriors) as continuing to ape the code of chivalry that he had found in his interpretation of the Middle Ages. Sometimes Nick used to quote Tim O'Brien that: 'War is mystery and terror and adventure and courage and discovery and holiness and pity and despair and longing and love. War is nasty, war is fun, war is thrilling, war is drudgery. War makes you a man; war makes you dead.'[75]

He never really confronted that final line apart as I have indicated when he did begin to think more about the business of war – but this was only at the end of his life. Despite or perhaps because of his trenchant criticism of Elshtain there is something terribly moving in his final thoughts on her.

---

[72] Rengger, 'A global ethic and the hybrid character of the moral world', *Ethics and International Affairs* (2012), pp. 27–31.

[73] Rengger, *The Anti-Pelagian Imagination*, p. 140.

[74] I think here of his affection for Theo Farrell, Christopher Coker, and many others.

[75] Tim O'Brien, *The Things They Carried* (Boston: Houghton Middlin, 1990).

He ends his second essay on Elshtain (after her death) in the following way: 'I was waiting in anticipation of how Jean would have responded to this thought. Alas, now I will only be able to wonder.'[76] I wonder what he would make of my claim that he had begun to move to a form of pacifism – albeit as I mentioned earlier – one that was in true Rengger style somewhat lightly worn.

---

[76] Rengger, 'Elshtain 2. Violence and the two sovereigns', in Rengger, *The Anti-Pelagian Imagination*, p. 141.

10

Just War as Tradition in a Civil International Order

Valerie Morkevičius[1]

Introduction

Nicholas Rengger's just war thought defies simple classification. His work clearly stands as a critique of both the legalist and revisionist approaches, which he deems overly optimistic about human nature and human capacities, and thus ultimately overly optimistic about the possibility that human institutions could work effectively to 'solve' the problem of war. Nor can Rengger be easily categorized as a just war thinker in the classical vein – while he clearly appreciates theological approaches both past and present, it would be a stretch to say that his work is primarily grounded in theology. Even contemporary neo-classical approaches to just war thinking face Rengger's critique as rather too state-centric in their approach. In Rengger's thinking, questions of just war are part and parcel of the broader project of international relations (IR). Rengger's broader approach to thinking about IR also transcends the usual paradigmatic pigeon-holes. Despite his deep scepticism about the robustness of international order, Rengger nonetheless calls contemporary realism to task for its insufficient interest in the problem of order. Likewise, he finds classical realists to be kindred spirits in many respects, but cautions against accepting their view of politics as tragedy.

---

[1] This chapter was meant to have been written by my friend and colleague, Amy Eckert, who would have produced a far more brilliant piece than I have managed to do in her stead. Sadly, she passed away suddenly and all too soon in the summer of 2020.

Rengger's fundamental scepticism takes nothing for granted, questioning everything. For some, this might leave the impression that Rengger is perhaps better at asking questions than answering them, better at pointing out the pitfalls in others' arguments about the ethics of war than at mapping out a way around them. I would argue, however, that this is precisely Rengger's *point*. We begin to go astray the moment we think ourselves to be standing on firm ground. Those of us asking questions about what is right and wrong in war are certainly seeking a kind of Truth. We want to know what is Just. Rengger's relentless scepticism is unsettling because it demands that we accept that none of us will ever quite get to such an understanding. But this isn't a blank cheque to succumb to nihilism, or to relativism, or even to some sort of tragic acceptance of our imperfectability. Instead, Rengger sees scepticism as opening opportunities for dialogue and deliberative discussions with others in which we leave open the possibility that our own original position may be incorrect and thus in need of modification. It is this scepticism which serves as the foundation for Rengger's conception of a 'civil international order'. We can't reach the ultimate answers – and thus we can't construct utopias – but there is value in grappling with the questions nonetheless. Rengger's refusal to accept the 'tragic' view of IR embodies this belief that discomfort with the recognition of our limited philosophical eyesight and practical capabilities can't be used as an excuse for shrugging off our human responsibility to keep thinking and acting.

To attempt to better clarify what Rengger's sceptical approach to just war entails, this chapter is organized around three key questions. What is just war thinking in Rengger's view? What challenges face the just war tradition today? How should we respond to them? In sketching out answers to these questions, I draw on a close reading of Rengger's work on just war (and IR theory more broadly) to suggest some practical ways in which we can not only make our peace with not being able to find the Truth, but even find ways to nevertheless thrive in its pursuit.

What is just war thinking?

Fundamentally, for Rengger, just war thinking is a tradition of 'practical morality'.[2] Good judgement, he argues, was always at the heart of the classical just war tradition 'rather than the language of justice in war per se'.[3]

---

[2] Nicholas Rengger, 'The judgment of war: on the idea of legitimate force in world politics', *Review of International Studies* 31 (2005), pp. 143–61 (149). Elsewhere, Rengger describes it as 'an aid to practical reflection'. Nicholas Rengger, 'On the just war tradition in the twenty-first century', *International Affairs* 78, 2(2002), pp. 353–63 (355).
[3] Rengger, 'The judgment of war', p. 144.

It therefore demands that we engage in casuistry, using our best judgement to do what we can to act justly even in difficult contexts. 'Although war is a realm of extremes, it is still the general human moral realm not some separate realm,' Rengger writes, and so the nature of what justice requires in war is not fundamentally different than what justice demands in other contexts.[4] What the just war tradition is asking us to do, then, is to think about what it is 'to do justice to ourselves and our common moral concerns even at the extremes of human life and conduct'.[5] In this, Rengger draws inspiration from Oliver O'Donovan's assertation that the just war tradition 'is in fact, neither a "theory", nor about "just wars", but "*a proposal for doing justice in the theatre of war*"'.[6] The idea of justice, after all, suggests something abstract and final, while judgement is always an act in progress, a practical response to the real world around us.

Contemporary just war thinkers inhabit three distinct camps. There are those who explore the ethics of the use of force from a base within the historical just war tradition – scholars such as James Turner Johnson (whom Rengger cites frequently, and whose language of just war thinking as practical morality he invokes).[7] Then there are those thinkers who continue down the path Michael Walzer forged, similarly insisting that just war thinking is a form of practical morality, but drawing on common sense and applied philosophy to develop arguments about the nature of justice in war, rather than a commitment to canonical sources.[8] Rengger refers to this as the juridical approach. Finally, there are those who advance arguments of a revisionist sort (Cécile Fabre comes to mind), whose approach is perhaps most similar to analytical philosophy. These thinkers Rengger describes as cosmopolitan.

Rengger's assertion that the just war tradition is best understood as a 'practical' moral system clearly indicates that he has more in common with the traditionalists or the Walzerian legalists. After all, Rengger makes it quite clear that he finds the cosmopolitan revisionists' approach far too idealistic. In his writing, he sets himself apart from those who would argue that just war thinking as a tradition is primarily organized around justice – a perspective that lends itself to an expansive view of the possibilities for the just use of

---

4   Ibid., p. 153.

5   Ibid., p. 157.

6   O. O'Donovan, *The Just War Revisited* (Cambridge: Cambridge University Press, 2003), p. vii, in Rengger, 'The judgment of war: on the idea of legitimate force in world politics', p. 152, emphasis in original.

7   James Turner Johnson, 'A practically informed morality of war: just war, international law, and a changing world order', *Ethics and International Affairs* 31, 4 (2017a), pp. 453–65.

8   Michael Walzer, 'On reciprocity and practical morality: a response to Sagan and Valentino', *Ethics and International Affairs* 33, 4 (2019), pp. 445–50.

force in the world as, after all, there are always a great deal of wrongs to be righted. Instead, he argues, it is better to think of the tradition as aiming 'to prevent injustice', rather than securing justice.[9] This subtle reframing reminds us that just war thinking should always remain sceptical about the potential of violent force to achieve good ends, even as it recognizes that such force may sometimes be necessary.

What does it mean to take just war thinking as a project aimed at preventing injustice, rather than securing it? The answer to this question is emblematic of Rengger's underlying sceptical approach to politics. It can also help us evaluate Rengger's relationship with both the traditional and legalist schools of just war thinking. In Rengger's view, the teleocratic turn in both domestic and international politics is not one to be embraced. And teleocratic approaches to politics are indeed everywhere. To some extent, teleocratic conceptions of politics are unavoidable – but Rengger cautions against allowing them to become more dominant.[10] Ultimately, this has led to a 'clash of teleocracies' in the contemporary international order, where each side's assumption that it has the monopoly on the proper understanding of the right aims of government endangers the very idea of civil association.[11]

Rengger rejects all such teleocratic claims, arguing that 'in general terms people cannot be trusted with too much power, and expanding the power of the state – or, indeed, of other agencies as proxies for states – to make war, even for very good reasons, necessarily (and not just contingently) will give them too much power'.[12] To allow teleocratic conceptions of politics to progress 'unchecked or unbalanced' is to undermine the very foundation of civil liberty, ultimately rendering civil politics impossible.[13] Pushing back against such teleocratic thinking is to be highly sceptical about claims that this or that war is necessary to advance the cause of justice. In other words, we must recognize that while force may sometimes be necessary to stop another from using force unjustly, force is a tool unlikely to *generate* real justice on its own, for both pragmatic and philosophical reasons.

Rengger's scepticism regarding teleocratic claims seems to position him closer to traditional just war thinkers than to contemporary legalists. This is for two reasons. First, traditional just war thinkers generally share Rengger's overall scepticism about teleocratic claims regarding the ends of the state in general, and just cause for war in particular. Augustine, after all, cautioned that the earthly city can never achieve true justice – although it can indeed

---

[9]   Rengger, 'The judgment of war', p. 157.
[10] Nicholas Rengger, *Just War and International Order: The Uncivil Condition in World Politics* (Cambridge: Cambridge University Press, 2013a), p. 167.
[11] Ibid., p. 173.
[12] Ibid., p. 175.
[13] Ibid., p. 176.

establish a reasonably just community, within the limits of human capacity. The peaceful communal order that the state creates is imperfect – as all human institutions must be by definition – but for Augustine it is nonetheless worth protecting.[14] As we will see in the concluding section, for Augustine as for Rengger, it is the value found in this human capacity to make the world around us better – never perfect – that prevents scepticism from collapsing into nihilism or tragedy.

Second, as Rengger points out, legalist just war thinkers tend to be statist, treating the state as the natural and obvious locus of right authority. Traditionalist just war thinkers, on the other hand, link right authority to the preservation of a more or less just domestic order in a way that destabilizes the connection between just authority and the state.[15] This insistence that right authority remains an open question further reinforces traditionalists' scepticism about any teleocratic claims that might be made on behalf of the state.[16] It is worth noting when one of Rengger's favourite traditionalists, Jean Bethke Elshtain, strayed away from this scepticism after 9/11, Rengger reacted by arguing that a better way forward would lie 'in the direction of a more civil and less statist form of politics', what he termed a 'nomocratic form of politics'.[17] When we stretch beyond attempting to respond practically and within our means to the problems before us towards various ideas of how we might radically overcome those problems, we slip into an ultimately doomed utopianism – a path which might very well wreak more havoc than the original problems ever would have.

Just war thinking in practice

How do we put such a sceptical, non-teleocratic, just war tradition into practice? Rengger's vision of a well-judged war (as opposed to a *just* war) demands that we carefully '*weigh* judgments about threat, proportionality, and the like against one another'.[18] Such political judgement can never be reduced

---

[14] Augustine, *City of God* (London: Penguin Books, 1984), XV, 4, p. 60.

[15] Valerie Morkevičius, 'Sovereignty and authority in the work of James Turner Johnson', in Eric D. Patterson and Marc LiVecche (eds), *Responsibility and Restraint: James Turner Johnson and the Just War Tradition* (Middletown, RI: Stone Tower Press, 2020), pp. 97–124 (99, 113).

[16] Indeed, much of Rengger's work reflects Michael Oakeshott's philosophical struggle against the progressive march of teleocratic thinking in modern societies, a theme which several other chapters in this volume take up in depth, including Chris Brown's chapter. In his arguments on just war, Rengger is consistent in pushing against any form of idealism or perfectionism.

[17] Nicholas Rengger, *The Anti-Pelagian Imagination in Political Theory and International Relations: Dealing in Darkness* (London and New York: Routledge, 2017), p. 141.

[18] Rengger, 'The judgment of war', p. 155, emphasis in original.

to a list of principles that must be ticked off to declare a particular war just or unjust. While accepting that 'in some contexts it will be unquestionably helpful to have a list of categories that we need to think about', Rengger counsels that 'in others it will not and in any event, it is important not to give greater weight than is necessary to the excessively juristic aspects of the contemporary just war tradition'.[19] As 'tools, not masters', the categories serve as open invitations to ask questions and to reflect.[20]

The just war tradition thus calls on us to take a 'deliberative posture', meaning that everything must be questioned – starting with the location of right authority. Rengger suggests that in constructing the tradition on 'the twin poles of authority and judgment' classical just war thinkers intended us to question even right authority, taking nothing for granted.[21] To this end, Rengger approvingly cites James Turner Johnson's work, with its emphasis on right authority and right intention. Too many contemporary just war thinkers, Rengger worries, have come to elide right authority with the state, treating that association almost as a given. On the other hand, Rengger asserts, the just war tradition more properly understood 'makes no assumption about the *moral* primacy of the state'.[22]

Although it is certainly true that in the modern world, 'authority, to be sure, normally flows from well-constituted government', Rengger cautions that nonetheless 'not all such government has "right authority" in all circumstances'.[23] This caution matters because, as Rengger points out, the assumption that right authority is properly limited to the realm of states not only ignores the rightful justice claims of some non-state actors, but also blinds us to the fact that right authority has always been contested – meaning that our contemporary world with its fears of sub-state and trans-national violence is really not so different from the past at all.

Since the mid-1990s, some just war thinkers along with liberal IR scholars have come to put their faith in international institutions, and the international community itself. While this move might seem to decentre the state, Rengger observes that states still remain the dominant actors, as it is states who make up these institutions. Furthermore, Rengger, always a sceptic about the possibility of stable cooperation, critiques such faith on pragmatic grounds. What evidence do we have that international institutions can really transcend the interests and politics of the states who make them up?

---

[19]   Ibid., p. 154.
[20]   Ibid., p. 154.
[21]   Ibid., p. 154.
[22]   Ibid., p. 153, emphasis in original.
[23]   Ibid., p. 154.

Rengger also raises an ethical red flag. Those who wish to centre international society around institutions rather than states tend to award such institutions a special kind of legitimacy – in the language of just war thinking, they are bestowed with right authority. But for Rengger, treating the international community as the obviously appropriate bearer of legitimate authority begs the question 'not only how such a "community" should be constituted but *what* kind of authority it would require and *how* it might acquire it'.[24] This concern reflects Rengger's earlier critique of communitarian approaches to international society, which he saw as rather circular. If international society is 'born in the mind' – if it comes into existence because we have voluntarily created and accepted certain norms – how do we adjudicate debates over the nature of those normative commitments?[25] And if such norms are assumed to have arisen out of actual practice (or at least are knowable to us because they reflect what states usually do), how could such norms possibly serve as an ethical yardstick measuring anything other than habits of entrenched self-interest?[26]

Rengger's scepticism about the nature of international society and its norms leads him to argue that we must be cautious about the desire to lift the responsibility for war-making from the shoulders of states. Entrusting war to institutions might seem to solve certain problems of authority and intent, but Rengger's scepticism urges us to think about the potential ethical and practical consequences of such a move. After all, the attempt to institutionalize 'common purposes', even laudable ones, pushes us 'in a profoundly problematic and teleocratic direction', a direction that Rengger strenuously counsels us to avoid.[27] Indeed in his view, just war thinking should serve as 'a powerful critic of the tendency of political authority – all political authority, in all contexts – to use force to achieve its aims' while simultaneously accepting the realist claim that 'politics will always be about the use of force in some context or other'.[28] Right authority is always possessed by someone for something, and the sceptical just war thinker must ask in each case if the possessor and the purpose are truly properly aligned.

Beyond questioning the locus of right authority, the deliberative approach to just war thinking reveals Rengger's underlying scepticism in another way. Of course, we must be sceptical about human motivations – hence the just war tradition invites us to consider whether we have the right intent in using force – but we must also be fundamentally sceptical about the power

---

[24] Ibid., p. 156, emphasis in original.
[25] Nicholas Rengger, 'A city which sustains all things? Communitarianism and international society', *Millennium* 21, 3 (1992), pp. 353–69 (360, 362).
[26] Ibid., p. 365.
[27] Rengger, *Just War and International Order*, p. 132.
[28] Rengger, 'The judgment of war', p. 160.

of human reason to give accurate insight into those motivations. 'Not that we cannot reason', Rengger writes, 'but we cannot expect too much of our reason'.[29] We cannot assume that our list of ethical principles includes all the concerns we ought to think about, nor can we assume that we have really weighed them properly and fairly against each other, nor can we assume that we even have all the necessary facts at our disposal. There is a good deal more uncertainty in the world and in our powers of reasoning than many of us are comfortable with – but it is better to learn to live with that uncertainty than to look for ways out, whether of a rationalist or teleocratic nature. Just war thinking in the tradition of Augustine can help us remain consistently sceptical 'about the claims we make for ourselves'.[30] After all, Augustine himself was highly doubtful about the extent of human reason. It's not just that we can be deceived by others, but that we may even deceive ourselves about our own internal motivations. The same epistemological uncertainty that characterizes our attempt to understand the outside world applies to our inner worlds as well.

Intriguingly, Rengger's scepticism also points us to ways in which the just war tradition as it has evolved from its Western Christian roots can be applied in a diverse world, where various political communities draw from different political theories and different religions. Other just war thinkers have developed a variety of ways of responding to the critique that the tradition's rootedness means it cannot speak to other traditions, whether by attempting to develop secular premises for its principles (as Michael Walzer has, for example) or by arguing there is an underlying 'universal tradition of moral reasoning' that can be found not only in the Western tradition, but in a wide variety of others as well (as Terry Nardin does).[31] Still others have adopted an Aristotelian approach, focusing on virtues presumed to be universal.

But Rengger finds all of these to be lacking, whether because their assumptions are indefensible or because they see human character as too perfectible. Instead, Rengger suggests that if our thinking is characterized by a 'bracing scepticism and horror of war', we will naturally be open to the sort of truly deliberative conversations that can help us find common grounds with those whose traditions differ.[32] This openness should facilitate authentic 'conversation and dialogue – about similarities and differences, rules and responsibilities, conduct becoming and unbecoming'.[33] Importantly, this

---

[29] Rengger, *Just War and International Order*, p. 128.
[30] Rengger, 'The judgment of war', p. 159.
[31] Ibid., p. 159.
[32] Ibid., p. 159.
[33] Rengger, *Just War and International Order*, p. 171.

dialogue would have to be based on an '*openness to* pluralism', rather than a mere embrace of pluralism itself.[34] Underlying this embrace of pluralism is, unsurprisingly, Rengger's habitual scepticism: 'no practice is "universal" except in its own terms and no theory that claims universality can be an appropriate consideration of a practice'.[35]

For Rengger, a willingness to accept plurality as a fact of our world does not 'by any stretch of the imagination imply that one approach cannot be correct and others incorrect, though it might be a pertinent reminder of the necessity for scholarly humility', although it can leave open the possibility that in some cases, '*different* answers to certain questions can be true'.[36] In this, Rengger accepts what he calls 'the necessary logic of the hybrid character of the moral world', in which we simultaneously recognize that 'the thick commitments of particularity' are what really bind us morally, but 'that such commitments stand side by side with the requirements of living with others who do not share them – in our own communities and in others'.[37] To balance these two aspects of moral life – our habitual practice and our obligation to exercise reason to justify our actions – requires the exercise of judgement, tempered (as always) by a healthy dose of scepticism about our own underlying principles and our own reasoning skills.

We must, in other words, engage in dialogue by making 'real attempts to produce agreement, change minds or, anyway, seriously consider alternative or rival views'.[38] Following Oakeshott's understanding of pluralism, Rengger suggests such conversations are possible even between individuals definitively rooted in differing civilizational frameworks – not because there is some underlying universal civilization, but because 'civilized people, whatever their culture will recognize what the conversation requires', namely 'non-domineering and non-manipulative' modes of communication.[39] Here lies the heart of Rengger's idea of civil politics, 'a politics composed of limits and self-enacted restraints'.[40] By recognizing its own limits, this civil approach to politics naturally rejects the teleocratic approaches that Rengger so decries.

---

[34] Nicholas Rengger, 'Pluralism in international relations theory: three questions', *International Studies Perspectives* 16, 1 (2015a), pp. 32–9 (35), emphasis in original.

[35] Nicholas Rengger, Review of *Moral Constraints on War: Principles and Cases by Bruno Coppieters and Nick Fotion*, in *International Affairs* 79, 2 (2003a), pp. 643–4 (644).

[36] Rengger, 'Pluralism in international relations theory: three questions', p. 36, emphasis in original.

[37] Nicholas Rengger, 'A global ethic and the hybrid character of the moral world', *Ethics and International Affairs* 26, 1 (2012c), pp. 27–31 (30).

[38] Nicholas Rengger, *International Relations, Political Theory, and the Problem of Order: Beyond International Relations Theory?* (London; New York: Routledge, 2000a), p. 193.

[39] Nicholas Rengger, 'The boundaries of conversation: a response to Dallmayr', *Millennium* 30, 2 (2001), pp. 357–64 (359).

[40] Rengger, *Just War and International Order*, p. xii.

Rengger's commitment to openness – the willingness to accept that our own beliefs may be incorrect – means that we must be willing to debate not only the means by which we might achieve certain ends, but the ends themselves, with the full awareness that a stable agreement on those ends may not be forthcoming.

This perspective naturally differs from superficially similar arguments about how differing ethical and moral frameworks might meaningfully engage with each other. For example, Rengger decries Rawls' approach, which imagines we might be able to come to some sort of rational, universal agreement as to appropriate international norms as a form of 'dystopic liberalism'.[41] And while Rengger does not specifically engage Habermas, one can easily imagine that he would likewise find his constructivist approach to communicative ethics, which imagines the possibility of constructing a universal philosophical framework, as equally problematic. The Habermasian perspective, after all, relies on the presumption that a settled agreement on the right ends of politics is not only desirable, but possible. In short, Rengger's scepticism about the hope of some sort of universal agreement on norms means that we can never reasonably imagine a world in which we will no longer have sincere, deeply held disagreements about what is right – so there will never be an end point to the sort of open-minded dialogue Rengger proposes.

What challenges face the just war tradition today?

While Rengger's approach to just war thinking, as outlined earlier, is certainly unique, Rengger himself often frames his project as one of recapturing the pragmatic and sceptical habits of thought evidenced by early just war thinkers, particularly Augustine. Not unsurprisingly, then, Rengger looks with dismay at several emerging trends in contemporary just war thinking, particularly as these potentially dangerous shifts are driven not by those hostile to just war thinking, but by just war thinkers themselves and their academic allies, including liberal institutionalists. Rengger argues that three trends characterize contemporary just war thinking, particularly since the mid-20th century: secularization, legalization, and liberalization. Combined, these trends are pushing just war thinking in a dangerous direction, towards the expansion of justifications for the use of force.

The trend towards secularization in just war thinking is not entirely new. To some extent this process has been underway since at least the 18th century, as the most prominent strands of just war thought shifted from theology to law and philosophy. Historically, this secularization process is tied to the

---

[41] Rengger, *The Anti-Pelagian Imagination*, pp. 65–6.

evolution of international law, a development where Grotius' work stands at the crossroads between the classical, theologically inspired tradition and the modern, secular, and rather more legalistic version. Rengger notes that this trend intensified during the period of just war's 're-discovery' in the mid-20th century, when the tradition's 'dominant face' became decidedly 'secular and at least in broad terms sympathetic to liberal ideas'.[42]

Of course, the secularization of just war thinking parallels the broader secularization of political theory and ultimately Western societies. But such modernizing, secularizing reforms to the just war tradition have not come without a cost. As Rengger puts it, 'the way in which Walzer "revives" or ... "recaptures" the just war tradition does violence to some of the central insights of earlier versions of the tradition, insights that might be able to help us to overcome' some of the current issues caused by the juristic form of reasoning so popular in today's discourse.[43] The problem, as Rengger sees it, is that the legalist paradigm inevitably 'sets up the just war as fundamentally state-based and connected with the language of rights as it has evolved and developed within liberal modernity'.[44] By contrast, the theological tradition, aimed as it was at individuals and individual decision-making, is in Rengger's view more open to the possibility of right authority inhabiting a variety of political structures.

Aside from the way in which this secularization has problematically facilitated the legalization of the tradition (more on that in the next section), secularization has also encouraged the tradition to frame the state in teleocratic ways.[45] While Rengger never quite explicitly unpacks this assertion, his interest in Augustine likely offers insight into his line of reasoning. Augustine, after all, saw the state as a necessary bulwark against disorder. The state (or, less anachronistically, the polity) serves the good in so far as it helps us to regulate our interactions with each other and our neighbours – but it is a decidedly human institution and cannot, therefore, be a good *in itself*. Here again we see echoes of Rengger's scepticism. To accept a teleocratic framing of the state is to believe that the state should be directed towards the achievement of some good. But as Rengger (and Augustine) would caution us, the state can never really achieve such an aim. At best, individuals can work through the institutions of the state to

---

[42] Rengger, 'On the just war tradition in the twenty-first century', p. 355. See also Rengger, 'The judgment of war', p. 150.

[43] Rengger, 'The judgment of war', p. 144.

[44] Ibid., p. 150.

[45] Nicholas Rengger, 'The wager lost by winning? On the "triumph" of the just war tradition', in Anthony F. Lang, Jr, Cian O'Driscoll, and John Williams (eds), *Just War: Authority, Tradition, and Practice* (Washington, DC: Georgetown University Press, 2013c), pp. 283–98 (286).

avoid or mitigate injustice, but human institutions will always fall short of actually establishing justice. Thus, insofar as secularized just war thinking sees the ethics of force 'primarily in teleocratic terms as an instrument for the elimination of injustice', it has gone a step too far, promising something it can never deliver.[46]

One of the primary consequences of secularization, Rengger suggests, has been the increasing dominance of legalism in just war thinking. To put it bluntly, legal thought has become 'the baseline, if not the be all and end all of moral thinking in politics'.[47] This trend extends beyond the academy. Military and political elites, particularly in the West, now view the just war tradition though 'principally legal, rather than ... moral or ethical terms'.[48] As this legalistic way of thinking about justice and war 'has become sedimented more generally in the wider political culture', just war's ability to really speak to the moral complexities of contemporary conflict has become strained.[49]

One key problem Rengger identifies with the legalistic trend in contemporary just war thinking, particularly in public discourse, is the assumption that morality and legality are 'one and the same'.[50] But as Rengger reminds us, this simply isn't true, even on the domestic level. After all, anyone can easily think of examples where obeying the law would be immoral, and thus where disobeying could even be a moral imperative (consider Nazi race laws, for example). And if this is true domestically, 'then it must be equally (if not more) true in the sphere of international law', which raises the question of what framework we can use to adjudicate those cases where our moral and legal obligations conflict.[51] The problem is, however, that in having done away with its underlying ethical and moral foundations, contemporary legalist just war thinking cannot offer a very useful response to such questions.

Another problem with legalist approaches to just war thinking, in Rengger's view, is that they undermine what he sees as one of the strengths of the classical just war tradition – its emphasis on ' "casuistic", case-based' reasoning.[52] Good judgement can never simply be reduced to the question of legality, although of course, it may take legality into account. Thinking in legal terms encourages us to see each aspect of a particular war discretely, divorcing *jus ad bellum* from *jus in bello*, and also analyzing each principle

---

[46] Ibid., p. 291.
[47] Rengger, 'The judgment of war', p. 151.
[48] Rengger, 'On the just war tradition in the twenty-first century', p. 355.
[49] Rengger, 'The judgment of war', p. 150.
[50] Nicholas Rengger, 'Political theory and the judgment of war', *Contemporary Politics* 13, 3(2007), pp. 243–55 (250–1).
[51] Ibid., p. 251.
[52] Rengger, *Just War and International Order*, p. 156.

(cause, intent, proportionality, authority, and so on) separately. But Rengger strenuously cautions against such a practice, warning us against using just war principles as checklists and arguing that the distinction between *jus ad bellum* and *jus in bello* should not be treated as a ' "load bearing" distinction'.[53] Any particular conflict must be judged holistically, and the practice of deciding *how* each principle should be weighed against the others is an act of judgement in itself.

The secularization and legalization of just war thinking are further tied to a third trend: liberalization. As with the history of the secularization of just war thought, its liberalization is also part and parcel of a broader historical trend in Western political thought. Since the Enlightenment, liberal thinkers have come to believe 'in the capacity of individuals and societies to reshape the character of politics' and to fix its problems – including the problem of war itself.[54] Liberals, in Rengger's eyes, take for granted an understanding of history as a story of progress – of the gradual reform of individuals and societies towards the better. If this is true, then the 'most obvious and egregious challenges' to building a fairer world ought to be overcome, particularly 'physical brutality and oppression, practiced by the strong against the weak'.[55]

While non-violent means can certainly be invoked to achieve such aims, 'in the background there would have to be the possibility of the use of force to enforce compliance with international norms, or, in other words, it would require "intervention" in international relations'.[56] When contemporary just war thinkers, influenced by liberal thought, shift away from Augustinian scepticism towards 'a more rationalistic and more optimistic assessment both of the proclivities of individuals and groups, including states, and of our ability to create and set up institutional procedures that can manage a permissive attitude to the use of force' they enter into dangerous territory.[57]

While proponents of the liberal democratic peace might argue that at least between democracies the problem of war has been solved, Rengger remains sceptical: 'that liberals have been hostile to war is unquestionably true, that they have waged it with uncommon zeal is equally true'.[58] If democracies don't fight among themselves, he asserts, it's because they have nothing to fight with each other about, as their interests do not conflict so severely. On the other hand, Rengger argues that the tendency of liberals and just war thinkers to embrace a broader array of justifications for the use of force

---

[53] Rengger, 'The judgment of war', p. 154.
[54] Rengger, *Just War and International Order*, p. 54.
[55] Ibid., p. 103.
[56] Ibid., p. 103.
[57] Ibid., p. 132.
[58] Rengger, *International Relations, Political Theory, and the Problem of Order*, p. 123.

stems from the belief that today's world is a radically different one, a world fraught with hitherto unimaginable threats that must be addressed head on. The resulting deep concern with the disorder liberals see outside the zone of liberal democratic states drives an interventionist foreign policy whose result in the 21st century seems to have generated quite a bit of war in exchange for very little democratic progress.

Altogether, these modern trends towards the secularization, legalization, and ultimately the liberalization of just war thinking have added up to the belief among some just war thinkers that the set of justifiable conditions for the use of force ought to be further expanded.[59] Rengger voices some surprise at this development, as in his view, the just war tradition 'is supposed to be about the *restraint* of war'.[60] Elsewhere, Rengger describes the trend towards a more expansive justification of war in less sanguine terms, as 'the imperial temptation'[61] and the 'greatest treason'.[62] Ironically, this expansion has been driven not by proponents of realpolitik, but by those who view IR through a liberal lens and – perhaps even more counterintuitively – by just war thinkers themselves. Specifically, Rengger notes that the call to broaden the scope of permissible uses of force is driven 'by strong supporters of the just war tradition (which has always excoriated preventive war) and strong supporters of the international rule of law (which has always outlawed it)'.[63]

This recognition that the threat comes from within generates the tone of deep disappointment which permeates Rengger's discussion of this topic. This is poignantly evident in his critique of Jean Bethke Elshtain, a fellow Augustinian thinker whose work he clearly admires. In his critique of her passionate response to 9/11 in *Just War Against Terror*, Rengger puts it bluntly. Elshtain's willingness to sign off on the more or less permanent use of force in the name of the 'global common good' fails, in Rengger's view, to recognize 'the impermanence of power and the fragility of virtue', representing instead a willingness to 'take up the ring of power'.[64] With this reference to *The Lord of the Rings*, Rengger reminds us of the hubris in believing that we can be trusted to use our power wisely. Here is where Elshtain – and too many other just war thinkers – have let Rengger down

---

[59] Rengger, *Just War and International Order*, p. xii.
[60] Ibid., p. xii, emphasis in original.
[61] Rengger, 'The judgment of war', p. 156.
[62] Rengger, *Just War and International Order* p. 132. See also N. Rengger, 'The greatest treason? On the subtle temptations of preventive war', *International Affairs* 84, 5(2008), pp. 949–61.
[63] Rengger, *Just War and International Order*, p. 10.
[64] Nicholas Rengger, 'Just war against terror? Jean Bethke Elshtain's burden and American power', *International Affairs* 80, 1(2004), pp. 107–16 (116).

by forgetting that a 'wise Augustinian would suggest such uses both will and should be limited and rare'.[65]

In particular, Rengger identifies two directions in which some just war thinkers are pushing at the boundaries of just cause: humanitarian intervention and preventive war. By addressing these two different types of uses of force in one breath, as it were, Rengger reveals the uncomfortable (if not shocking) way in which justifications for both humanitarian intervention and preventive war are cut from the same teleocratic cloth. This discomfiting realization should prompt those who support humanitarian intervention, but not preventive force, to seek 'a principled way of distinguishing the two practices'.[66]

Nevertheless, Rengger clearly has more sympathy for those advancing the logic of humanitarian intervention than for those attempting to justify preventive war. After all, those who argue forcibly for the moral imperative of humanitarian interventions are at root well-intentioned, desiring to protect human rights and human lives. Such scholars are 'genuinely committed to thinking through ways in which human beings might be able to regulate their collective affairs more benignly, more effectively, and with less likely violations of the things we hold most dear'.[67] But, Rengger warns, 'by seeking to institutionalize such claims … contemporary international society is running the risk that undid Dr. Frankenstein: making a creature that will exceed anybody's ability to control or direct it'.[68] Once we begin to countenance non-defensive uses of force, where will it end? What might be the unintended consequences?

Instead, Rengger argues, we should be 'very suspicious about many (if not all) claims for humanitarian intervention'.[69] There are a good many wrongs that could stand to be righted in the world, and we must think carefully about whether or not *force* is the appropriate way to go about righting them. After all, force is a costly tool whose success is uncertain. Furthermore, given that there are significant disputes in the international community as to what sets of human rights matter most, opening the door to humanitarian interventions for the sake of causes liberal democracies deem important also means opening the door to humanitarian interventions other types of polities might see as valuable. In addition, echoing a concern famously raised by Alan Kuperman's work on humanitarian interventions, Rengger worries that any such mechanism might create what amounts to a system of

---

[65] Ibid., p. 116.
[66] Amy Eckert, 'The just war tradition: restraint on the use of force or partner in crime?' *International Studies Review* 17 (2015), pp. 457–9 (458).
[67] Rengger, *Just War and International Order*, p. 133.
[68] Ibid., p. 10.
[69] Ibid., p. 123.

perverse incentives to create circumstances where the institutional process will be used.[70] For all of these reasons, then, it is prudential to maintain an attitude of scepticism towards intervention in other states.

For advocates of the preventive use of force, Rengger has less patience. While one could argue that humanitarian intervention intersects with the classical just war tradition's concern with punishing wrongdoing, it is hard to see how preventive war could ever be justifiable within the traditional framework.[71] As with humanitarian intervention, the inspiration to call for a broadening of the realm of just cause is underpinned by the belief that the world has changed radically of late, particularly since 9/11.[72] But even *if* we accepted the claim that today's world is radically different than that of the past, Rengger asserts, there would still be 'very good reasons for not developing a doctrine of justifiable preventive war'.[73] First of all, from a pragmatic point of view, Rengger wonders what hope there is for an effective and fair mechanism that would 'guarantee that states will not abuse the institutional processes set up to establish "humanitarian interventions" or "justifiable preventive wars"', given that states themselves are part of the problem.[74]

Second, Rengger reminds us that there are ethical reasons we ought to shy away from preventive war. The just war tradition, in its classical form, denies the legitimacy of preventive force, instead demanding that force always be the last resort. But this call to restraint – and the exploration of other options – isn't only because force is 'intrinsically bad', but also because it is ultimately unpredictable.[75] Given Rengger's scepticism about the powers of human reason, this critique is unsurprising. It is true, of course, that even in wars of necessity we cannot be sure that our use of force will achieve our desired ends. But there is a significant moral difference. In one case, war has been forced upon us by another, while in the case of preventive war, we have chosen to take on the risk of war all on our own. If we get it wrong, the responsibility is entirely ours.

Third, Rengger voices an epistemological concern laden with ethical implications. When launching a preventive war, how can we be sure that the threat we fear would really come to pass if we did not act? Given the proportionality requirement that we weigh the harms of war against the good we hope to achieve, this is an ethically urgent question. After all, 'events are always uncertain and projected ones even more so than any other sort'.[76] For

---

[70] Ibid., p. 124.
[71] Ibid., p. 115.
[72] Ibid., p. 117.
[73] Ibid., p. 123.
[74] Ibid., p. 123.
[75] Ibid., p. 126.
[76] Ibid., p. 128.

this reason, Rengger cautions that a benefit of 'the existing prohibition is that it at least requires actual harms before we act; thinking we know harms are on the way is all too easy but may be mistaken; but then, if we have taken "preventive action", we have let the genie of war out of its bottle and will have the devil's own time putting it back'.[77]

How should just war thinking respond to such challenges?

Rengger's work goes beyond mere critique to suggest some practical ways that we might respond to the recent sea change in the tenor of just war thinking. On the one hand, we could respond by adopting new disciplinary or methodological approaches, whether by drawing on theology or IR realism. On the other, we could respond by adopting new habits of thought, embracing scepticism about the uniqueness of our own era and even our own powers of reason.

One implication of Rengger's line of argument is that we should attempt to reclaim some of the half-forgotten insights of the classical tradition. Writing on the intersection between theology and IR, Rengger argues that the 'conversation between theology and IR should be renewed and indeed deepened'; it is likely he would argue the same applies to the narrower field of just war thinking.[78] Taking this injunction seriously could mean following in the footsteps of James Turner Johnson, Daniel Brunstetter, Cian O'Driscoll, and others who are working to resurrect the classical tradition by building explicitly on the work of canonical just war thinkers. Such an approach would naturally combat all three of the worrisome trends Rengger identifies, but its theological overtones might limit the breadth of those who participate in the conversation. This is particularly the case as Rengger reminds us that when we think about religion in IR, we are grappling with questions of 'truth or falsity', for which we need some sort of external framework if we are to evaluate truth claims coming from different traditions (or different thinkers within a single tradition) in any meaningful way.[79] In lieu of such a common framework, perhaps the best we will be able to do is to seek 'to do

---

[77] Ibid., p. 128.

[78] Nicholas Rengger, 'On theology and international relations: world politics beyond the empty sky', *International Relations* 27, 2(2013b), pp. 141–57 (153). Rengger also takes up the implications of theology for understanding the 'crisis of the modern' in international relations in his last article, Nicholas Rengger, 'Between transcendence and necessity: Eric Voeglin, Martin Wight, and the crisis of modern international relations', *Journal of International Relations and Development* 22 (2019a), pp. 327–45.

[79] Nicholas Rengger, 'Eternal return? Modes of encountering religion in international relations', *Millennium* 32, 2(2003b), pp. 327–36 (335).

justice' to all the various ways we can encounter religion – 'philosophical, historical, practical and many others' – allowing for a humble scepticism as to whether or not our own particular lens is really the most fitting.[80] This leaves us with the uncomfortable – but realistic – realization that we will never actually get to some sort of final, complete, universally acceptable knowledge of Truth. But rather than seeing the pursuit of truth as a fruitless task, we should instead recognize that the impossibility of reaching a final conclusion may actually be a good thing – such 'epistemological scepticism' serves as 'the motor behind the development of modern philosophy'.[81]

Another disciplinary approach we could consider adopting is to inject just war thinking with a bit of IR realism as a way to tame the overly optimistic, idealistic direction the tradition is taking. Classical realists, after all, accept that 'humans are frail, limited beings', whose best efforts to establish order (or justice or peace) do not always succeed.[82] From this point of view, 'politics is indeed finite and limited', a perspective that encourages restraint.[83] Unlike their neorealist counterparts, Rengger argues, classical realists take the problem of order seriously, and do recognize a thin sort of international society. This makes their perspective both more reflective of reality and more amenable to ethical reflection. By contrast, 'neo-realism is and can only be silent on all of the most important questions facing contemporary world politics, since only a normative defence of "order" (even understood as they do) could justify the actions and policies they usually claim to recommend'.[84]

Still, classical realism is not without its shortcomings. Rengger cautions us against accepting the view that the character of IR is inherently tragic.[85] Following Michael Oakeshott, Rengger suggests that the concept of 'tragedy' isn't quite the right way of thinking about the reality of IR. When we class all of it as tragic, we remove the possibility for both the sincere moral evaluation of our actions and even, ultimately, for human action itself. Instead, Rengger wants us to think about how we can learn from the 'precariousness of our situation', from 'human life and its vicissitudes as it is and they are', some way of thinking about practical ways 'of making the world a better or a safer place'.[86] In other words, we must somehow learn from the realists a healthy scepticism about the capacity of humans

---

[80] Ibid., p. 336.
[81] Vassilios Paipais, 'Between faith and scepticism: Nicholas Rengger's reflections on the hybridity of modernity', *International Relations* 34, 4, pp. 627–733 (629).
[82] Rengger, *International Relations, Political Theory, and the Problem of Order*, p. 60.
[83] Ibid., p. 60.
[84] Ibid., p. 75.
[85] Nicholas Rengger, 'Tragedy or scepticism? Defending the anti-Pelagian mind in world politics', *International Relations* 19, 3(2005a), pp. 321–8 (323).
[86] Ibid., p. 327.

to make good decisions, as well as the limits on the possibility of order in the international system, without falling prey to the temptation to throw up our hands and say that the world simply is as it is, and can neither be changed nor judged for it.

Beyond drawing on such disciplinary approaches, Rengger's work suggests we can also combat the teleocratic turn in just war thinking by adopting a more sceptical frame of mind, particularly by questioning the uniqueness of our own era and the power of reason. Rengger frequently urges his readers to think a bit more critically about the historical moment in which we find ourselves. Arguing that 'the world of post-9/11 is very much the world of pre-9/11, indeed of pre-1989 (and even pre-1945) in many respects', he asserts that while of course things have changed – they always do – 'what has changed does not warrant the kinds of evaluative claims – and political decisions – that have been, and are being, attributed to it'.[87] To defend this point, Rengger rejects the usual claims that are made about the significance of 9/11. In Rengger's telling, 9/11 doesn't mark a turning point in the amount of conflict in the world, as 'world politics has always been conflictual – though not necessarily violent – and riven by major differences of interest and power and it still is'.[88] It also doesn't herald a revival of the clash of civilizations. (Rengger is deeply sceptical that such a lens does much to help us understand IR, and even if it did, civilizational and cultural differences have long served as touchpoints for violent confrontation, even before 9/11.[89]) And 9/11 certainly does not mark the return of hard power to the world stage, for in truth, it never left. Ultimately, Rengger argues that those who call for a drastic revision of the restraint inherent in just war thinking 'on a belief that the world of international politics has changed … in kind, rather than just in degree', are ultimately 'rethinking in a profoundly problematic and teleocratic direction'.[90] All this suggests that we must be deeply sceptical about arguments that rely on the assumption that our day and age *needs* a new way of thinking because our times our profoundly unique.

Appreciating the breadth and depth of continuity in world politics – even though of course the times 'are always a-changing' – serves the important function of giving us critical distance from the events of our own time. This recognition can help us see that allowing our attention to be drawn obsessively to the analysis of 'the problems of the moment' like moths to the flame is likely to make us 'prisoners of the assumptions of the moment',

---

[87] Rengger, *Just War and International Order*, p. 6.
[88] Ibid., p. 17.
[89] Ibid., p. 18.
[90] Ibid., p. 133.

some of which likely sparked those problems in the first place.[91] What's more, if our present is not radically different from our past, then we can draw on the wisdom of past thinkers to help us reason through our current circumstances. We can, as Rengger would put it, 'distance' ourselves from our problems, 'to see how people distant in time or space or both sought to identify and grapple with their problems'.[92] Furthermore, this recognition of the fundamental continuity of history is a natural inoculation against claims that this or that crisis or revolution in military affairs warrants a radical re-envisioning of our moral frameworks.

Lastly, we could also stand to be more sceptical about our own powers of reason. In Rengger's judgement, the contemporary effort to 'replace Augustinian scepticism with a much more "rationalist" approach to the tradition' is an act of hubris.[93] As we imagine what principles we would like statesmen, soldiers, and citizens to keep in mind as they make decisions about war, it would behoove us to remember that we will always be operating in an environment of imperfect information, clouded by our emotions. If we fail to take this reality into account, we run the risk of being tempted to expand the range of circumstances in which it would be justifiable to use force on the mistaken assumption that we really will be able to distinguish necessary from unnecessary cases, not to mention cases where we are truly acting with right intent from those where we are not. If we allow ourselves to become too optimistic about our motivations and our ability to actualize them, we may be creating a set of principles whose consequences will be deeply destabilizing. As Rengger puts it, 'the real danger of this version of the just war is ... [that] it runs the risk of turning it into an ideology, and more, a messianic one'.[94]

The good news is that, despite the urgent sense that just war thinking is heading full-stream down the wrong track, Rengger believes its teleocratic trajectory is '*not* a destiny but rather a choice, or a series of choices'.[95] We can choose to see the world around us through more realistic lenses; we can choose to recognize the limits of our institutions, theories, and even our reason. After all, Rengger's scepticism is neither tragic nor deterministic. His approach is to question, to challenge, to push against the boundaries of certainty. In so doing, Rengger believes, we really can come to learn something certain, to uncover some corner of truth. And that provides a foundation on which we can build practical responses to real world problems.

---

[91] N. Rengger, 'Political theory and international relations: promised land or exit from Eden?', *International Affairs* 76, 4 (2000), pp. 755–70 (769–70).

[92] Ibid., p. 770.

[93] Rengger, *Just War and International Order*, p. 128.

[94] Rengger, 'The judgment of war', p. 157.

[95] Rengger, *Just War and International Order*, p. 177, emphasis in original.

PART IV

AFTERWORD

11

Rengger, History, and the Future of International Relations

Richard Whatmore

The relevance of history

Nick Rengger had a vision of the practice of international relations (IR) transformed by engagement with intellectual historians and political philosophers. What this entailed in full never became clear because of his early death. That there was a mission and a vision is clear from the chapters here collected. How would Rengger have responded to them? 'My goodness,' he can be heard saying, 'I had no idea I was so interesting.' Unquestionably, he would have been delighted, honoured, and stimulated, the latter especially because of the critical tone taken by so many of the engagements with his work. He might well have asserted, in response to negative commentary upon his last book *The Anti-Pelagian Imagination*, that it needed to be seen in the same way that Jean-Jacques Rousseau saw his *Contrat social* of 1762, which is to say that it was altogether unfinished, part of a longer work entitled *Institutions politiques*, and that therefore readers needed to wait for the culminating volume tying everything together. The tragedy of course, in the case of both Rousseau and Rengger, is that neither work will ever be completed.

What would Rengger most have appreciated? First, the engagement with his own claims with a view to their refinement through the work of fellow-travelling luminaries, such as Gillian Rose; texts Rengger was committed to but rarely cited, such as Max Weber's 'Politics as a vocation'; and work he would have drawn much from, such as the New Right theorist Alain de

Benoist.[1] Second, the attempts to work out how far perceived holes in his argument were due to a mis-reading of the greatest influence upon him, Michael Oakeshott, or indeed mistaken evaluations of the work of those he ultimately termed Pelagians and anti-Pelagians alike. Third, the making of his own philosophy and its practical implications both plainer and sharper as a potential research tool, specifically by developing Rengger's ideas about prudence and judgement. Finally, working out more clearly what he was actually arguing and what the implications of his arguments might be.[2]

If Rengger would have acknowledged these chapters as a fitting tribute to the work he had undertaken, admired the scholarship in evidence and the eminence of the commentators, he would part-jokingly have asked what a mere intellectual historian was doing in their midst. 'You've got nothing to say about the present so why are you here?' he might have whispered with a smile on his face during a conference tea-break or lunch. In response, it might be said that I spent a lot of time with Rengger for what, we were all unaware, proved the final years of his life. The reason was partly his interest in history in general and the history of ideas more specifically. He was fast friends with the leading intellectual historian Michael Bentley and once plotted the creation of a St Andrews variant of the Chicago Committee on Social Thought, a proposal stymied only by the anti-interdisciplinary stance taken by the then Head of History at the university. One of the scholars Rengger always praised to the heavens was David Armitage, for all of his works but particularly the 2004 essay 'The fifty years' rift: intellectual history and international relations'.[3] Rengger had been first employed at St Andrews within the History faculty; the School of International Relations was a subsequent innovation. As such, Rengger was among the most interdisciplinary of figures working in IR and among the most historically minded.

What did this historical mindedness entail for Rengger's work? It is difficult to chart Rengger's use of and debt to history because his own knowledge was so wide-ranging. He attended classes in classical Greek in order to better understand Thucydides. He was steeped in Roman rhetoric and saw himself as an orator and rhetorician. One of his goals, he once told me, was to give lectures at Gresham College. It is clear from his use of Augustine and the heresies he combatted, Donatism, Pelagianism, and

---

[1]   Kate Schick, ' "Keep your mind in hell, and despair not": Gillian Rose's anti-Pelagianism', this volume; John-Harmen Valk, 'Poetics and politics: Rengger, Weber, and the *Virtuosi* of Religion', this volume; Michael C. Williams, 'Conservatism, civility, and the challenges of international political theory', this volume.

[2]   Valerie Morkevičius, 'Just war as tradition in a civil international order', this volume.

[3]   David Armitage, 'The fifty years' rift: intellectual history and international relations', *Modern Intellectual History* 1, 1 (2004), pp. 97–109.

Manicheanism, that he was equally knowledgeable with regard to the various theologies of the medieval Christian church. Rengger's Durham PhD was concerned with the 18th century, with David Hume and Immanuel Kant, and entitled *Reason, Scepticism and Politics: Theory and Practice in the Enlightenment's Politics*. Professionally, he worked on the international crises and justifications of war that emerged in the 19th and 20th centuries. If his knowledge of history was so wide-ranging and so extensive, was it a general store of knowledge to be drawn upon? Or was there a message in history for the present and, more especially, that ought to be used to reshape IR as a discipline?

Engaging with anti-Pelagianism

All of the contributors to this volume have engaged to a greater or lesser extent with this issue. One of the difficulties is that Rengger was truly a polymath, giving the impression that he had started reading at birth and never stopped to draw breath. Here is an example from an email of 2015, originally sent to a soon-to-be lamented colleague Alex Danchev, and for a reason that cannot be recalled copied to me:

> Alex, one small snippet which you may know, or not, (or may not care about) but it amused me. While I am not a wild fan of popular culture (certainly not the modern variety), I do like certain fictional genres, including detective fiction. One of my top three writers in this areas is the US writer Rex Stout, who wrote a huge amount of stuff in his 88 years (including some early poetry and novels that were very unusual for their time) and became for a while a celebrated public intellectual in the US, chairing the war writers board during world war two and clashing memorably with the House UnAmerican activities committee when they accused him of being a communist by responding that' I hate communists as much as you do, the chief difference is I know what a communist is and you do not'. He was, I think, an old style American radical (like Mencken, but of the Left rather than the Right). His chief claim to fame, however, is his series of novels and novellas featuring his two chief protagonists, Nero Wolfe and Archie Goodwin. They have attracted a huge legion of fans (including Jacques Barzun, P. G. Wodehouse, Ian Fleming, Agatha Christie, and, more recently, P. D. James, A. S. Byatt and [not that I am citing myself in the same breath] me). But among them was, apparently, Magritte. A friend (a member of the Wolfe pack, the part scholarly/part fan association dedicated to Stout's work) mentioned to me that some of his paintings were titled by allusions to Stout's Wolfe novels (eg 'The Companions of Fear' which was the French translation of Stout's second Wolfe Novel, 'The

League of Frightened men'. There are apparently others, but he did not elaborate).[4]

Rengger had interests in Montaigne and Magritte, Wittgenstein and Wolfe, Cicero and Agatha Christie. Such learning in all fields and genres of the humanities and indeed the social sciences too makes it all the more difficult to pin Rengger down, something made more challenging still by the allusive and conversational style that he deployed, as noted in several chapters in this collection. He was ever, as Ian Hall perfectly puts it in this volume, 'a Socratic gadfly'.[5]

With regard to history though, is it possible to be more specific in Rengger's case? History seems to be significant as it arises from two sources. First, through Rengger's engagement with his mentors who were themselves the most historically minded of theorists, Michael Oakeshott and Martin Wight. Second, through his engagement with historic luminaries from Aristotle and after. The latter, Anthony F. Lang, Jr argues, in 'Rengger the reluctant rule follower' is actually the way to see Rengger, someone seeking to formulate prudential rules of action for use in disparate circumstances.[6] This point will be returned to as history surely was for Rengger, as Lang asserts, a means to the cultivation of character, a weapon in the battle to sharpen prudential knowledge. How Rengger's sense of prudence and political judgement was indebted to Oakeshott, Leo Strauss, Eric Voegelin, and Martin Wight is explored perceptively by Chris Brown, Ian Hall, Noël O'Sullivan, and Sophia Dingli in this collection. The influence of such figures, and that of Judith Shklar as Rengger aged, was substantial and never-wavering.[7]

Noël O'Sullivan and Sophia Dingli make the point that behind all of Rengger's work was the Straussian insight concerning ancient political thought affirming 'the impossibility of reason ever creating political consensus about the nature of justice'.[8] More significant still, they assert, was Oakeshott's distinction outlined in his book of 1975 *On Human Conduct* between an enterprise association directed towards a specific endpoint and a civil association founded on rules for maintaining the association without prescribing higher objectives or ways of living. Rengger was following

---

[4]   Nicholas J. Rengger, Email to Alex Danchev copied to Richard Whatmore (2015b), Monday, 15 June 2015.
[5]   Ian Hall, '"A dangerous place to be"? Rengger, the English School, and international disorder', this volume.
[6]   Anthony F. Lang, Jr, 'Rengger the reluctant rule follower', this volume.
[7]   Caroline Kennedy-Pipe, 'Rengger and the "Business of War"', this volume.
[8]   Noël O'Sullivan and Sophia Dingli, 'Rengger's anti-Pelagianism' , this volume.

Oakeshott in attacking contemporary politics as a purposive association pursuing the development of liberalism, democracy, a particular sense of the national interest or war as a crusade. What Oakeshott rejected as teleocratic thinking Rengger too found wanting, especially in the form of politicians in nation-states drawing upon the moral claims of the just war tradition to justify going to war. O'Sullivan and Dingli cite a paragraph of Rengger's which really gets to the heart of what he was about:

> Taken together, I want to suggest (and I think Oakeshott wanted to suggest) that all of these things have created in modern states an orientation that is heavily disposed to see itself in terms of an enterprise association, and a central component of this understanding is the ordering of a society for 'war'. Of course, the common enterprise for which force may be used will shift over time; it may be obviously material in one generation – access to the goods and services of the empire, the 'expansion of England'; and so forth – and more ideational in another – 'intervention for humanitarian purposes' perhaps, as we shall see. Nonetheless, central to the understanding of a modern state as an enterprise association is a willingness to see a 'common purpose' for which, under at least some circumstances, force is an entirely appropriate response; as Oakeshott says, the habits learned through endless preparation for war are retained in times of relative peace.[9]

Rengger agreed with Oakeshott that the five 'modes of experience' deployed to make sense of reality – the practical, the historical, the scientific, the aesthetic, and the philosophical – if confused could end up being overwhelmed by a deluded and spurious approach to politics and ethics that nevertheless attracted adherents on the grounds of an asserted objectivity. The most dangerous field in which such fakery could be found was IR itself as Rengger said, once more quoting Oakeshott directly: 'Perhaps it is in the sphere of international relations that the project of a science of politics has made itself most clear … From Grotius to the United Nations a continuous attempt has been made to elaborate the principles of a science of peace.'[10]

It was Oakeshott then that made Rengger a sceptic. One of more revealing claims made by Ian Hall, Chris Brown, and Caroline Kennedy-Pipe is that Rengger turned into a cynic after 9/11 and the unravelling of the debate

---

[9] Nicholas J. Rengger, *Just War and International Order: The Uncivil Condition in World Politics* (Cambridge: Cambridge University Press, 2013a), p. 33.

[10] Michael Oakeshott, *Religion, Politics and the Moral Life*, edited by Timothy Fuller (London: Yale University Press, 1993), p. 104; Nicholas Rengger, *The Anti-Pelagian Imagination in Political Theory and International Relations: Dealing in Darkness* (London and New York: Routledge, 2017), p. 162.

about the legitimacy of the Bush/Blair so-called 'war on terror' within intellectual circles. Ian Hall makes the point that in writings of the 1990s up to the appearance in 2000 of *International Relations, Political Theory, and the Problem of Order*, Rengger argued that the emergence of modern states created two forms of rules for politics. One set could be traced to Augustine, whose goal was 'the minimizing of disorder, conflict and instability'. A second tradition associated with figures as diverse as Kant and Marx instead sought to impose a new 'pattern of authority' which solved the problem of state conflict at its root, establishing some version of perpetual peace in some cases entailing the abolition of the state itself. Rengger was forever an enemy of the second tradition of progressivists, teleocrats, liberal positivists, and cosmopolitans because he felt that in seeking to get rid of war altogether or in seeking to specify the legitimate use of war, they were inadvertently promoting the wild schemes of nation-state politicians. With more verve after 2000, however, Rengger assaulted those who were turning the international arena into a zone of fantasy politics and fake morality. To illustrate this point, Chris Brown helpfully quotes *Just War and International Order*:

> '[for] most of the modern period ... the scope of justifications for the use of force has in fact – and contrary to a widely believed narrative – been expanding not contracting, and the most influential tradition that is supposed to be about the restraint of war (the just war tradition) has in fact been complicit in this.'[11]

Brown goes on to underline how angry Rengger was about Michael Walzer's defence in *Just and Unjust Wars* of the abandoning of the rules of war on the grounds of emergency or necessity. For Rengger, Walzer was straightforwardly abandoning traditions of argument themselves underpinned by the application of justice-seeking practical moral judgement:

> in a very important sense constituted by and through its rules, and they cannot be 'trumped' or overridden by any particular social or contextual circumstance. That, indeed, is what it means, I think, to see the just war tradition as Walzer at least claims to do as a casuistic tradition. Any given action, the bombing of German cities, for example would have to be examined in the context of the 'rules' which are not merely laws, and nor are they fixed, but they certainly have a centre of gravity around a common set of precepts. Political communities may have a putative right of defence under these precepts, for example, but

---

[11] Nicholas J. Rengger, *Just War and International Order*, p. xii.

such a right is always conditional on other precepts being met and is never absolute.[12]

The point of Rengger's final work of 2017 *The Anti-Pelagian Imagination in Political Theory and International Relations* was to identify the second and more dangerous tradition with Pelagius. Proper work in IR had to be grounded in anti-Pelagian impulses, and could be found in the scholarship of thinkers as diverse as Chris Brown, William Connolly, John Gray, Carl Schmitt, Stephen Toulmin, Leo Strauss, Michael Oakeshott, Judith Shklar, George Santayana, and Jean Bethke Elshtain. At the same time, Rengger showed how far the malaise had spread, even to those who considered themselves to be enemies of Pelagian liberal internationalism and radical cosmopolitanism. Teleology, perfectibility, and utopianism were infecting intellectual discourse and the beast needed to be named. No better example can be found than Rengger's ridiculing of Jean Bethke Elshtain's justification of the war on terror as a corollary of the moral role of the United States across the globe. Once more it is worth following our authors, this time O'Sullivan and Dingli, in quoting Rengger in full:

> surely there is more than a touch of 'imperial grandiosity' in [Elshtain's] belief that the United States is the guarantor of human dignity in the contemporary world and that it is the special responsibility of the United States, because of both its political character and the temper of the times, to act as the 'indispensable nation'. 'We, the powerful', as she puts it, have first perhaps to examine the sources of our own power rather than merely assuming that it is 'ours' to deploy in the service of justice as we wish. As Augustine [of whom Elshtain is such a great admirer] recognized very well, part of the 'seductive lure' of 'imperial grandeur' is the belief that we can do great good with our great power, but the reality is likely to be that, as always, power corrupts.[13]

Caroline Kennedy-Pipe's 'Nick Rengger and the "Business of War"' provides more evidence still for Rengger's ultimately deep scepticism about the moral and political world he was inhabiting. Rengger's deep scepticism translated into a real fear that warmongers and imperialists were once more in charge of the field, using the old tricks of presenting themselves as moralists, patriots, and true representatives of the people and the global good all meshed together.[14]

---

[12] Nicholas J. Rengger, *Just War and International Order*, p. 154.
[13] Rengger, *The Anti-Pelagian Imagination*, p. 128.
[14] Nicholas J. Rengger, 'The greatest treason? On the subtle temptations of preventive war', *International Affairs* 84, 5 (2008), pp. 949–61.

The problem that is emphasized in almost all of the chapters here collected is uncertainty about the source of Rengger's negative verdict upon present politics and IR theory. For Ian Hall, Chris Brown, and Noël O'Sullivan/Sophia Dingli this is the ultimate difficulty, the question that Rengger, were he still with us, would be faced with over and over. Kennedy-Pipe makes the fascinating suggestion that the position Rengger ultimately arrived at was Christian pacifism giving his anti-Pelagianism a moral gloss. This line is supported by something that several members of faculty at St Andrews noted about Nick, that he attracted large numbers of PhD students who were themselves devout and indeed evangelical in their rejection of contemporary morals and politics on the grounds of religious commitment. This also fits with a point made by O'Sullivan and Dingli, that in John Gray's *Black Mass: Apocalyptic Religion and the Death of Utopia* (2007) Rengger traced what he called Gray's excess of pessimism to viewing all religious belief as apocalyptic, neglecting the variety and utility of many forms of Christian morality. Lang and Valk insightfully discover a related source that might help to explain Rengger's late perspectives in the form of Charles Taylor's *A Secular Age* (2007). Here the actions of the Good Samaritan are justified as an act of judgement in response to pain rather than the unfolding of a commitment to a moral framework of rules. For Lang, Rengger was a student of the exercise of judgement, ultimately meaning an Aristotelian defender of an education in the virtues.

If the sources of Rengger's arguments was unclear, there were other problems too. For Chris Brown, Rengger's Pelagians and their enemies were straw men. The distinction between perfectibilists and anti-perfectibilists was black and white. Brown cites his own case as illustrative, being a member of the anti-Pelagian brigade while accepting the views of fully-paid-up members of the opposite party:

> I defended Steven Pinker's position [in *The Better Angels of our Nature*, 2007 and *Enlightenment Now* 2019] that violence and intolerance have become less salient over time. The story Pinker tells is of a long-term decline of violence in all its forms, war, civil war, domestic oppression, racism, and prejudice. Because Pinker is not by training a student of things international many scholars in international relations were sceptical of his data, yet well-established IR scholars such as Joshua Goldstein [in *Winning the War on War*, 2011] and John Mueller [in *The Remnants of War*, 2007] have come to much the same conclusion.[15]

For Hall, Rengger ultimately 'catalogues various versions of anti-Pelagianism, but crucially, does not justify it, either historically or philosophically – or indeed theologically'. In the case of other critics of moral progress in history, such as

---

[15] Chris Brown, 'Rengger's War on Teleocracy', this volume, p.124.

Herbert Butterfield or Wight, the source of the argument was the crooked timber of humanity. For Hall, Rengger's ultimately empirical grounding upon knowledge of the 20th century was insufficient.[16] For O'Sullivan and Dingli similarly, Rengger lacked a theory of prudence that might have been derived from Hume or Stuart Hampshire. Hall's worry is that Rengger amounted to a Cassandra ever lacking the means of convincing her audience.

The importance of the history of political thought

Is there anything else to be said? Hall makes the insightful point that what distinguished Rengger's first book, *Political Theory, Modernity and Postmodernity* (1995), was an obsession with history and the paths not taken. Rengger was, as several commentators have noted, a close reader of Alasdair McIntyre. More still though, he was interested in the authors of the so-called Cambridge School of the history of political thought, Quentin Skinner, J.G.A. Pocock, and John Dunn, and beside them the related older work of R.G. Collingwood, the contemporary work of Michel Foucault and that of their philosopher-ally Richard Rorty. Hall argues that this meant that Rengger was of the view that we live in epistemological traps that can't be broken down and that limit the options open to historical actors.

Hall does not go on to say what was the precise nature of the trap that moderns found themselves to be unable to break out of. Here too the historians of political thought helped him and it is this that has been insufficiently recognized. Skinner, Pocock, and Dunn are all critics, as we would now put it, of globalization. All three felt that the political traditions of the present were in numerous respects more limited than those of the past. The project of the history of political thought was one of recovery in the hope of expanding the political horizons of moderns and also of recognizing the nature of the modern historical predicament. The latter was bleak being much less coherent, much less certain to survive and much less obviously healthy than might be supposed by apologists for modernity untrained in intellectual history. Dunn revealed the peculiarities, limitations, and fragilities of modern forms of democracy against a backdrop of states that proclaimed international peace while being addicted to economic warfare. Skinner recovered the lost traditions of liberty defining freedom from domination in early modern Europe, sometimes termed republican traditions of political aspiration. Pocock reconstructed the Commonwealth tradition of political argument that condemned life in commercial societies as narrow and selfish, dividing the purposive self and causing unhappiness while politics become more elitist and corrupt. Alien traditions remained visible through vestiges,

---

[16] Rengger, *The Anti-Pelagian Imagination*, pp. 163–8.

such as the Commonwealth obsession with the right to bear arms in the United States, which could be identified and then misunderstood. Distinct critiques of global capitalism were formulated along concrete descriptions of the roads not taken but that might become options in politics again. Rengger could not have agreed more with the historical method and the conclusions arrived at through the embrace of history.

Richard Ned Lebow has argued against Rengger's reliance upon history on the grounds that 'the future need not resemble the past' and that 'the so-called lessons of history can ... [have] the unfortunate potential to make our expectations of a fear-based world self-fulfilling'.[17] The latter argument is problematic because it is hard to see precisely how assessments of the possible realization of negative political outcomes in practice become more likely the more they are contemplated. Surely the more obvious tendency, emphasized by Rengger after 2001, is historically ignorant political actors sleepwalking into disaster. Rengger once made the serious joke about Blair and Bush that if they had ever read Montesquieu on the impossibility of translating one form of government with a history in one place into a different place with an alternate history, events in Iraq and Afghanistan would not have unfolded as they did. Rengger considered latter-day politicians and theorists to be at kindergarten level in their knowledge of the past. This explained in part their errors and the horrors that accompanied ignorance. Lebow's first point about the future not resembling the past Rengger also found ridiculous. Unless human nature changed, of course it would. That nothing was new in politics was a lesson that needed to be recognized anew and taught to every generation of students.

If Rengger's realism was historical it was also based on the eavesdropping upon the conversations of those who had understood politics deeply in the past. Rengger's conversations, far more even than those of Oakeshott or Wight, took seriously the arguments of the historical actors he was engaging with for the good reason that he believed that their insights about their own time contained lessons for our own. To be more precise, it was vital to recover a lost perspective upon the present. Consider Rengger's definition of the anti-Pelagian mindset once more:

> [A modern anti-Pelagian] ... will acknowledge, with the realist, the intractability of the practical world, but refuse the realist's accommodation to the logic of that world, and rather seek to understand it from the outside, as it were. Such an individual might

---

[17] Richard Ned Lebow, 'Tragedy, politics and political science', in R.N. Lebow and Toni Erskine (eds), *Tragedy and International Relations* (London: Palgrave Macmillan, 2012), pp. 69–70.

also accept, with many who seek to reform the world, that sometimes reform will occur and that sometimes it should be welcomed, but they would also refuse the claim that such reform either would be or should be necessarily permanent, and that somehow the world of human conduct will itself change. And, again, they will stand outside the logic of the world. And that, perhaps, is the point with which we might close. The world of international relations will look very different when viewed through the lens of the anti-Pelagian imagination: not because many of the features of the world will be unfamiliar, but because the logic of how they are understood and what follows from that understanding will be very different. And, at bottom, the difference is a moral one; the sceptical anti-Pelagian imagination offers a world viewed from the perspective of a different scale of values. That is its opportunity – and its challenge.[18]

The fact is that Rengger's modern anti-Pelagian sounded very much like an exponent of the science of the legislator of the Enlightenment era which he worked upon at the start of his career.

Why is this important? It is because Rengger's anti-Pelagian stance mirrored that of the historian and political theorist István Hont. Hont's work, published in essay form from the 1980s onwards and then collected together in the book *Jealousy of Trade* in 2005 inspired a large number of scholars interested in IR, including figures Rengger followed closely, such as David Armitage.[19] Raymond Geuss has written that the best way to understand Hont is to draw a parallel with Nietzsche's self-description as looking at the world 'with the eyes of a "cold angel" who "sees through the whole miserable spectacle", yet neither bears reality any ill-will, nor finds the world in the least bit "cozy"... István was impervious to the siren-songs of coziness, [to] explicit or tacit theodicies, to naive belief in progress, and to the self-congratulatory forms of wishful thinking that are particularly characteristic of modern liberal democracies'.[20] Geuss could have been describing Rengger.

Hont was famous for drawing a direct parallel between the 18th-century international predicament and that of the present. In both cases he argued that politics were failing, the difference being that in the present the extent of the myopia was marked and myths of progress abounded. One way of

---

[18] Rengger, *The Anti-Pelagian Imagination*, p. 168.
[19] István Hont, *Jealousy of Trade: International Competition and the Nation State in Historical Perspective* (Cambridge, MA: Belknap Press of Harvard University, 2005).
[20] Raymond Geuss, 'István Hont, 1947–2013', *The Point* (20 December 2013), available at: https://thepointmag.com/politics/istvan-hont-1947-2013/

seeing Hont is to focus on the meaning of the Enlightenment. For 18th-century authors the Enlightenment meant the development of political philosophies capable of preventing fanatics and enthusiasts from deluding the people into supporting politicians embracing mad projects that would end in war. The creation of philosophies capable of preventing fanaticism had been the great achievement of the 17th century in putting an end to the wars of religion that had torn the European continent apart. The intellectual world of politics, Hont argued, changed radically at the end of the 17th century. The Treaty of Westphalia failed as soon as the ink was dry upon the document because of changes in the capacity of states to pursue global commerce. In a simple sense, Westphalia created Enlightenment if the latter term is employed to signify putting an end to the carnage of religious wars. How could existing borders be maintained, however, when, as David Hume – a hero for Hont as for Rengger – said that commerce had become a reason of state? Hume argued that: 'Trade was never esteemed an affair of state till the last century; and there scarcely is any ancient writer on politics, who has made mention of it.' Even those he termed 'the Italians' – he was thinking chiefly about Machiavelli – 'have kept a profound silence with regard to it'. The world was now transformed because the pursuit of trade had become 'the chief attention, as well of ministers of state, as of speculative reasoners'. The source of the change for Hume was 'the great opulence, grandeur, and military achievements of the two maritime powers'. This rise of two states 'seem first to have instructed mankind in the importance of an extensive commerce'.[21]

Hume's maritime powers were the Dutch Republic and England. Their military power revealed means of maintaining states through the aggressive pursuit of commerce backed up by armed force. Such strategies for national greatness were in Hume's view from the late 17th century being adopted to a greater or less extent by all European states. Hume argued that the norms of IR were transformed from the time when states started to compete with one another for the control of markets. Such a development was vital in strategic terms because of the military revolution that in the 17th century had changed the way that states went to war. In order to maintain themselves states had to invest in the latest military technology. Vast armies carrying guns became the norm with the most important element being the engineers responsible for cannon, mortar, and siege. Paying for such technologies to prevent defeat in war relied upon generating revenues

---

21 David Hume, 'Of civil liberty', in *Essays Moral, Political, Literary, edited and with a Foreword, Notes, and Glossary by Eugene F. Miller, with an appendix of variant readings from the 1889 edition by T.H. Green and T.H. Grose, revised edition* (Indianapolis: Liberty Fund, 1987), p. 88.

through commerce. The capacities of states to do this radically improved when immediate revenue generation through public credit became an option. Again, this occurred in the late 17th century. Paying national debts necessitated economic success as extensive trade required expansive markets generating revenues for the state over time. Public credit also required a greater level of trust among creditors in the polity. Such forces translated into a lust for empire in the sense of empire for markets. Creating economic empires became practically realizable because of the gulf in power between commercial and non-commercial states and because of the pressure upon states to expand their markets.

Thomas Hobbes, Hont claimed, needed to be understood as the last Renaissance theorist because he found solutions to problems in pure politics. Political projects alone in Hobbes' civil science could bring peace. After Marx, by contrast, the intellectual world changed also because the crazy claim became commonplace that the solution to the problem of war domestically and internationally was to abolish politics and the state altogether through the productiveness of socialist and communist economies. Hont was a product of Cold War Hungary and defected to Britain in the mid-1970s. The true study of politics, he argued, lay between Hobbes and Marx, between solely political solutions and purely economic solutions. Combining both meant returning to the 18th-century study of political economy. Hont held that the study of IR had declined since authors – from Mandeville and Fénelon to Hume, Rousseau, and Smith to Kant and Hegel – had accepted that war between human communities could only be prevented by politics in the old sense of natural jurisprudence and political economy operating in conjunction with one another. Rengger's view of the limits of contemporary disciplinary subjects was never as bleak as that of Hont. Rengger would never go as far as Hont in his critique of IR and political philosophy, which for Hont could not hold a candle to analyses of the same topics in the 18th century, before the disciplines had been created. Hont's argument that a new historically grounded discipline, which Hont termed political economy, was required to vanquish Rengger's Pelagianism would have itself been described as a Pelagian impulse by Rengger. At the same time, the substance of Hont's analysis of IR would have been accepted by Rengger.

Hume's great insight in Hont's view was that in the new international era of war for trade the rich would tend to eat up the poor. Imperial dominion might not require invasion in the old Roman sense but might rather entail the use of state-sponsored companies controlling local politics. Local legislators and politicians in weak or poor states might see themselves as governors of sovereign entities but this was not the case in reality if their economies were effectively governed from a foreign metropole. As the gap between the economic superpowers and the lesser states was growing all of the time, few states in the modern world, however stable they might perceive themselves to be, were safe from internal and external trauma. More and more states would have their domestic politics determined by an economically dominant foreign power. Few states in Europe in the 18th century were therefore safe. A host of traditional powers, from Sweden and the Dutch Republic to Venice, Genoa, and Poland-Lithuania declined rapidly, being unable to turn themselves into commercial powers or expand their markets. Poorer states entered a prolonged period of crisis. Traditional survival strategies for small states, which had ranged from economic specialization to alliances to confederation and above all national patriotism or manliness ('virtù'), were no longer sufficient. It was no longer the case that small-state patriotism, last evinced by the Dutch against the Spanish empire, could create a new polity. Several small states ceased to exist. Others found their domestic politics perpetually interfered with by larger commercial powers, who suddenly had an interest in the economic activities of their neighbours. Rome as a model became less relevant to moderns. Modern states that followed Carthage, for the first time in history, found new means of becoming rich and of establishing empire. The major question was whether they too could maintain themselves or whether they would sooner or later fall before even larger states with more extensive natural resources.

The result of such developments was constant war between the larger states for commercial dominion. War tended to be carried out by economic means rather than by military action. Smaller states found their own domestic politics were suddenly dependent upon the views of the ambassadors from the major powers. Forms of xenophobia arose in which foreigners and rival states were blamed for the economic condition of one's own state. In free states where the populace was involved in electing magistrates and legislators, it was discovered that blaming foreigners for the economic condition of the country rather than national politicians could translate into electoral victory. Trade and war generated gargantuan profits for particular groups in society. In the British case opposition arose towards 'the monied interest', those whose wealth derived from investment in government stocks or who exploited the commercially dependent elements of empire for personal gain. A major worry of commentators concerned about the commercialization of societies was that the monied interest were dangerous because their wealth was so liquid. Rather than being forced to remain in a state in time of crisis, because of reliance upon the immoveable wealth of land, the monied interest could move their assets across borders and ruin the economies of states in so doing. A still greater fear was voiced by Adam Smith in arguing that a monied interest could establish what he called a 'mercantile system', a corrupt nexus of bankers and merchants and the politicians they bribed who made legislation for their own profit against the public good. Smith asserted that the 'unnatural and retrograde order' of modern Europe, the addiction to war and empire, could be blamed upon the mercantile system.[22]

Following the insights of Hume and of Smith, Hont argued that almost every theorist of the 18th century saw themselves to be experiencing an unparalleled period of upheaval and crisis. Global wars were being fought for trade and empire. This was a new historical development. Few exponents of the science of the legislator or natural jurisprudence expressed any optimism about the future. IR were being reshaped so that a small number of giant states sustained by trading empires were increasingly dominant; they were fighting ever more brutal wars to maintain or extend their dominion. In addition, new forms of enthusiasm and fanaticism which had characterized the wars of religion were now abroad in domestic political life. As Hume got older, especially from the close of the Seven Years' War, he worried that fanaticism in the form of a lust for empire and a lust for liberty had translated from theology into everyday politics. Modern Puritans, he worried at the end of his life, were once again turning the world upside down.

Hont did not use the terminology but from an 18th-century perspective what was being experienced was an end of Enlightenment. This was very much Rengger's view too. The strategies developed to restore states to peace and prevent violent conflict on the basis of religious difference were no longer working. This was why Hume and so many philosophers between the 1770s and the 1810s were certain that they had failed the task of adjusting their theories to a new international economic and political reality characterized by fanaticism. Hume and Smith were obsessed with stopping those who saw the world from an enthusiastic perspective because this translated into faith in dangerous projectors proffering easy or universal solutions to problems. Hont followed Hume's and Smith's perspective and applied it to the present in arguing that we continue to live in a world experiencing the end of Enlightenment. Few states are sovereign in the senses understood by Hobbes. Current debates popular among populists, patriots, and nationalists about self-rule and being in control of your own national destiny would have been seen as entirely fake by our ancestors. From Hont's perspective we have become very bad at identifying and dealing with enthusiasts, projectors, and fanatics. We also failed in Smith's and Hume's generation to challenge the mercantile system of corrupt commerce. The great tragedy of the early 19th century was that the most corrupt mercantile system, the demise of which had been predicted by every major theorist from Montesquieu to Kant, proved so good at combining war and empire that it became a model polity for fellow states.

---

[22] Adam Smith, *An Inquiry into the Nature and Causes of the Wealth of Nations* (London: W. Strahan and T. Cadell, 1776), Book III, Ch. 1, Vol. I, p. 380.

Britain remained a mercantile system whose legislation was the product of what Jeremy Bentham called 'sinister interests'. Yet as an empire it was redefined as the quintessential liberal polity. Bentham's once high hopes turned altogether utopian of social institutions capable of 'grinding rogues honest', of emancipating your colonies, or of doux-commerce leading to perpetual peace. At some point, critics of Britain's market-guzzling empire argued, the old logic of poor states undercutting richer states would kick in, or Britain would go bankrupt by war or further colonial rebellion and the mercantile system would collapse. This has now come to pass. Rather than seeing an end to political fanaticism and the mercantile system, however, European variants have been replaced by even more powerful mercantile systems. The difference between the 18th century and the present is the acknowledgement that the mercantile systems in the contemporary world have the capacity to destroy the planet. Hont's critique of contemporary theorists who failed to see past and present as he did overlaps altogether with Rengger's Pelagians. With different emphases, Hont's and Rengger's work was profoundly related to the point of being near Janus-faced.

Rengger and the future of international relations

Rengger's then was very much a Humean/Hontian 18th-century perspective upon IR. It is bleak but clear-sighted. Corruption and Caesar figures, mobocracy and populism, the manipulation of electorates and public information, xenophobia and the blaming of the ubiquitous 'other', violence and revolution: all become explicable and norms of modern politics rather than states of exception. The Enlightenment ended and has yet to be restored. There has been an ongoing failure to stop wars of religion from breaking out in secular politics. Things have become still worse with the progress of globalization. Hont found his lodestar in the work of Hume and Smith, being uncorrupted by the presumption of purely political solutions to problems or the presumption that political problems could be abolished by economic progress. Reconstructing their intellectual world became urgent on the grounds that the 18th-century authors had a clearer sense of our problems than we do ourselves because they shared them independently of obfuscating 19th- and 20th-century political ideologies.

Again, Rengger would never have gone so far. It needs to be admitted that he never found his lodestar, even in the work of Oakeshott. Rengger was above all a brilliant critic, a vocal sceptical voice necessary to any conversation. What his conservatism entailed in a positive sense is difficult to work out. It did entail civility and moderation, above all the respect for ongoing conversations grounded on the assumption that no party, even if they were convinced they were correct in the present, could be presumed to have the right answer in perpetuity. History tended to change everything. Power always corrupted, especially the virtuous. This was why Rengger's conservatism had something of the 1950s about it, being closer to that of Harold Macmillan, himself a friend of Oakeshott's, than Margaret Thatcher's. Rengger was an opponent of assertions of objective truths and unquestionably certain politics peddled by exponents of free markets and property rights at all costs as much as by radical socialists; he remained with Montaigne an enemy to projectors of every stripe and pedlars of easy solutions or those which lacked negative consequences.

As he got older there can be no doubt that the sense of the failures of IR as a subject was felt more keenly by Rengger, just as domestic and international politics became more ideological and overfull of projectors. Ideological turns were explicable in times of crisis and social division. The kinds of moderation and civility that Rengger valued, he was aware, tended to be the product of a post-crisis environment, when war or catastrophe had done their tragic work. The challenge faced by IR as a subject was to teach that the circumstances of tragedy and the possibility of war had to be rekindled day to day, in the hope of identifying projectors and fanatics before their actions destroyed communities and international worlds anew. In short, disaster itself had operated in the past as a transition mechanism to the more moderate, civil, and unified politics that Rengger admired. Theorists of IR had to find transition mechanisms that were not reliant upon war. This was no small order.

His own contribution to the task saw international theory as a way of energizing the moral imagination to develop non-teleocratic habits of human interaction. His anti-Pelagianism was not merely an imaginative, historically minded way of renewing theoretical speculation about the international, but above all a sceptical *ethos* of engagement with the dilemmas of world politics. Such an ethos seeks neither to change the world nor submit to its fixity, and in that sense, it is marked by a historical sensibility that does go beyond both tragedy and utopianism, as the subtitle to this volume suggests. Ultimately, theory, history, and the moral imagination come together in Rengger to offer a different vision of the same world from a perspective that combined realist sobriety, playful irony, and moral integrity.[23]

Rengger would have said himself that beyond his own sense of the reality of international politics he had not managed to persuade others sufficiently to foster scepticism and moderation together. Perhaps the key message of this collection is that pinning Rengger down is beyond us and is likely to remain so. Rengger showed us how to spot incoherence and fakery and fanaticism dressed up as liberal or conservative moderatism. Rousseau was often called the critic's critic, accepting that it was next to impossible to take

---

[23] I thank Vassilios Paipais for conversations on this point.

foolproof steps for the public good in a fallen world. What Rousseau did was to show the pitfalls in the schemes that portrayed themselves as being indisputably for the good of all. Rengger did the same. He had a vision of an up-to-date and nuanced subject called IR altogether intertwined with history. Glimpses of his vision are everywhere.

Bibliography

Abensour, Miguel (2008) 'Persistent utopia', *Constellations* 15, 3, pp. 406–21.

Abrahamsen, Rita, et al. (2020) 'Confronting the international political sociology of the New Right', *International Political Sociology* 14, 1, pp. 94–107.

Allhoff, Fritz, Adam Henscke, and Bradley Jay Strawser, eds (2015) *Binary Bullets: The Ethics of Cyberwarfare* (Oxford: Oxford University Press).

Allison, Graham T. (2017) *Destined for War: Can America and China Escape Thucydides' Trap* (London: Scribe UK).

Arendt, Hannah (1959a) 'Reflections on Little Rock', *Dissent* 6, 1, pp. 45–56.

Arendt, Hannah (1959b) 'Reply to critics', *Dissent* 6, 2, pp. 179–81.

Arendt, Hannah (1963) *Eichmann in Jerusalem: A Report on the Banality of Evil* (New York: Viking Press).

Aristotle (2000) *Nicomachean Ethics*, edited by Roger Crisp (Cambridge: Cambridge University Press).

Armitage, David (2004) 'The fifty years' rift: intellectual history and international relations', *Modern Intellectual History* 1, 1 pp. 97–109.

Asad, Talal (2009) 'Free speech, blasphemy, and secular criticism', in Talal Asad, Wendy Brown, Judith Butler and Saba Mahmood, *Is Critique Secular? Blasphemy, Injury and Free Speech*, The Townsend Papers in the Humanities, No. 2. (Berkeley, CA: Townsend Center for the Humanities, University of California), pp. 20–63, available at: http://escholarship.org/uc/item/84q9c6ft

Asad, Talal (2012) 'Thinking about religion, belief, and politics', in Robert A. Orsi (ed), *The Cambridge Companion to Religious Studies* (Cambridge: Cambridge University Press), pp. 36–57.

Asad, Talal (2018) *Secular Translations: Nation-State, Modern Self, and Calculative Reason* (New York: Columbia University Press).

Augustine (1984) *City of God* (London: Penguin Books).

Augustine (2001) *The Confessions* (London: Everyman's Library).

Bain, William (2007) 'Are there any lessons of history? The English school and the activity of being an historian', *International Politics* 44, 5, pp. 513–30.

Bain, William (2020) *Political Theology of International Order* (Oxford: Oxford University Press).

Bassin, Mark (2015) 'Lev Gumilev and the European New Right', *Nationalities Papers: The Journal of Nationalism and Ethnicity* 43, 6, pp. 840–65.

Baylis, John and Nicholas Rengger, eds (1992) *Dilemmas of World Politics: International Issues in a Changing World* (Oxford: Oxford University Press).

Bellamy, Alexander J. (2002) 'Pragmatic solidarism and the dilemmas of humanitarian intervention', *Millennium: Journal of International Studies* 31, 3, pp. 473–97.

Benjamin, Walter (2007) *Illuminations* (New York: Schocken Books).

Berenskoetter, Felix (2018) 'Deep theorizing in International Relations', *European Journal of International Relations* 24, 4, pp. 814–40.

Berki, Robert N. (1981) 'Oakeshott's concept of civil association: notes for a critical analysis', *Political Studies* 29, 4, pp. 570–85.

Bevir, Mark and Ian Hall (2017) 'International relations', in Mark Bevir (ed), *Modernism and the Social Sciences* (Cambridge: Cambridge University Press), pp. 130–54.

Bevir, Mark and Ian Hall (2020) 'The English school and the classical approach: between modernism and interpretivism', *Journal of International Political Theory* 16, 2, pp. 153–70.

Bonner, Ali (2018) *The Myth of Pelagianism* (Oxford: Oxford University Press).

Brown, Chris (2007a) 'Tragedy, "tragic choices" and contemporary international political theory', *International Relations* 21, 1, pp. 5–13.

Brown, Chris (2007b) 'From humanised war to humanitarian intervention: Carl Schmitt's critique of the just war tradition', in Louiza Odysseos and Fabio Petito (eds), *The International Political Thought of Carl Schmitt* (London: Routledge), pp. 56–79.

Brown, Chris (2010/2012) *Practical Judgement in International Political Theory: Selected Essays* (London: Routledge).

Brown, Chris (2013) 'Just war and political judgement', in Anthony F. Lang, Jr, Cian O'Driscoll and John Williams (eds), *Just War: Authority, Tradition and Practice* (Georgetown, DC: Georgetown University Press).

Brown, Chris (2017) 'Political thought, international relations theory and international political theory: an interpretation', *International Relations* 31, 3, pp. 227–40.

Brown, Chris (2018) 'Michael Walzer', in Daniel Brunstetter and Cian O'Driscoll (eds), *Just War Thinkers: From Cicero to the 21st Century* (London: Routledge).

Brown, Chris (2019) 'In response', in Mathias Albert and Anthony F. Lang, Jr (eds), *The Politics of International Political Theory: Reflections on the Work of Chris Brown* (London: Palgrave Macmillan), pp. 243–55.

Brown, Chris (2020) 'From serpents and doves to the war on teleocracy', *International Relations* 34, 4, pp. 616–20.

Brown, Chris (2021) 'Justified: just war and the ethics of violence and world order', in Lothar Brock and Hendrik Simon (eds), *The Justification of War and International Order* (Oxford: Oxford University Press), pp. 435–48.

Brown, Chris, Terry Nardin, and Nicholas Rengger, eds (2002) *International Relations in Political Thought: Texts from the Ancient Greeks to the First World War* (Cambridge: Cambridge University Press).

Brown, Peter (2013) *Augustine of Hippo*, 45th anniversary edition, (Berkeley: University of California Press).

Brunstetter, Daniel R. and Cian O'Driscoll, eds (2018) *Just War Thinkers: From Cicero to the 21st Century* (Abingdon: Routledge).

Bull, Hedley (1972) 'International relations as an academic pursuit', *Australian Outlook* 26, 3, pp. 251–65.

Burnham, James (1941) *The Managerial Revolution: What is Happening in the World* (New York: John Day Co.)

Butler, Judith (2005) *Giving an Account of Oneself* (New York: Fordham University Press).

Butler, Judith, Ernesto Laclau, and Slavoj Žižek (2000) *Contingency, Hegemony, Universality: Contemporary Dialogues on the Left* (London and New York: Verso).

Butterfield, Herbert (1949) *Christianity and History* (London: G. Bell and Sons).

Butterfield, Herbert and Martin Wright, (eds) (2019 [1966]) *Diplomatic Investigations: Essays in the Theory of International Politics*, new edition (Oxford: Oxford University Press).

Buzan, Barry (1993) 'From international system to international society: structural realism and regime theory meet the English school', *International Organization* 47, 3, pp. 327–52.

Buzan, Barry (2014) *An Introduction to the English School of International Relations: The Societal Approach* (Cambridge: Polity).

Chiaruzzi, Michele (2016) *Martin Wight on Fortune and Irony in Politics* (New York: Palgrave).

Clark, Stephen (1989) *Civil Peace and Sacred Order* (Oxford: Clarendon Press).

Clover, Charles (2016) *Black Wind, White Snow: The Rise of Russia's New Nationalism* (New Haven, CT: Yale University Press).

Coker, Christopher (2015) *The Improbable War: China, the United States and the Logic of Great Power Conflict* (London: Hurst & Co.)

Connolly, William E. (1993) *The Augustinian Imperative: Reflections on the Politics of Morality* (London: Sage).

Corrigan, Richard W. (1981) *Tragedy: Vision and Form* (London: Harper & Row London).

Dallmayr, Fred (2001) 'Conversation across boundaries: political theory and global diversity', *Millennium: Journal of International Studies* 30, 2, pp. 331–47.

De Benoist, Alain (1993/1994) 'The idea of empire', *Telos* 98–99, pp. 80–93.

De Benoist, Alain (1996) 'Confronting globalization', *Telos*, 108, pp. 117–37.

De Benoist, Alain (2017/1977) *View From the Right* (London: Arktos).

Den Uyl, Douglas (1991) *The Virtue of Prudence* (London: Peter Lang Publishing Inc.)

Der Derian, James, ed (1995) *International Theory: Critical Investigations* (Basingstoke: Macmillan).

Derrida, Jacques (1994) *Specters of Marx: The State of the Debt, the Work of Mourning, and the New International* (New York: Routledge).

Dingli, Sophia (2020) 'Conceptualising peace and its preconditions: the anti-Pelagian imagination and the critical turn in peace theory', *Journal of International Political Theory* 17, 3, pp. 468–87.

Dinniss, Heather Harrison (2012*) Cyber War and the Laws of War* (Cambridge: Cambridge University Press).

Doyle, Michael (2011) *Striking First Preemption and Prevention in International Conflict* (Princeton, NJ: Princeton University Press).

Drolet, Jean-François and Michael C. Williams (2018) 'Radical conservatism and global order: international theory and the new right', *International Theory* 10, 2, pp. 285–313.

Drolet, Jean-François and Michael C. Williams (2019) 'The view from MARS: American paleoconservatism and ideological challenges to the liberal international order', *International Journal* 74, 1, pp. 15–31.

Drolet, Jean-François and Michael C. Williams (2021a) 'Realism, radical conservatism, and the evolution of post-war international theory', *Review of International Studies* (advance online), pp. 1–22.

Drolet, Jean-François and Michael C. Williams (2021b) 'From critique to reaction: the New Right, critical theory, and international relations', *Journal of International Political Theory* (advance online), pp. 1–17.

Dugin, Alexander (2012) *The Fourth Political Theory* (London: Arktos).

Dunn, John (1990) *Interpreting Political Responsibility* (Cambridge: Cambridge University Press).

Dunne, Tim (1995) 'The social construction of international society', *European Journal of International Relations* 1, 3, pp. 367–89.

Dunne, Tim (1998) *Inventing International Society: A History of the English School* (Basingstoke: Macmillan).

Dunne, Tim and Ian Hall (2019) 'Introduction to the new edition', in Herbert Butterfield and Martin Wight (eds) *Diplomatic Investigations: Essays in the Theory of International Politics*, new edition (Oxford: Oxford University Press), pp. 1–36.

Eckert, Amy (2015) 'The just war tradition: restraint on the use of force or partner in crime?', *International Studies Review* 17, pp. 457–9.

Elshtain, Jean Bethke (1997) *Augustine and the Limits of Politics* (Notre Dame, IN: Notre Dame Press).

Elshtain, Jean Bethke (2003) *A Just War Against Terror* (New York: Basic Books).

Epp, Roger (1998) 'The English school on the frontiers of international society: a hermeneutic recollection', *Review of International Studies* 24, 5, pp. 47–64.

Erskine, Toni and Richard Ned Lebow (2012) *Tragedy and International Relations* (Basingstoke: Palgrave Macmillan).

Evans, Trevor and Peter Wilson (1992) 'Regime theory and the English school of international relations: a comparison', *Millennium: Journal of International Studies* 21, 3, pp. 329–51.

Fagan, Madeleine (2013) *Ethics and Politics after Poststructuralism* (Edinburgh: Edinburgh University Press).

Feibleman, James (1962) *In Praise of Comedy: A Study of its Theory and Practice* (New York: Russell & Russell).

Finlayson, Alan (2020) 'YouTube and political ideologies: technology, populism and rhetorical form', *Political Studies* (online), pp. 1–17.

Finnemore, Martha (2018) 'Ethical dilemmas in cyberspace', *Ethics & International Affairs* 32, 4, pp. 457–62.

Fox, Robin Lane (2015) *Augustine: Conversions to Confessions* (New York: Basic Books).

Francis, Samuel T. (1984) *Power and History, The Political Thought of James Burnham* (Lanham, MD: University Press of America).

Francis, Samuel T. (1992) 'Nationalism: old and new', *Chronicles*, June, pp. 18–22.

Francis, Samuel T. (1993) 'Winning the culture war', *Chronicles*, December, available at: www.chroniclesmagazine.org/article/winning-the-culture-war/

Francis, Samuel T. (1999) *James Burnham: Thinkers of Our Time* (London: Claridge Press).

Francis, Samuel T. (2000) 'Paleoconservatism and race', *Chronicles*, 1 December, pp. 9–12.

Francis, Samuel T. (2005) *Leviathan and its Enemies* (Washington, DC: Washington Summit Publishers).

Frei, Christoph (2001) *Hans J. Morgenthau: An Intellectual Biography* (Louisiana: Louisiana State University Press).

Gamble, Andrew (2015) 'Oakeshott and totalitarianism', in Terry Nardin (ed), *Michael Oakeshott's Cold War Liberalism* (New York: Palgrave Macmillan), pp. 83–98.

Geuss, Raymond (2005) *Outside Ethics* (Princeton, NJ: Princeton University Press).

Geuss, Raymond (2013) 'István Hont, 1947–2013', *The Point*, 20 December, available at: https://thepointmag.com/politics/istvan-hont-1947-2013/

Gierke, von Otto (2002) *Community in Historical Perspective*, edited by Antony Black (Cambridge: Cambridge University Press).

Gillespie, A. Michael (2008) *The Theological Origins of Modernity* (Chicago: University of Chicago Press).

Goldstein, Joshua (2011) *Winning the War on War* (New York: Dutton).

Goodhart, David (2018) *The Road to Somewhere* (London: Hurst).

Gottfried, Paul (1995) 'Reconfiguring the political landscape', *Telos* 103, pp. 11126.

Gottfried, Paul (2001) *After Liberalism: Mass Democracy in the Managerial State* (Princeton, NJ: Princeton University Press).

Gottfried, Paul (2007) *Conservatism in America* (London: Palgrave).

Gould, Harry (2017) 'Prudence, relevance and the scholastic disposition', *International Studies Review* 19, 4, pp. 707–10.

Grader, Sheila (1988) 'The English school of international relations: evidence and evaluation', *Review of International Studies* 14, 1, pp. 29–44.

Gray, John (2007) *Black Mass: Apocalyptic Religion and the Death of Utopia* (New York: Farrar, Strauss and Giroux).

Gray, John (2008) *False Dawn: The Delusions of Global Capitalism* (New York: New Press).

Gray, Rosie (2017) 'Behind the internet's anti-democracy movement', *The Atlantic*, 10 February.

Gross, Michael L. and Tamar Meisels, eds (2017) *Soft War: The Ethics of Unarmed Conflict* (Cambridge: Cambridge University Press).

Guilhot, Nicolas, ed (2011) *The Invention of International Relations Theory: Realism, the Rockefeller Foundation, and the 1954 Conference on Theory* (New York: Columbia University Press).

Guilhot, Nicolas (2018) *After the Enlightenment: Political Realism and International Relations in the Mid-Twentieth Century* (Cambridge: Cambridge University Press).

Habermas, Jürgen (2000) *The Postnational Constellation* (Cambridge: Polity Press).

Hall, Ian (2001) 'Still the English patient? Closures and inventions in the English school', *International Affairs* 77, 4, pp. 931–42.

Hall, Ian (2002) 'History, Christianity and diplomacy: Sir Herbert Butterfield and international relations', *Review of International Studies* 28, 4, pp. 719– 36.

Hall, Ian (2006) *The International Thought of Martin Wight* (New York: Palgrave).

Hall, Ian (2012) *Dilemmas of Decline: British Intellectuals and World Politics, 1945–1975* (Berkeley and Los Angeles, CA: University of California Press).

Hall, Ian and Nicholas Rengger (2005) 'The Right that failed? The ambiguities of conservative thought and the dilemmas of conservative practice in international affairs', *International Affairs* 81, 1, pp. 69–82.

Hampshire, Stuart (1996) *Innocence and Experience* (London: Penguin).

Hampshire, Stuart (1998) 'Justice is conflict: the soul and the city', *Tanner Lectures on Human Values* 19, pp. 148–71.

Hawley, George (2016) *Right Wing Critics of American Conservatism* (Lawrence: University Press of Kansas).

Hegel, Georg Wilhelm Friedrich (1977) *Phenomenology of Spirit* (Oxford: Clarendon Press).

Henize, Eric and Rhiannon Neilsen (2020) 'Limited war and the return of reprisals in the law of armed conflict', *Ethics & International Affairs* 34, 2, pp. 175–88.

Hoffman, Mark (1987) 'Critical theory and the inter-paradigm debate', *Millennium: Journal of International Studies* 16, 2, pp. 231–50.

Honig, Bonnie (1993) *Political Theory and the Displacement of the Political* (London: Cornell University Press).

Hont, István (2005) *Jealousy of Trade: International Competition and the Nation State in Historical Perspective* (Cambridge, MA: Belknap Press of Harvard University).

Horton, John (2010) 'Realism, liberal moralism and a political theory of modus vivendi', *European Journal of Political Theory* 9, 4, pp. 431–48.

Hotam, Yotam (2007) 'Gnosis and modernity: a post-war German intellectual debate on secularisation, religion and "overcoming" the past', *Totalitarian Movements and Political Religions* 8, 3–4, pp. 591–608.

Hume, David (1792) *Of the Independence of Parliament*, available at: http://press-pubs.uchicago.edu/founders/documents/v1ch11s4.html

Hume, David (1987) *Essays Moral, Political, Literary*, edited and with a Foreword, Notes, and Glossary by Eugene F. Miller, with an appendix of variant readings from the 1889 edition by T.H. Green and T.H. Grose, revised edition (Indianapolis: Liberty Fund).

Hutchings, Kimberly (2013) 'A place of greater safety? Securing judgement in international ethics', in Amanda Russell Beattie and Kate Schick (eds) *The Vulnerable Subject: Beyond Rationalism in International Relations* (Basingstoke: Palgrave Macmillan), pp. 25–42.

Ignatieff, Michael (1993) *Blood and Belonging: Journeys into the New Nationalism* (New York: Vintage).

Ignatieff, Michael (1998) *The Warrior's Honor: Ethnic War and the Modern Conscience* (New York: Vintage).

Ignatieff, Michael (2001) *Virtual War* (New York: Vintage).

Jackson, Robert H. (1990) 'Martin Wight, international theory and the good life', *Millennium: Journal of International Studies* 19, 2, pp. 261–72.

Jackson, Robert. H. (2000) *The Global Covenant: Human Conduct in a World of States* (Oxford: Oxford University Press).

James, Alan (1982) 'Michael Nicholson on Martin Wight: a mind passing in the night', *Review of International Studies* 8, 2, pp. 117–23.

Jeffrey, Renee (2008) *Evil as Thoughtlessness, Human Suffering in an Age of Terror* (New York: Palgrave Macmillan).

Johnson, James Turner (2005) *The War to Oust Saddam Hussein: Just War and the New Face of Conflict* (Lanham, MD: Rowman & Littlefield).

Johnson, James Turner (2017a) 'A practically informed morality of war: just war, international law, and a changing world order,' *Ethics and International Affairs* 31, 4, pp. 453–65.

Johnson, James Turner (2017b) 'Three perspectives on just war', *International Relations* 31, 4, pp. 511–22.

Jonas, Hans (1992) *The Gnostic Religion: The Message of the Alien God and the Beginnings of Christianity* (London: Routledge).

Jones, Roy E. (1981) 'The English school of international relations: a case for closure', *Review of International Studies* 7, 1, pp. 1–13.

Jonsen, R. Albert and Stephen Toulmin (1988) *The Abuse of Casuistry: A History of Moral Reasoning* (Berkeley: University of California Press).

Kaldor, Mary (2006) *New and Old Wars: Organized Violence in a Global Era* (Cambridge: Polity).

Kaplan, Robert (1996) *The Ends of the Earth: A Journey at the Dawn of the Twentieth Century* (New York: Random House).

Keegan, John (1976) *The Face of Battle: A Study of Agincourt, Waterloo and the Somme* (London: Pimlico).

Kennedy-Pipe, Caroline (2013) 'The Manichean temptation: moralising rhetoric and the invocation of evil in US foreign policy', *International Politics* 50, 5, pp. 623–38.

Kennedy-Pipe, Caroline (2020) 'Nicholas Rengger and two wars', *International Relations* 34, 4, pp. 621–6.

Kennedy-Pipe, Caroline and Nicholas Rengger (2006a) 'BISA at thirty: reflections on three decades of British International Relations Scholarship', *Review of International Studies* 32, 4, pp. 665–78.

Kennedy-Pipe, Caroline and Nicholas Rengger (2006b) 'Apocalypse now? Continuities or disjunctions in world politics after 9/11', *International Affairs* 82, 3, pp. 539–52.

Kennedy-Pipe, Caroline and Nicholas Rengger (2012) 'The new assassination bureau: on the "robotic" turn in contemporary warfare', *Carnegie Ethics Online Monthly Column*, November, available at: www.carnegiecouncil.org/publications/ethics_online/0075

Kochi, Tarik (2012) 'Being, nothing, becoming', in Matthew Stone, Illan rua Wall, and Costas Douzinas (eds), *New Critical Legal Thinking: Law and the Political* (London: Birkbeck Law Press), pp. 138–54.

LaCapra, Dominick (2001) *Writing History, Writing Trauma* (Baltimore: John Hopkins University Press).

Lang, Jr, Anthony F. (2007a) 'The violence of rules: rethinking the 2003 war against Iraq', *Contemporary Politics* 13, 3, pp. 257–76.

Lang, Jr, Anthony F. (2007b) 'Morgenthau, agency and Aristotle', in Michael C. Williams (ed), *Reconsidering Realism: The legacy of Hans J. Morgenthau in International Relations* (Oxford: Oxford University Press), pp. 18–41.

Lang, Jr, Anthony F. and Amanda Beattie, eds (2008) *Torture and Terrorism: Rethinking the Rules of International Security* (London: Routledge).

Lang, Jr, Anthony F., Nicholas Rengger, and William Walker (2006) 'The role(s) of rules: some conceptual clarifications', *International Relations* 20, 3, pp. 274–94.

Lasswell, Harold (1936) *Politics: Who Gets What, When, How* (New York: Whittlesey House).

Lebow, Richard Ned (2003) *The Tragic Vision of Politics: Ethics, Interests, and Orders* (New York: Cambridge University Press).

Lebow Richard Ned (2005) 'Tragedy, politics and political science', *International Relations* 19, 3, pp. 329–36.

Lebow, Richard Ned (2007) *Coercion, Cooperation, and Ethics in International Relations* (Abingdon: Routledge).

Lebow, Richard Ned (2012) 'Tragedy, politics and political science', in R.N. Lebow and Toni Erskine (eds), *Tragedy and International Relations* (London: Palgrave Macmillan), pp. 63–71.

Lewis, Clive S. (1942) *The Screwtape Letters* (London: Geoffrey Blis).

Linklater, Andrew and Hidemi Suganami (2007) *The English School of International Relations: A Contemporary Reassessment* (Cambridge: Cambridge University Press).

Little, Richard (1995) 'Neorealism and the English school: a methodological, ontological and theoretical reassessment', *European Journal of International Relations* 1, 1, pp. 9–34.

Lloyd, Vincent W. (2008) 'Interview with Gillian Rose', *Theory, Culture and Society* 25, 7–8, pp. 201–18.

Lucas, Jr, George (2016) *Ethics and Cyberwarfare: The Quest for Responsible Security in an Age of Digital Warfare* (Oxford: Oxford University Press).

McIntyre, Alasdair (1981) *After Virtue: A Study in Moral Theory* (London: Duckworth).

McMahan, Jeff (2009) *Killing in War* (Oxford: Oxford University Press).

McMahan, Jeff (2015) 'Syria is a modern-day holocaust: we must act', *The Washington Post*, 30 November 2015, available at: www.washingtonpost.com/news/in-theory/wp/2015/11/30/syria-is-a-modern-day-holocaust-we-must-act/

McMahon, Darren M. (2001) *Enemies of the Enlightenment: The French Counter-Enlightenment and the Making of Modernity* (Oxford: Oxford University Press).

Mearsheimer, John (2019) 'Bound to fail: the rise and fall of the liberal international order', *International Security* 43, 4, pp.7–50.

Milbank, John (2006) *Theology and Social Theory: Beyond Secular Reason*, 2nd edition (Oxford: Blackwell).

Milbank, John (2013) *Beyond Secular Order: The Representation of Being and the Representation of the People* (Chichester: Wiley Blackwell).

Milbank, John and Adrian Pabst (2016) *The Politics of Virtue: Post-Liberalism and the Human Future* (London and New York: Rowman and Littlefield).

Mohler, Armin (2018) *The Conservative Revolution in Germany, 1918–1932* (Washington, DC: Washington Summit).

Morgenthau, Hans J. (1947) *Scientific Man vs Power Politics* (London: Latimer House).

Morkevičius, Valerie (2020) 'Sovereignty and authority in the work of James Turner Johnson', in Eric D. Patterson and Marc LiVechhe (eds), *Responsibility and Restraint: James Turner Johnson and the Just War Tradition* (Middletown, RI: Stone Tower Press), pp. 97–124.

Moses, Jeremy (2018) 'Peace without perfection: the intersections of realist and pacifist thought', *Cooperation and Conflict* 53, 1, pp. 42–60.

Mouffe, Chantal (1993) *The Return of the Political* (London: Verso).

Mueller, John (2007) *The Remnants of War* (Ithaca, NY: Cornell University Press).

Nardin, Terry (1983) *Law, Morality, and the Relations of States* (Princeton, NJ: Princeton University Press).

Nash, George H. (1996) *The Conservative Intellectual Movement in America, 1945–1980* (Wilmington, DE: Intercollegiate Studies Institute).

Nicholson, Michael (1981) 'The enigma of Martin Wight', *Review of International Studies* 7, 1, pp. 15–22.

Nussbaum, Martha (2001/1986) *The Fragility of Goodness: Luck and Ethics in Greek Tragedy and Philosophy* (Cambridge, Cambridge University Press).

Oakeshott, Michael (1960) 'Introduction to Leviathan', in *Hobbes on Civil Association* (Indianapolis: Liberty Fund).

Oakeshott, Michael (1983) *On History and Other Essays* (Oxford: Basil Blackwell).

Oakeshott, Michael (1991/1975) *On Human Conduct* (Oxford: Clarendon Press).

Oakeshott, Michael (1993) *Religion Politics and the Moral Life*, edited by Tim Fuller (New Haven, CT: Yale University Press).

Oakeshott, Michael (1996) *The Politics of Faith and the Politics of Scepticism*, edited by Timothy Fuller (London: Yale University Press).

Oakeshott, Michael (1999) 'The tower of Babel', in Michael Oakeshott, *On History and Other Essays* (Indianapolis: Liberty Fund), pp. 179–210.

Oakeshott, Michael (2010/1991/1962) *Rationalism in Politics and Other Essays* (London: Methuen & Co.)

Oakeshott, Michael (2014) *Notebooks, 1922–86*, edited by Luke O'Sullivan (Exeter: Imprint Academic).

Oakeshott, Michael (2015/1966/1933) *Experience and Its Modes* (Cambridge: Cambridge University Press).

Oakley, Jacob (2020) *Waging Cyberwar: Technical Challenges and Operational Restraints* (New York: Springer).

O'Brian, Tim (1990) *The Things They Carried* (Boston: Houghton Mifflen).

O'Donovan, Oliver (2003) *The Just War Revisited* (Cambridge: Cambridge University Press).

Ohlin, Jens David, et al. (2015) *Cyber War: Law and Ethics for Virtual Conflicts* (Oxford: Oxford University Press).

Open letter (2002) 'What we are fighting for', *The Washington Post*, 12 February 2002, available at: https://www.washingtonpost.com/wp-srv/nation/specials/attacked/transcripts/justwar_letter020102.html

Owen, David and Tracy B. Strong (2004) 'Introduction', in David Owen and Tracy B. Strong (eds) and Rodney Livingstone (trans), *Max Weber, The Vocation Lectures* (Indianapolis: Hackett Publishing Company), pp. ix–lxii.

Paipais, Vassilios (2016) 'Overcoming "Gnosticism"? Realism as political theology', *Cambridge Review of International Affairs* 29, 4, pp. 1603–23.

Paipais, Vassilios (2019) 'First image revisited: human nature, original sin and international relations', *Journal of International Relations and Development* 22, 2, pp. 364–88.

Paipais, Vassilios (2020) 'Between faith and scepticism: Nicholas Rengger's reflections on the "hybridity" of modernity,' *International Relations* 34, 4, pp. 627–733.

Passmore, John (2000) *The Perfectibility of Man* (Indianapolis: Liberty Fund.

Pinker, Steven (2011) *The Better Angels of our Nature* (New York: Viking Books).

Pinker, Steven (2019) *Enlightenment Now* (London: Penguin).

Pitkin, Hannah F. (1973) 'The roots of conservatism: Michael Oakeshott and the denial of politics', in Lewis A. Coser and Irving Howe (eds), *The New Conservatives: A Critique from the Left* (New York: Quadrangle), pp. 243–88.

Pomerantsev, Peter (2015) *Nothing is True and Everything is Possible: The Surreal Heart of the New Russia* (New York: Public Affairs).

Popper, Karl R. (1961) The *Poverty of Historicism*, 3rd edition (London: Routledge and Kegan Paul).

Ramberg, Bjorn (2009) 'Richard Rorty', in Edward N. Zalta (ed), *The Stanford Encyclopedia of Philosophy*, Spring 2009 edition, available at: https://plato.stanford.edu/archives/spr2009/entries/rorty/

Rawls, John (1993) *Political Liberalism* (New York: Columbia University Press).

Reiss, Timothy J. (1980) *Tragedy and Truth: Studies in the Development of a Renaissance and Neoclassical Discourse* (New Haven, CT: Yale University Press).

Rengger, Nicholas (1987) *Reason, Scepticism and Politics: Theory and Practice in the Enlightenment's Politics*, PhD diss., Department of Politics, University of Durham.

Rengger, Nicholas (1988a) 'Going critical? A response to Hoffman', *Millennium: Journal of International Studies* 17, 1, pp. 81–99.

Rengger, Nicholas (1988b) 'Serpents and doves in classical international theory', *Millennium: Journal of International Studies* 17, 2, pp. 215–25.

Rengger, Nicholas (1989) 'Incommensurability, international theory and the fragmentation of Western political culture', in J.R. Gibbins (ed), *Contemporary Political Culture: Politics in a Postmodern Age* (London: Sage), pp. 237–50.

Rengger, Nicholas (1992a) 'Culture, society, and order in world politics', in John Baylis and Nicholas J. Rengger (eds), *Dilemmas of World Politics: International Issues in a Changing World* (Oxford: Oxford University Press), pp. 85–103.

Rengger, Nicholas (1992b) 'A city which sustains all things? Communitarianism and international society', *Millennium: Journal of International Studies* 21, 3, pp.353–69.

Rengger, Nicholas (1994) 'From Köningsberg to Alexandria (and back): classical thought, global ethics and world politics', *Paradigms* (now *Global Society: Journal of Interdisciplinary International Relations*) 8, 1, pp. 36–58.

Rengger, Nicholas (1995a) *Political Theory, Modernity and Postmodernity: Beyond Enlightenment and Critique* (Oxford: Blackwell).

Rengger, Nicholas (1995b) 'Trust, prudence and history: John Dunn and the tasks of political theory', *History of Political Thought* 16, 3, pp. 416–37.

Rengger, Nicholas (1996a) *Retreat from the Modern: Humanism, Postmodernism and the Flight from Modernist Culture* (London: Bowerdean Publishing Company).

Rengger, Nicholas (1996b) 'On cosmopolitanism, constructivism and international society: some reflections on British international studies at the fin de siècle', *Zeitschrift für Internationale Beziehungen* 3, H. 1, pp. 183–99.

Rengger, Nicholas (1997) 'The ethics of trust in world politics', *International Affairs* 73, 3, pp. 469–87.

Rengger, Nicholas (1998) 'The beginning of the end of modernity? Honour, ethics and the practices of civil war at the fin de siècle', *Civil Wars* 1, 2, pp. 38–51.

Rengger, Nicholas (2000a) *International Relations, Political Theory, and the Problem of Order: Beyond International Relations Theory?* (London and New York: Routledge).

Rengger, Nicholas (2000b) 'Political theory and international relations: promised land or exit from Eden?', *International Affairs* 76, 4, pp. 755–70.

Rengger, Nicholas (2001a) 'The boundaries of conversation: a reply to Dallmayr', *Millennium: Journal of International Studies* 30, 2, pp. 357–64.

Rengger, Nicholas (2001b) 'European communities in a neo-medieval global polity: the dilemmas of fairyland?', in Morten Kelstrup and Michael C. Williams (eds), *International Relations Theory and the Politics of European Integration* (London: Routledge), pp. 57–71.

Rengger, Nicholas (2002) 'On the just war tradition in the twenty-first century', *International Affairs* 78, 2, pp. 353–63.

Rengger, Nicholas (2003a) 'Review of *Moral Constraints on War: Principles and Cases by Bruno Coppiters and Nick Fotion*', *International Affairs* 79, 2, pp. 643–4.

Rengger, Nicholas (2003b) 'Eternal return? Modes of encountering religion in international relations,' *Millennium: Journal of International Studies* 32, 2, pp. 327–36.

Rengger, Nicholas (2004) 'Just a war against terror? Jean Bethke Elshtain's burden and American power', *International Affairs* 80, 1, pp. 107–16.

Rengger, Nicholas (2005a) 'Tragedy or scepticism? Defending the anti-Pelagian mind in world politics', *International Relations* 19, 3, pp. 321–8.

Rengger, Nicholas (2005b) 'The judgment of war: on the idea of legitimate force in world politics', *Review of International Studies* 31, pp. 143–61.

Rengger, Nicholas (2007) 'Political theory and the judgment of war,' *Contemporary Politics* 13, 3, pp. 243–55.

Rengger, Nicholas (2008) 'The greatest treason? On the subtle temptations of preventive war', *International Affairs* 84, 5, pp. 949–61.

Rengger, Nicholas (2012a) 'Tragedy or scepticism? Defending the anti-Pelagian mind in world politics', in Toni Erskine and Richard Ned Lebow (eds), *Tragedy and International Relations* (Basingstoke and New York: Palgrave Macmillan), pp. 53–62.

Rengger, Nicholas (2012b) 'Politics and international relations', in Mervyn Davies, Oliver D. Crisp, Gavin D'Costa, and Peter Hampson (eds), *Christianity and the Disciplines: The Transformation of the Disciplines* (London: Bloomsbury), pp. 167–82.

Rengger, Nicholas (2012c) 'A global ethic and the hybrid character of the moral world', *Ethics and International Affairs* 26, 1, pp. 27–31.

Rengger, Nicholas (2013a) *Just War and International Order: The Uncivil Condition in World Politics* (Cambridge: Cambridge University Press).

Rengger, Nicholas (2013b) 'On theology and international relations: world politics beyond the empty sky', *International Relations* 27, 2, pp. 141–57.

Rengger, Nicholas (2013c) 'The wager lost by winning? On the "triumph" of the just war tradition', in Anthony F. Lang, Jr, Cian O'Driscoll, and John Williams (eds), *Just War: Authority, Tradition, and Practice* (Washington, DC: Georgetown University Press).

Rengger, Nicholas (2014) 'Post-secular global order: metaphysical not political?', in Luca Mavelli and Fabio Petito (eds), *Towards a Post-secular International Politics: New Forms of Community, Identity, and Power* (London: Palgrave), pp. 65–80.

Rengger, Nicholas (2015a) 'Pluralism in international relations theory: three questions', *International Studies Perspectives* 16, 1, pp. 32–9.

Rengger, Nicholas (2015b) 'Email to Alex Danchev copied to Richard Whatmore', 15 June.

Rengger, Nicholas (2017) *The Anti-Pelagian Imagination in Political Theory and International Relations: Dealing in Darkness* (London and New York: Routledge).

Rengger, Nicholas (2019a) 'Between transcendence and necessity: Eric Voegelin, Martin Wight and the crisis of modern international relations', *Journal of International Relations and Development* 22, 2, pp. 327–45.

Rengger, Nicholas (2019b) 'Practical judgement: inconsistent – or incoherent?', in Mathias Albert and Anthony F. Lang, Jr (eds), *The Politics of International Political Theory: Reflections on the Works of Chris Brown* (Basingstoke: Palgrave), pp. 55–68.

Rengger, Nicholas and Mark Hoffman (1992) 'Modernity, postmodernism and international relations', in Joe Doherty, Elspeth Graham, and Mo Malek (eds), *Postmodernism and the Social Sciences* (Basingstoke: Palgrave Macmillan), pp.127–47.

Rengger, Nicholas and Ben Thirkell-White (2007) 'Still critical after all these years? The past, present and future of critical theory in international relations', *Review of International Studies* 33, S1, pp. 3–24.

Rengger, Nicholas and Caroline Kennedy-Pipe (2008) 'The state of war', *International Affairs* 84, 5, pp. 891–902.

Ricoeur, Paul (1974) *Political and Social Essays*, edited by David Stewart and Joseph Bien (Athens, OH: Ohio University Press).

Ricoeur, Paul (1991) *Lectures 1, Autour du politique* (Paris: Éditions du Seuil).

Roberson, Barbara, ed (1998) *International Society and the Development of International Relations Theory* (London: Pinter).

Rorty, Richard (1980) *Philosophy and the Mirror of Nature* (Princeton, NJ: Princeton University Press).

Rose, Gillian (1981) *Hegel Contra Sociology* (London: Athlone).

Rose, Gillian (1992) *The Broken Middle: Out of Our Ancient Society* (Oxford: Blackwell).

Rose, Gillian (1993) *Judaism and Modernity: Philosophical Essays* (Oxford and Cambridge, MA: Blackwell.

Rose, Gillian (1995) *Love's Work: A Reckoning with Life* (New York: Schocken Books).

Rose, Gillian (1996) *Mourning Becomes the Law: Philosophy and Representation* (Cambridge: Cambridge University Press).

Rose, Gillian (1999) *Paradiso* (Menard Press).

Sabbagh, Dan (2020) 'Hackers HQ and space command: how UK defense budget could be spent', *The Guardian Online*, 18 November, available at: www.theguardian.com/uk-news/2020/nov/18/hackers-hq-and-space-command-how-uk-defence-budget-could-be-spent

Sabbagh, Dan and Patrick Butler (2020) 'Boris Johnson agrees 16bn rise in defense spending', *The Guardian Online*, 18 November, available at: www.theguardian.com/politics/2020/nov/18/boris-johnson-agrees-16bn-rise-in-defence-spending

Scheuerman, William (2007) 'Was Morgenthau a realist? Revisiting scientific man vs. power politics', *Constellations* 14, 4, pp. 506–30.

Scheuerman, William (2009) *Morgenthau* (Cambridge: Polity Press).

Schick, Kate (2012) *Gillian Rose: A Good Enough Justice* (Edinburgh: Edinburgh University Press).

Schick, Kate (2013) 'Gillian Rose and vulnerable judgement', in Amanda Russell Beattie and Kate Schick (eds), *The Vulnerable Subject: Beyond Rationalism in International Relations* (London: Palgrave Macmillan), pp. 43–61.

Schick, Kate (2018) '"The tree is really rooted in the sky": beside difficulty in Gillian Rose's political theory', in Joshua B Davis (ed), *Misrecognitions: Gillian Rose and the Task of Political Theology* (Oregon: Cascade Books), pp. 87–106.

Schmitt, Michael N., ed (2017) *Tallinn Manual 2.0 on the International Law Applicable to Cyber Operations* (Cambridge: Cambridge University Press).

Sedgwick, Mark (2009) *Against the Modern World: Traditionalism and the Secret Intellectual History of the Twentieth Century* (Oxford: Oxford University Press).

Shearman, Nancy (2005) *Stoic Warriors: The Ancient Philosophy of the Military Mind* (Oxford: Oxford University Press).

Shklar, Judith (1964) *Legalism: Law, Morals and Political Trials* (Cambridge, MA: Harvard University Press).

Shklar, Judith (1990) *The Faces of Injustice* (New Haven, CT: Yale University Press).

Skinner, Quentin (1978) *The Foundations of Modern Political Thought: Volume 2, The Age of Reformation* (Cambridge: Cambridge University Press).

Slaughter, Anne-Marie (2001) *A New World Order* (Princeton, NJ: Princeton University Press).

Sleat, Matt (2016) 'Realism, liberalism and non-ideal theory or, are there two ways to do realistic political theory?', *Political Studies* 64, 1, pp. 27–41.

Slobodian, Quinn (2018) *Globalists: The End of Empire and the Birth of Neoliberalism* (Cambridge, MA: Harvard University Press).

Smith, Adam (1776) *An Inquiry into the Nature and Causes of the Wealth of Nations* (London: W. Strahan and T. Cadell).

Spektorowski, Alberto (2010) 'The New Right: ethno-regionalism, ethnopluralism and the emergence of a neo-fascist "Third Way"', *Journal of Political Ideologies* 8, 1, pp. 117–34.

Suganami, Hidemi (1983) 'The structure of institutionalism: an anatomy of British mainstream international relations', *International Relations* 7, 5, pp. 2363–81.

Sullivan, Andrew (2017) 'The reactionary temptation', *New York Magazine,* 1 May.

Sylvester, Christine (2016) 'Creativity', in Aoileann Ni Mhurchu and Reiko Shindo (eds), *Critical Imaginations in International Relations* (Abingdon: Routledge), pp. 56–69.

Taylor, Charles (2007) *A Secular Age* (Cambridge, MA: Belknap Press of Harvard University Press).

Taylor, Charles (2011) *Dilemmas and Connections: Selected Essays* (Cambridge, MA: Belknap Press of Harvard University Press).

Teitelman, Benjamin (2020) *War for Eternity: Inside Steve Bannon's Far Right Circle of Global Power Brokers* (New York: Harper Collins).

Toulmin, Stephen (1992) *Cosmopolis: The Hidden Agenda of Modernity* (Chicago: University of Chicago Press).

Tsirigotis, Anthimos Alexandros (2017) *Cybernetics, Warfare and Discourse: The Cybernetisation of Warfare in Britain* (New York: Springer).

Valeriano, Brandon and Ryan Maness, eds (2015) *Cyber War versus Cyber Realities: Cyber Conflict in the International System* (Oxford: Oxford University Press).

Valeriano, Brandon and Ryan Maness (2018) 'International relations theory and cyber security: threats, conflicts and ethics in an emergent domain', in Chris Brown and Robyn Eckersley (eds), *The Oxford Handbook of International Political Theory* (Oxford: Oxford University Press), pp. 259–72.

Vallor, Shannon (2016) *Technology and the Virtues: A Philosophical Guide to a Future Worth Wanting* (Oxford: Oxford University Press).

Versluis, Arthur (2014) 'A conversation with Alain de Benoist', *Journal for the Study of Radicalism* 8, 2, pp. 84–5.

Vigezzi, Brunello (2005) *The British Committee on the Theory of International Politics (1954–1985): The Rediscovery of History* (Milano: Edizioni Unicopoli).

Voegelin, Eric (1952) *The New Science of Politics: An Introduction* (Chicago: University of Chicago Press).

Voegelin, Eric (2005) *Science, Politics and Gnosticism* (Wilmington, DE: ISI Books).

Waldman, Thomas (2020) *Vicarious Warfare, American Strategy and the Illusion of War on the Cheap* (Bristol: Bristol University Press).

Walker, R.B.J. (1992) *Inside/Outside: International Relations as Political Theory* (Cambridge: Cambridge University Press).

Waltz, Kenneth N. (1979) *Theory of International Politics* (Reading, MA: Addison Wesley).

Walzer, Michael (2015) *Just and Unjust Wars: A Moral Argument with Historical Illustrations*, 5th edition (New York: Basic Books).

Walzer, Michael (2019) 'On reciprocity and practical morality: a response to Sagan and Valentino,' *Ethics and International Affairs* 33, 4, pp. 445–50.

Ware, Owen (2004) 'Dialectic of the past/disjuncture of the future: Derrida and Benjamin on the concept of messianism', *Journal for Cultural and Religious Theory* 5, 2, pp. 99–114.

Weber, Max (1946) *From Max Weber: Essays in Sociology*, edited by H.H. Gerth and C. Wright Mills (New York: Oxford University Press).

Weber, Max (1978) *Economy and Society: An Outline of Interpretive Sociology*, Vols. 1–2, edited by Guenther Roth and Claus Wittich (Berkeley, CA: University of California Press).

Wendt, Alexander (1999) *Social Theory of International Politics* (Cambridge: Cambridge University Press).

Wheeler, Nicholas J. (1996) 'Guardian angel or global gangster: a review of the ethical claims of international society', *Political Studies* 44, 1, pp. 123–35.

White, Stephen K. (1991) *Political Theory and Postmodernism* (Cambridge: Cambridge University Press).

Wight, Martin (1991) *International Theory: The Three Traditions*, edited by Brian Porter and Gabriele Wight (Leicester: Leicester University Press).

Wight, Martin (2005) *Four Seminal Thinkers in International Theory: Machiavelli, Grotius, Kant, and Mazzini*, edited by Gabriele Wight and Brian Porter (Oxford: Oxford University Press).

Wight, Martin (2019/1966) 'Why is there no international theory?', in Herbert Butterfield and Martin Wight (eds), *Diplomatic Investigations: Essays in the Theory of International Politics*, new edition (Oxford: Oxford University Press), pp. 37–54.

Williams, Bernard (2005) *In the Beginning was the Deed: Realism and Moralism in Political Argument* (Princeton, NJ: Princeton University Press).

Williams, Michael C. (2005) *The Realist Tradition and the Limits of International Relations* (Cambridge: Cambridge University Press).

Wolff, Ernst (2011) *Political Responsibility for a Globalised World: After Levinas' Humanism* (Bielefeld: Transcript).

Index

www.ingramcontent.com/pod-product-compliance
Lightning Source LLC
Chambersburg PA
CBHW070617030426
42337CB00020B/3825